CURRENCY
KINGS

CURRENCY
KINGS

HOW BILLIONAIRE TRADERS MADE THEIR FORTUNE TRADING FOREX AND HOW YOU CAN TOO

BEN ROBSON

NEW YORK   CHICAGO   SAN FRANCISCO   ATHENS
LONDON   MADRID   MEXICO CITY   MILAN
NEW DELHI   SINGAPORE   SYDNEY   TORONTO

1 2 3 4 5 6 7 8 9   LCR   22 21 20 19 18 17

ISBN 978-1-259-86300-4
MHID   1-259-86300-X

e-ISBN 978-1-259-86301-1
e-MHID   1-259-86301-8

This publication is designed to provide accurate and authoritative information in regard to the subject matter covered. It is sold with the understanding that neither the author nor the publisher is engaged in rendering legal, accounting, securities trading, or other professional services. If legal advice or other expert assistance is required, the services of a competent professional person should be sought.
    —*From a Declaration of Principles Jointly Adopted by a Committee of the American Bar Association and a Committee of Publishers and Associations*

Library of Congress Cataloging-in-Publication Data

Names: Robson, Ben (Financial analyst) author.
Title: Currency kings : how billionaire traders made their fortune trading forex and how you can too / Ben Robson.
Description: 1 Edition. | New York : McGraw-Hill Education, 2017.
   Identifiers: LCCN 2017010959 (print) | LCCN 2017014920 (ebook) | ISBN 9781259863011 | ISBN 1259863018 | ISBN 9781259863004 (hardback) | ISBN 125986300X
Subjects: LCSH: Investments. | Futures. | Securities. | BISAC: BUSINESS & ECONOMICS / Investments & Securities.
Classification: LCC HG4521 (ebook) | LCC HG4521 .R6657 2017 (print) | DDC 332.4/5—dc23
LC record available at https://lccn.loc.gov/2017010959

McGraw-Hill Education books are available at special quantity discounts to use as premiums and sales promotions or for use in corporate training programs. To contact a representative, please visit the Contact Us pages us at www.mhprofessional.com.

CONTENTS

ACKNOWLEDGMENTS

"There's a book in everyone," I was once told. And this is mine. The journey to writing this book started long before I embarked upon a career in the financial markets. And there are many people who have helped shape the course of my life and who deserve a share of the credit for this piece of work.

I will start with mentors: Clive Hawes, Larry O'Connell, Michelle Garnier-Chedotal, Lorna Almonds-Windmill, Jonathan Cook, Barry Hannen, David Foley and Simon Raybould.

If I then move on to those who have helped me at various stages during my financial markets career (some are mentioned above), then I would like to add Richard Plane, Richard Craddock, and Frank Lentini. There are others who added color and opinion to *Currency Kings* for which I'd like to thank Mark Davison, Mark O' Neill, Ross Donaghue, Peter Nesden, Moorthy Sadasivam, Vinish Ramanathan, Vivek Premkumar, John Ramkin, Jim Berlino, Rakesh Daryani, Harish Pawani, and Badre Maktari. A special thank-you to David Hastings and Tradermade for creating some charts and to Edward Wright for my portrait photo.

I especially wish to thank my agent, Jeanne Glasser Levine. Also, Donya Dickerson, Daina Penikas, Marci Nugent, Mauna Eichner and Lee Fukui, and the team at McGraw-Hill for all their hard work in getting this book to press.

Lastly, a small word for my family. To my wife Saskia and my daughters Sophie and Paloma. Thank you for your patience.

INTRODUCTION

I have been lucky enough to be involved in the forex (FX) market for more than 20 years. I say lucky because I have always found the market fascinating, dynamic, and often exhilarating. It is a massive market—some $5.3 trillion in FX transactions is traded each day. The market ebbs, it flows, and then in an instant, it can spike and retrace or continue to move in truly Brownian fashion. There are so many factors that may influence a pair of currencies, and there are thousands of traders pitching their wits (and cash) in the relentless pursuit of profits and perhaps perfection.

There are some who argue that luck plays a great part in the success or failure of any particular trader or philosophy. There are several theories that support this contention. And it is perhaps applicable to the vast majority of FX participants. But there is a breed of traders who reject this generalization and quite rightly base their educated, risk-adjusted wagers on something a bit more certain than luck. Some of these people either are already Currency Kings or are on the right track to become future Currency Kings.

If I were to fully define what I mean by a Currency King, it would be an individual who has made multimillions or billions in the FX marketplace by scaling up a legitimate competitive advantage. The marketplace in my mind encompasses spot, futures, forwards, and options as products and also technology and innovation as a means to access and penetrate the market either in a trading capacity or as an enabler of trading. The traders, speculators, market makers, and technology providers you will read about have all made fortunes in the FX marketplace, and some are integral to the market as it is today.

Going back through my 20-plus years as a foreign exchange dealer and trader, there are people, places, and events that have led me to believe that markets can be beaten. In a transactional sense, wealth is transferred from A to B and markets are efficient, as Professor Eugene Fama and his "efficient market hypothesis" suggests. But there are many instances when markets are inefficient or predictable to a degree, where the odds of a payoff are not equal and therefore favor one particular outcome over another, and there are traders out there who consistently beat the odds. I have witnessed this, and it has inspired me.

From my very early days at Goldman Sachs, I found the energy of the establishment and the people phenomenal. Goldman Sachs has some of the very largest and most successful hedge funds trading through its market making desks—in effect, these are super smart people executing colossal orders for super smart people. Without doubt, in my mind, some of these funds had compelling competitive advantages, and for many the competitive advantage was accessed through the simple principle of hard work. Some of the global macro funds employed exceptionally intelligent people to do their research. It may be a simple analogy, but a concert pianist doesn't become a concert pianist without spending many hours a day plying his or her trade. Similarly, to get a sniff of being a top global macro hedge fund trader, one needs, among other things, intelligence, dedication, and application, not to mention some of the other significant qualities such as courage, tenacity, and discipline.

During my time at Prudential Bache, I encountered other types of traders—no less fascinating than the global macro funds that traded through Goldman's books—and these were trend following commodity trading advisors (CTAs). What struck me about CTAs—of which there were many—was how aligned in direction and frequency their trading was. Some days, there would be very little activity, and then on others it was one-way traffic all day long. It led me to conclude that many of the "black box" programs were remarkably similar. What also struck me was that on those busy days, the market tended to "go with the flow." Hence many dealing desks had what is termed "flow traders" whose role was to follow some of the "directional" FX flows.

The late 1990s and the early 2000s saw the arrival of many online market makers and the beginnings of "retail" FX trading. This allowed many smaller customers to access the FX market through small brokers. The unfortunate statistic for retail traders is that about 80 percent of them lose money. My experience working at CMC Markets in Hong Kong would probably suggest that the winning percentage was slightly higher, but that was due mainly to the fact of leverage restrictions imposed by the Hong Kong regulator. What CMC Markets and many other retail brokers did, especially in their early years, was take the opposite side to many retail clients' trades. In some instances, positions could become quite large, and so the strategy was not without risk. Those who take risks are often rewarded, which was the case for CMC.

As the retail trading fraternity grew, and regulators became more aware of small brokers taking on large FX risks, the practice of straight-through processes (or agency brokering) became the modus operandi of many retail brokerages. Brokers would simply take a spread or commission as the trade passed "straight through" to a bank. It turned out to be a positive evolution in the market as banks would fight to be "top of book" (in other words, to offer the best executable bid or offer price) in aggregated liquidity pools and distribute their liquidity through retail brokers and electronic communication networks to end clients.

The reward for the banks was to warehouse the risk in greater scale than their retail counterparts. Bigger balance sheets equated to more risk taking. If a bank could supply pricing to several retail brokerages, it could collect the trades and therefore potentially collect the 80 percent of losing trades. The natural progression of this evolution was for non-bank market makers and ultimately high-frequency traders to join the bandwagon and fight to provide top-of-book liquidity to retail brokerages. In the case of HFTs, however, in many cases the strategy was to be a maker and taker of liquidity, often capitalizing on pricing latency between two counterparties to make nearly instantaneous profits. In the zero-sum game of FX, huge fortunes were made by these three distinct types of brokers and market makers, some of whom listed on worldwide stock exchanges on the back of this trade. Retail traders were the losers of course.

Continuous advancements in technology and innovation have been at the forefront of the FX market for the last two decades. Computer power has in many respects replaced brain power and sleight of hand. In an arena heavily influenced by HFTs, millions of orders can be placed (and canceled) in millionths of a second, and computers are so powerful and rapid that one could argue that markets are in fact nowadays practically efficient. And yet, there are still avenues for arbitragers without supercomputers to make money. Finding a legitimate competitive advantage may be tougher these days, but it can still be done. Smart people will always find a way to make money.

My own experience as a proprietary trader led me to establish four basic principles that I believe lead to trading success. These are covered in the first chapter, but put very simply, they involve doing some detailed work on your trading philosophy, working out whether you have a legitimate competitive advantage, and seeing whether you can scale it up while constantly being aware of your risks.

As an example, I will cite an arbitrage trading business I ran out of Singapore and Dubai. My team and I had worked out that there were some forward pricing anomalies in certain currency pairs. Our competitive advantage was that we had some very good banking relationships and received superlative pricing from our banks. Our challenge was to maintain both the banking relationships and pricing and at the same time take advantage of pricing inefficiencies. We had two of the four ingredients to create a highly profitable trading business. It was scalable up to a point, and the risks were limited to our counterparties, which were mitigated by using a prime broker. It turned out to be a very successful venture—but not enough to make us Currency Kings. Scale was the limiting factor. On another eminently scalable arbitrage, our firm lacked the capital to support the trade to any large degree. The point I wish to make here is that we found opportunities to make money, and there are still opportunities today.

I am convinced that if you have the four basic principles stacked in your favor, you can make outsize trading returns. You do not have to be the smartest kid on the block either, as many great currency traders have only a very basic education. There are plenty of traits that quality traders exhibit that can easily be learned. Others will come with application. Trading discipline is perhaps one of the key concepts that define whether you will be successful over the longer term.

My goal in this book is to give examples of traders, products, and ways in which you can make money in the FX marketplace, point out the many obstacles that you will face in your pursuit of profits, and give advice on how you can train yourself to think smart and trade smart. One observation I have made in my financial markets experience is that traders both big and small often employ too much risk. Another, more so nowadays, is that they trade too frequently. It is also well documented that the majority of traders are quick to take profits and slow to cut losses.

By committing to a disciplined strategy and sticking to it, you will find that in most cases, trading performance will improve. Understanding the risks and dangers of trading is fundamental to staying in the game. You can beef up your tactics by learning from the Currency Kings.

The last point I wish to make is that if you are serious about trading, it is possible to win. As with most things, if you wish to do it well, it requires preparation, time, effort, and dedication. It also requires continuous focus, guts, tenacity, and coolness under pressure. Trading is not a walk in the park. It is the business of making money, and that must be front and center in your mind. If you are at all blasé in your approach, then you will lose.

If the performance metric of winners to losers is to improve, then it starts with adopting a serious attitude. And that means doing the work. Discovering your method of trading will then come naturally to you. By avoiding some of the obstacles in your path you will improve your profitability. If along that path you discover that you have a genuine competitive advantage, then you are well on the way to winning. How much so depends on the competitive advantage and how scalable it is. But always be mindful about the risks you take. There are a lot of very intelligent ex-traders who have been incapable of managing their risks, and there have been a great many spectacular blowups.

The book *Currency Kings*, I hope, will act as a guide and an aide-mémoire to your trading activities. If the book inspires people to trade with a plan and with discipline, it will have achieved most of its goal; if it helps launch a new Currency King, it will have succeeded beyond my expectations.

The Four Basic Trading Principles

For the few who make millions or even billions in the currency market, there are many thousands who lose, and the failures or losses can be measured by the same amount. It is a zero-sum game in which there are more diabolical traders than talented ones. Some people hedge, some speculate, and some arbitrage; brokers siphon off commissions; and there are hidden fees in spreads, rollovers, and financing charges. It is virtually pointless to trade currencies on leverage if you do not have a genuine hedging requirement against some physical purchase or sale at a future date or if you lack a genuine competitive advantage. With a bit of good fortune, in the short term, virtually any trading style can make you money. In longer-term trading, with spreads, commissions, and other leakages, you will find that the "coin toss" is not fair. Probability implies you will lose money, unless of course you have a fail-safe system that beats the odds. It really is genuinely difficult to consistently make money trading currencies.

At the end of the day, however, making money is what trading currencies is all about—and making a lot of money at that. It is not about being part of the game. It's about winning. It's not about a visit to the casino and throwing a few chips on the table in a vague hope that your number comes up. It's about beating the odds and collecting more valuable chips.

The traders you will read about in this book have won the game already, and some continue to win it, but not without great effort. There is no easy way to become a Currency King. The individuals highlighted here have all "done the work." And that is what we must all aspire to do. Almost all of them had, or have, a legitimate competitive advantage—a brilliant and unique idea— or they were early adopters or creators of technology. While they are speculators, they are not reckless gamblers—that is, they use appropriate risk controls to efficiently and successfully run their businesses. Lastly, their businesses are scalable, and scale is what turns small ideas into multi-million-dollar profits.

I will take it for granted that you either have had or will have a brilliant idea that you think will make you millions in the currency markets. The idea is one thing, but the following questions must be asked:

- How well have you researched that idea?

- Has it already been done, and has it been done better by somebody else?

- What are the barriers to entry? Capital? Lack of information? Competition? Regulators? Size?

My point is that research is important. Luckily, ideas are free! If you look at hundreds of brilliant traders from all financial trading disciplines, whether they be in equities, bonds, commodities, or currencies, you'll see that they tend to be some of the smartest people in the room. The days are long gone when aggressive traders quoted "the dollar versus the deutsche mark" and wildly spread prices to their advantage. Computer technology has transformed dealing rooms from buzzing noisy squawk-box cauldrons to rapid and efficient centers, more resembling libraries for their quietness, where hundreds of millions of dollars are traded at the click of a mouse and profits are measured in fractions. Currency trading has become so sophisticated that in some currency pairs, prices are now quoted to the sixth decimal, a far cry from even 10 years ago, when pip value was derived from the fourth decimal on major currency pairs. Efficient systems have allowed for the erosion in spreads, and computers have replaced humans in dealing rooms. Algorithms and risk managers are the new traders. And believe it or not, profits can still be made from the sixth decimal (1 tick on the sixth decimal is equivalent to $1 in every 1 million euros versus U.S. dollars traded).

Maybe it's too late for you to go to MIT, the University of Chicago, Harvard, or Stanford, but whatever idea you are developing, you must have a solid plan, and that plan has to be researched and tested. If it's a technical analysis scenario, it must be tested over perhaps millions of time frames. With macro ideas, years of historical data must be sifted through, and a thorough knowledge of geopolitical relationships and tensions is required, not to mention an encyclopedic economic appraisal of whatever countries are involved. With options, pricing is of the utmost importance because the multiple variables can shave percentages off profits (or add them) if even one of those variables is out of whack.

Work is required. Work, work, work!

In the retail space, it would pay for the average investor to read a quality, unbiased FX guide, such as *Currency Kings*, before attending any brokerage sponsored FX seminar or event. There are too many experts explaining how easy it is to make money in the FX market. And there are too many followers (and losers). Trading leveraged FX allows for big profits but even bigger losses when you add spreads and slippage. Even if spreads were choice (no spread at all, with the same bid and offer price, and you "choose" to buy or sell), the average retail punter (a person who gambles, places a bet, or makes a risky investment) would still lose money. (I will explain why in Chapter 8.) Spread compression and competiveness for tight spreads among the brokerage space in Japan is about as impressive as it gets. Why? Because retail FX traders lose money. Retail brokers even run models on how long it will take the average client to blow up and what their average profit is per client. "Caveat emptor" is the motto for any-body who wishes to open a retail FX or contract for difference (CFD) account.

And what about the self-styled FX experts, all of whom seem to be in their early twenties to thirties? Generally, the experts work for the brokers, and some may quite genuinely feel that they are providing worthy information or insight. By and large, the expert advice is focused on technical analysis, and while it may often work in the short run, most statisticians would tell you that on the basis of probability, the analysis will be doomed in the long run.

Other experts work for themselves and often advertise their seminars in national newspapers for wonderful no-lose trad-ing systems and ideas. I have often seen five or six get-rich-quick seminar advertisements in the national Sunday newspapers, espe-cially in Asia. They normally promote the random disciple who has quadrupled his money in double-quick time. But they don't promote the loser who lost 75 percent of his capital. Shame! So why do these experts explain their "fail-safe systems" in semi-nars and not trade the money themselves? Well, it's a lot easier to have a crowd of followers who might pay to go to these experts' seminars or subscribe to their systems than to actually trade the systems themselves and potentially lose. These experts might also get kickbacks from the brokers they recommend. It is entirely possible, however, that if they align everybody the right way and engage these people to trade in the market, there may be benefits of scale that help them with their own trading. A first-in/first-out strategy before others join the trade is akin to front-running, if there is sufficient weight behind the trade.

The FX market is vast, and it will swallow up most people over the long run. This book aims to inspire every budding trader to help avoid that fate by approaching currency trading with dis-cipline and a strategy. If you can combine hard work with disci-pline, find a true competitive advantage, pledge sufficient capital, and keep controls in place, then you can truly win big. But before you risk your capital, you must be serious about your plan—otherwise, your venture into FX trading will be more painful and less enjoyable than a visit to a casino resort.

DOING THE WORK: FOCUSING YOUR EFFORTS ON DEVELOPING A WINNING STRATEGY

Hard work is the first principle of success. It is very important to follow up an idea by researching it and testing it. This applies across the board. It relates equally to technical analysis or options trading or to following a global macro strategy. You will have a better chance of winning if you have actually put some time into working out how you are going to win.

For example, George Soros has a phenomenal work ethic and is considered one of the greatest macro traders of all time. He has an uncanny ability to process information about the global economy, and he understands how countries' internal economic policies affect not only their domestic economies but also their relationships with other countries. This interaction between countries is constantly flowing with states of harmony and equilibrium moving across many factors to potential disharmony and disequilibrium. These factors can be as simple as interest rates, costs of labor, imports and exports, tariffs, and taxes. It is the pressures of disequilibrium that in his mind pave the way for movements in currencies, bonds, equities, and commodities.

Soros's ex-trading partner Jim Rogers is also renowned for his work ethic. In Jack Schwager's *Market Wizards*, Rogers, when describing how he approaches predicting whether a country will have inflation or deflation, mentions that he looks at money supply, government deficits, inflation figures, the financial markets, and government policy. Rogers left his partnership with Soros in the Quantum Fund in 1980. He then traveled around the world before writing of his experiences in his book *Investment Biker*. Whenever you hear Rogers speak, there is a certain straightforwardness, tangibility, and authenticity about what he says. His arguments, while sometimes unflatteringly forthright, are compelling because he is so well-read and he has traveled so widely. In many ways he is a Currency King himself, and he is definitely a man who has an incredible capacity to assimilate information.

Another ex-Soros partner and hedge fund manager, Victor Niederhoffer, is also famous for his thoroughness and quantitative skills. Niederhoffer, who is credited with helping many traders make hundreds of millions of dollars, examines relationships in just about anything, whether they be technical analyses or music scores, and he relates his findings to price movements in the financial markets. His brilliant book *The Education of a Speculator* is a must read. Sadly for Niederhoffer, his two successful funds, each making high double-digit returns for many consecutive years, abruptly closed after the market meltdowns in 1997 and 2007.

Billionaire John Henry, who is considered one of the greatest ever trend followers, started out hedging crops for farmland that he owned. His family farmed corn and soybeans, and Henry learned the basics of price risk and hedging with respect to their crops. He analyzed price action for data going back many years, and he created his own trading system. Devoid of human emotion, the system traded all commodity markets from either a long or a short perspective. He then tuned the system to trade currencies too, and he became a hugely successful currency trader, going on to run funds of many billions.

There are endless examples of how doing the work pays off. An unidentified genius has successfully worked out how to win at the Hong Kong races. Ben Mezrich's entertaining book *Bringing Down the House* chronicles how a group of MIT students figured out how to beat the casinos at blackjack. And think of the work and application of the many brilliant men and women in sports.

In a nonfinancial markets sense, working hard can get you a leg up too. Think about it. Work hard, get into a good school, and get a career in a profession of your choosing. Doing the work opens doors, which in turn opens more doors, which in turn opens more still. Many people have gone a long way by using connections as well. Dale Carnegie's *How to Win Friends and Influence People* is all about a strategy to do just that. There are hundreds of clubs and cliques that help their members get a leg up, whether it is old school clubs, university clubs, Masons, Rotary, religious clubs, industry clubs, and even FX market clubs. These can all help people get started. In the financial markets it certainly helps your career if you start off at the right bank, for example, and yes, there are alumni clubs for investment bankers too. However, a word of caution: if hard work gets you membership into these clubs, don't violate the principle of a legitimate competitive advantage (covered in full in the next section). Unfortunately, within the financial markets a few cliques and cartels of dealers have received the full scrutiny and force of the regulators for rigging prices in FX, gold, and interest rates.

Doing the work can get you to a place where you might be able to knock on the right door and network with the "right" people, but this is arguably a small competitive advantage only in a sycophantic sense. Is that really fulfilling? And can it possibly lead to making billions in the currency markets? I would argue "No!" on both counts. The people highlighted in this book are almost entirely self-made, and while one or two now wish to be remembered for philanthropy and not necessarily for the way in which they made their money, there isn't too much of a whiff of networking about any of them. Their brilliant minds, ruthlessness, cunning, courage, and belief in themselves are what make them stand out from the rest. Their work is associated with finessing their ideas and businesses and making money—lots of it. In Michael Kaufman's book *Soros*, he mentions that Soros rarely has friends other than in transactional relationships. There are no clubs involved, and very likely Soros is more often the "winner" in the relationship.

FINDING A COMPETITIVE ADVANTAGE

In the financial markets, competitive advantage can trigger out-size returns, so it always helps to have this competitive edge. But two things need to be said. One, the edge must be legitimate, and two, it must be real—that is, not just perceived. For example, a back-tested technical analysis strategy may yield excellent results. But the past is not now, nor is it the future. It may be a great strategy, but it is not a competitive advantage.

In itself, strategy is a good thing, and along with discipline, it forms a solid foundation for trading. In the example of the technical system, if human emotion and error can be eliminated from the equation—that is, if the trading strategy can be automated—then it is quite possible that the system may work, although it would be difficult to predict for how long and to what scale. To win big, there needs to be more: a certainty that allows a trader to trade with a winning confidence. That certainty is a competitive advantage.

Competitive advantage forms a large part of the winning process, and when it is coupled with scale, gains of significant magnitude can be made. In terms of time, competitive advantage may last only a matter of seconds to several months or even years. Therefore, the opportunity must be seized, and in order for that to be done, the context of the situation must be taken into account with respect to the trading strategy employed. The following chapters will explain in detail how each Currency King developed and exploited his competitive advantage.

As mentioned before, the foreign exchange market is massive, and the odds are stacked against individual traders. The playing field is not at all level, and traders will have to contend with spreads, commissions, slippage, and other hidden fees and charges. Add to this a lack of information and lack of knowledge of order books and flows and it's clear that most traders start off at a distinct disadvantage.

The Five Forces

A great deal of academic analysis has been written on competitive advantage, and of this, Michael Porter's "five forces" has been the preeminent guide. A Harvard Business School professor, Porter is considered a world expert on strategy and leading change. In essence, Porter has suggested that across all industries, the underlying drivers for profitability can be summarized by his five forces: the external factors outside of the ever present industry-specific competition (Porter's "industry rivalry") that company strategists must consider. These forces include the threat of new entrants, the threat of substitute products and services, the bargaining power of buyers, and the bargaining power of suppliers. Firms must consider these forces to ascertain whether they can compete and sustain a competitive edge.

With respect to the FX market, this theory holds especially well for the sell side—that is, banks and brokers. Traders and hedge funds would be considered the "buy-side bargainers."

If I take an example of retail FX brokerages as part of that market and apply Porter's five forces, then we see that the buy-side bargainers may wish for security of funds, competitive spreads, best execution, competitive margin rates, low financing charges, zero slippage on stop-losses, and transparent and fair rollover charges. Banks that supply pricing want to attract non-toxic flow in return for fine pricing. (They wish to internalize this flow from the many brokers they provide pricing to, effectively running a very large risk book.) Banks will also wish to extract a profit from prime brokering services. There are other non-bank price makers who may additionally add liquidity to attract flow. These providers may run flows or quickly off-load flows depending on the risk management algorithms they employ. New entrants will always be on the sidelines, and in order to gain market share, they will absolutely need to cater to the needs of clients. Of course, if equity markets are rallying, then CFD providers who offer CFDs on equities may act as competitors. Similarly, warrants have been popular in the past, as have binary products.

I would argue that there is at least one other force in the FX market, and that is the *force of the regulator*. Regulators can impose capital restrictions, margin restrictions, and onerous reporting obligations and also enforce costly operational functions that may inhibit new entrants to the market or, in some cases, squeeze existing companies from the market. In Japan, for example, margin rates were increased over the space of two years from 1 percent to 2 percent to 4 percent. This forced a lot of companies to leave the industry. In Hong Kong, paid-up capital requirements for a new broker are HK$30 million, or about US$4 million, which could be considered a barrier to entry.

The people who have lost money with disreputable FX brokers may welcome regulatory intervention as a good thing. That leaves several of the stronger original brokers, who continue to make outsize profits for their owners. For what I have described as a disadvantage to traders is actually an advantage to brokerages. It is a fairly well known fact that some retail brokerages really care only about clients that lose money because a lot of them run what are known as "B Books" on client flows. They analyze clients singularly and as a whole, and they identify and categorize those clients, hedging flow from the good traders and running a book on the not-so-good traders' business. Some people are so bad at trading that there are even some algorithms that can take this information and do exactly the opposite of what these clients are doing and then leverage those positions! Similarly, these brokers may go with the good flows.

Retail brokerages have good technology, good analytics of client information, and generally inexpensive staff. The first two allow them to offer very competitive pricing. Inexpensive staff can administer the business, sell the electronic product, and onboard clients. There are several retail FX billionaires, some of whom will be highlighted in Chapter 5.

Once again, apart from technology, information, and order flow, capital and staff can give larger-scale organizations a competitive advantage. There are definitely superior institutional platforms among the banks vying for higher rankings in the various FX polls that circulate. Capital allows those banks to run bigger risks on their hedging algorithms. Experienced traders can use institutional flows to generate profits for the banks. Experienced salespeople might leak information to other clients to generate greater order flows.

For those traders looking for a competitive edge, then, it pretty much boils down to superior technology, superior staff, best and speedy execution, innovation, flexibility, low transaction and financing costs, information, and secrecy. If we combine these with original thinking, strategy, and discipline, we have nearly all the ingredients for a competitive advantage— something that differentiates us from the average ill-informed, ill-disciplined, disorganized normal trader. Something that can help us win!

Information as a Competitive Advantage

The value of information goes back a long way. In 1815 Nathan Rothschild received the information one full day ahead of the British government's receiving it that Wellington had been victorious at the Battle of Waterloo. Although he didn't trade until after the news was made public, Rothschild subsequently bought up government bonds, figuring that the government would wish to borrow less after the war. His trade netted him a 40 percent profit. In today's financial markets, there is a difference between trading on publicly available information and trading on inside information. Trading on inside information is illegal, and regulators have cracked down severely on individuals who are deemed to have traded in such a manner. In contrast, there is nothing wrong with trading on publicly available information, and it is advantageous to receive that information in as timely a manner as possible.

Timely information can be critical, especially for high-frequency traders (HFTs) who can buy and sell in fractions of a second. If we are to believe the efficient market hypothesis—that all market information is reflected in the price—then HFTs seek to beat that hypothesis, by milliseconds, or as is now the case, millionths of a second. If they can trade the market on news before the news is widely read, the efficient market hypothesis doesn't hold for them the way it does for the rest of us slowpokes.

News travels a great deal faster than it did in 1815. Two hundred years later, we see Warren Buffett's fast-moving *Business Wire* newsfeed. Buffett actually restricted high-frequency traders from subscribing to the *Business Wire*. The split-second timing in which the high-frequency traders could turn news into trades was considered too much of a competitive advantage for this select group.

In the realm of HFTs, some may be arbitrageurs. Arbitrage traders look for price inefficiencies. They require speed of execution and a good deal of secrecy. There's no point in telling the world about the arbitrage because the market will become more efficient as more traders exploit the arbitrage. Other HFTs look for technological efficiencies by collocating servers at exchanges. Every millionth of a second is an edge. One trader at an HFT company described its trading strategy as "simultaneous hedging with a market-neutral strategy." (In FX vernacular this is largely known as *scalping*—a practice that causes a lot of rancor with the bank price providers.)

Keeping the Competitive Edge

There is a tendency for smart ex-investment bankers to set up or go to work for hedge funds and commodity trading advisors (CTAs), even more so now with regulatory scrutiny over banking bonuses. In general, the competitive advantage that hedge funds have stems from their intellectual property, their staff, and the confidentiality they offer. In all scenarios, an edge is only an edge if it remains an edge. For example, George Soros wrote about staying ahead of the curve in his book *Soros on Soros*. In generating multiyear outsize returns, he has always remained flexible, adaptive, and innovative, seizing opportunities as they have presented themselves.

It must be remembered that the market is bigger than an individual, a fund, or even an investment bank. The market is also a very humbling place. Divulging intellectual property or secrets to the market can expose overleveraged funds or undercapitalized and exposed brokers and banks to the bankruptcy bin. There are plenty of examples of this, some of which I cover later in this chapter in the section on risk management.

If you are really serious about winning, in addition to work and tenacity, you need to do everything you possibly can to give yourself a fighting chance. It is beneficial to find the right broker or bank not only for information flow but also for execution. It is important to have a disciplined approach to trading so that you are not bewildered when things don't go your way. It is advisable to be innovative and flexible rather than stubborn and resolute. In *Market Wizards*, Ed Seykota is quoted as saying, "There are old traders, there are bold traders, but there are no old, bold traders." Finally, it pays to have a little bit of luck. Because even dead certainties sometimes have a habit of losing.

SCALING UP A COMPETITIVE ADVANTAGE

FX trading is scalable. The market turns over $5 trillion or more each day, which leaves billions of dollars of profits up for the taking.

In short, scale in FX trading equates to leverage in a pure trading sense. It can also equate to the balance sheet in another sense.

The bottom line is that scaling is money or gearing that enables you to take more risk. Arguably it's best to put through a trade in a liquid currency that can absorb your trade without moving the market too much. This is as important when you put through the trade as it is when you ultimately take a profit (or loss). There is nothing worse than seeing losses compound (or profits erode) when stops get slipped or when markets mysteriously move against you when you take profit. And it goes without saying that the bigger the amount, the bigger the potential slippage. If you have a competitive advantage, scale is super important because it literally allows you to "do more." Doing more without alerting the market is also a competitive advantage. Having more than one broker or bank is also useful because you are less likely to be pitched if you are within your margin limits. If the trade is good and you have a competitive advantage and a no-lose (or very small chance of losing) scenario, leverage is the key to outsize profits.

There are some fantastic stories of billion-dollar trades resulting in massive gains for courageous investors. There are also as many horror stories. Scale is great, but it needs to be coupled with appropriate and effective risk management systems. The market is bigger and smarter than the individual, and the horror stories tend to involve the market discovering the competitive advantage of the traders, whose trades then ultimately failed as their edge disappeared.

Horror Stories

While this section is not meant to highlight traders who lost the lot with overleveraged positions, it is definitely noteworthy to emphasize the incredible scale that some markets offer. If we take silver as an example, then it is utterly amazing that Nelson Bunker Hunt and his brother William Herbert Hunt managed to accumulate silver holdings of 3.1 million kilograms (100 million ounces) in 1979. Effectively, they cornered the silver market and drove prices up from $11 per ounce to $50 per ounce, making billions on the way. Of course they overleveraged, and once the New York metals market (COMEX) raised margin rates, they were caught high and dry. Silver collapsed as they reduced their positions, and apart from losing a fortune, they then had to file for bankruptcy due to the lawsuits that ensued from speculators who had lost money because of the Hunts' market manipulation.

Another disastrous high-scale trade was that of Yasuo Hamanaka, former chief copper trader at Sumitomo Corporation. Known as "Mr. Copper" or "Mr. Five Percent" because of the size of his position in the market (and his attempts to corner it), Yasuo managed to rack up losses of $2.6 billion and then got eight years in jail for trying to hide those losses. His brokers at Winchester Holdings bought themselves apartments in Monaco with the millions they made from him.

And finally to gold, it only gets better. The then U.K. Chancellor of the Exchequer Gordon Brown's 1999 attempt at reverse alchemy stands outs as the largest billion-dollar bullion blunder in history. Brown started to sell gold at $282.4 per ounce in exchange for foreign currency deposits. The United Kingdom sold about 395 tons of gold at an average price of $275 per ounce shortly before a 12-year rally in the price of the precious metal. Brown's bet in gold would have achieved a marked-to-market loss of more than $15 billion by 2011. He got promoted to prime minister!

Cornering the FX Market

Cornering is illegal, but can you really corner the FX market? Arguably not in major currency pairs, but they can definitely be moved. When Stanley Druckenmiller approached George Soros with his short sterling-mark idea, he originally wished to short 4 billion GBP. Soros said "not enough," and the pair shorted

10 billion. The Bank of England held its bid for a short period of time, and then it caved in with the weight of waves and waves of short selling. The multiplier effect of a fund shorting 10 billion pounds, along with bank traders, other hedge funds, CTAs, and institutional herding, buried the pound and scarred the Conservative government of the time with notorious ignominy, while at the same time elevating Soros to the status of mythical hedge fund guru—and of course netting him a billion-dollar profit!

One particular trade that had a scalable limit was the Indian rupee onshore/offshore arbitrage. In a nutshell, there was an arbitrage between the onshore Indian rupee price as traded on the exchange and the offshore or non-deliverable forward price as offered by investment banks. Both rates settled at the same price on "fixing" day, with the "fix" set by the Reserve Bank of India (RBI). The reason this trade had a scale limit was that there were only a few brokers, perhaps seven or eight, who could offer the offshore price. These brokers were limited by their capital and their prime brokers' appetite for collecting large one-way bets on the Indian rupee. It is a trade I was involved in for about five years. The overall monthly position we calculated at about $10 to $15 billion. Bearing in mind that the arbitrage could yield about 1 to 2 percent per month, the profits from this trade across the market participants was anything between $100 million and $200 million per month, or up to $2,500 million per year, which is a nice trade! The trade was somewhat kiboshed by the banks widening their spreads and increasing margin rates—a sure way to destroy any arbitrage!

In less liquid pairs, someone will always call foul. In 1987, Andy Krieger managed to short hundreds of millions of New Zealand dollars using Bankers Trust's balance sheet and by trading options. His trade was arguably bigger than the entire money supply of New Zealand. The kiwi plummeted, and Krieger netted millions in profits for the bank. Allegedly all sorts of threats from the New Zealand government came Bankers' way. But the trade was legitimate, and so was the profit. The same goes for Soros and the Bank of England sterling-mark (GBP/DEM) trade. Unfortunately for Nelson Bunker Hunt, his competitive advantage was not deemed legitimate, the market knew his position, and he was decoupled by having taken too much leverage when the market went against him.

Carry Trades and Options

More scalable trades can be taken in liquid pairs, such as the U.S. dollar versus the yen and euro. A very popular trade for years has been known as the *carry trade*. The theory is pretty simple: invest in a country and currency where you get paid more interest and borrow in a country and currency where you pay less interest. The difference is the profit. This trade holds well if the currency stays stable. It is doubly good if the currency in which you invest appreciates and the currency in which you borrow depreciates. But all hell breaks loose if there is some catastrophic event that drives investors into safe haven currencies, such as the yen, and the carry trade collapses. (Two well-documented events in which carry trades dissolved are the 1998 Russia default and the 2008 subprime mortgage crisis.) There was even a name for the ubiquitous yen carry trader: "Mrs. Watanabe." We haven't heard as much about her since, but prior to 2008 she was almost a cartoon pinup of how to successfully trade virtually anything against the yen.

So how do you make a billion dollars in liquid currencies? How about this: place $100 million in margin, leverage up 100 times, and make 10 percent. The trouble is that your timing needs to be near perfect, and not all of us have $100 million where we would employ such insane amounts of leverage. Having said that, while I cannot attest to the margin he placed, I do know of one individual who held a multi-billion-dollar kiwi-yen position with a carry that arguably earned a billion dollars in interest a year. As I said, all is good until the carry trade falls out of bed.

This unfortunate trader took huge losses when the yen appreciated after the 2011 earthquake in Japan.

Options are a way in which to achieve scale, but remember that you have to cover the premium in order to make profits. While this is doable, there are lots of "Greeks" that need to be factored into the price. These include time (theta), volatility (vega), and interest rates (rho), not to mention delta (the change in an option's value as a result of the change in the underlying asset's price) and gamma (the change in an option's price resulting from a change in the delta of an option). Banks and brokers have a habit of mispricing these Greeks in their favor, which by and large means that 90 percent of options expire out-of-the-money or become profitless.

Why not sell options? Why not indeed? First, if you go down that track, profits are limited to premiums while losses are potentially limitless. This may be a strategy solely for the bold. Second, whomever you sell the option to needs to pay you enough for the risk you take on. Normally that will be a bank or broker, which may not pay you a fair price. Having said that, arguably one of the greatest Currency Kings of them all—Urs Schwarzenbach—does exactly that: he sells options. (More on him in Chapter 4.)

APPROPRIATELY AND EFFECTIVELY MANAGING RISK

In the previous section on scale, I wrote that if you are going to survive in the market, you will require appropriate and effective risk management for the size of your trade. For example, one of the fundamental preconditions of trading is to have a stop-loss in place. It is good discipline for a start, and it also gives an approximation of the extent of a potential loss because stops should be based on capital allocated to a trade. Trade without some notion of a stop, and you are asking for trouble. If you show overconfidence, you will quickly be taught a lesson. If you are lucky, you will make money. If you are courageous and lucky, perhaps you will make a lot of money. If you are courageous and unlucky, you will blow up.

Overleveraging and overtrading are probably the two mistakes that kill off most traders in the FX market. Overleveraging is often spurred by the fantasy that you are smarter than the market, and it affects small and big traders alike. Ultimately you are done in by relatively small market moves. If you are 50 times leveraged, then it takes only a 2 percent move in the market to wipe you out. The propensity for all manner of traders to overleverage has caused major catastrophes in all sorts of markets, and it will continue to do so. Leverage can magnify your gains, as when scaling a competitive advantage, but it can also compound your losses. It also erodes your capital because it amplifies the cost of spreads and commissions that you pay to brokers.

Likewise, overtrading and paying away the spread is another way to erode your capital. Often called "gambler's ruin," the term implies that if you continue to bet even on a fair toss of a coin, then ultimately brokers' commissions will eat into your capital until you are left with nothing.

A combination of overleveraging and overtrading is akin to trading suicide.

The only true way to make effective use of leverage and frequent trading is if you have a genuine competitive advantage, as discussed earlier in the chapter. Arbitrage and high-frequency market making or taking come close to representing an effective use of leverage. The simultaneous or near simultaneous buying and selling of a product—whether it be on the same market or slightly different markets to take advantage of favorable price discrepancies—is an excellent low-risk, market-neutral strategy, and it is hence relatively impervious (save for an out trade) to market movements. (Arbitrageurs and HFTs will be covered in Chapter 6.)

Leverage is the proverbial double-edged sword. Employ it successfully and you will make outsize, even spectacular, returns. Too much leverage, however, can have terrifying consequences in all manner of ways, both in life and in the financial markets. How many times have we heard when describing failure that so-and-so may have overextended himself a little?

A Vicious Cycle

For some reason a perverse human characteristic, closely linked to the fantasy that we are smarter than the market, often takes hold when losses start to accumulate. Humans run losses far, far more than they run profits. So by definition, far more people lose money than make it. Doubling down on poor trades, by and large, is akin to doubling the leverage employed in a trade. It has been a strategy used extensively by quant equity funds, particularly previous to the 2007 to 2008 subprime blowout. (Their value models at the time simply advised to buy undervalued stock in a falling market and in many cases sell overvalued stock. As other hedge funds deleveraged out of liquid stock to stave losses from subprime debt positions, perversely undervalued stocks became more undervalued and overvalued stocks continued to rise.) However, when the market sniffs a kill—a weak market participant in trouble because of overleverage—or a "black swan" event happens, that is, a statistically "virtually impossible" event—then all models advocating doubling down only help advance the destruction of capital and capitulation to either a margin call or a total wipeout.

For many years the strategy of many Wall Street investment banks was to reward traders for their courageous ability to trade big and take risk, which inevitably was paying for people to withstand the anxiety and pain of running both winning and losing positions. Lucky traders made money, took big positions, and got paid millions. Unlucky traders took big positions, lost money, got paid less money, and got sacked. This all sounds pretty fair until you add in the fact that unsuccessful traders usually ended up at other banks where they enjoyed the kudos of being big hitters, and so pretty soon they would employ the same strategy, taking on big risks leading to either one of the two outcomes mentioned above.

So, in the pre-subprime era, the ultimate financial markets job was to work for a Wall Street trading powerhouse. With bonuses in the region of 10 to 15 percent of profits, one successful year could pay for a lifetime on the beach. For all traders, taking bigger risks won every time: win, you get paid; lose, you work at another bank elsewhere (doubtless on a huge salary because banks are not allowed to disclose how good or bad you actually are when they are requested to give a reference).

And so the cycle continued.

We could well call it a "hubristic vicious cycle": supremely arrogant traders took enormous risks on behalf of investment banks, spurred on by overambitious CEOs, in turn spurred on by shareholders' aspirations and industry performance metrics. The asymmetrical reward to risk for traders was skewed massively in their favor.

The downside risks of big traders, maverick traders, or rogue traders have led to several high-profile bankruptcies in the last two decades and a little bit of jail time for a few. Trading led to the bankruptcy of Barings Bank (where the queen of England held a private account), Long-Term Capital Management (LTCM), Bear Stearns, and Lehman Brothers. It led to the high-profile dismissal or resignation of traders at Morgan Stanley (Howie Hubler), J.P. Morgan (Bruno Iksil), Societe Generale (Jerome Kerviel), and UBS (Kweku Adoboli). And in recent years it led to the blowup of brokerage MF Global. Billions may have been wiped off the value of the financial markets, but then in many ways, the financial markets demanded that kind of risk taking.

Risk Management Case Studies: LTCM and MF Global

The disastrous downfall of Long-Term Capital Management (LTCM) is an almost perfect case study for risk management (Roger Lowenstein's book *When Genius Failed* aptly describes the sensational rise and fall of the original super quant hedge fund). LTCM had several competitive advantages: certainly it was run by some of the smartest quants in Wall Street at the time, including Myron Scholes, who is famous for his part in devising the Black-Scholes options pricing model. LTCM had done the work and created superlative trading models as well. It also had plenty of cash (initially) to support its positions, and it had investment banks desperate to give it credit and leverage.

One of LTCM's favorite trades was selling *on-the-run bonds* and buying *off-the-run bonds* with the same expiry date and rate of interest (essentially the same bond issued on different dates, but with exactly the same characteristics and expiry). The on-the-run bonds tended to be more liquid and sold for a premium, but the price of the two bonds converged at expiry. Because of LTCM's high-profile alumni and the reverence with which LTCM's traders were treated in the market, LTCM was able to negotiate very inexpensive credit charges and extract huge amounts of leverage from its counterparties. It put on massive positions in this trade as well as other convergence strategies.

The calamitous capitulation of the fund and destruction of wealth can be considered more hubris than having a march on the capital markets. LTCM believed in its models, period. It doubled down and leveraged up. Events that it opined were not feasibly possible actually happened. LTCM blew up the way any other fund blows up when it overextends itself. The secrets of its positions and vulnerability hit the market, and the market took LTCM out. The market bought on-the-run bonds and sold off-the-run bonds on a scale that overwhelmed LTCM. The convergence didn't happen until after LTCM had been squeezed out of the market.

LTCM understood three-quarters of the ideas championed in this chapter correctly: doing the work, finding a competitive advantage, and scaling that competitive advantage. It made one fundamental error: it didn't model for fat-tail risk. Its models suggested that it was inconceivable that it should fail. But it did, by overleveraging itself. And none of its quants were able to manage its risk appropriately.

Equally intriguing is the case of MF Global because it involves the ignominious humbling of a giant risk taker and courageous trader, Jon Corzine, the former CEO of Goldman Sachs and governor of New Jersey. Ironically, Corzine and Goldman Sachs made a fortune the same year as they helped sort out LTCM's failure.

Some say Corzine came to MF Global as "personal redemption" for his feelings of guilt over being ousted from Goldman Sachs, where he had held the post of joint CEO with Henry "Hank" Paulson. But maybe it was simply a love for what he did, or thought he did, best—trading. Corzine, who had made much bigger bets and had won at Goldman Sachs, will be blighted forever more as the man who brought down MF Global in the financial markets' tenth-biggest bankruptcy. But how did he get this far, and why hadn't the city learned from the rogue traders and excessive risk taking of the past? Indeed, MF Global had already been rocked once, shortly after its 2008 float, with a $150 million loss on a rogue wheat trade by the little-known broker Evan Dooley.

MF Global had spent millions updating its archaic risk management systems and practices, and it had parted company with Chris Smith, the COO who had presided over the Dooley affair. It had also bolstered nearly every corporate governance function required in a properly regulated firm. All this came at a cost. Back-office personnel, systems, and tier upon tier of managers had replaced brokers and moneymakers. Bureaucracy and internal politics had ground profitability to a halt. It could have been a scene out of *Atlas Shrugged*.

At the time, Corzine's friend and business partner JC Flowers, who had bailed out MF Global in return for preference shares, was looking at an impending loss on a bad investment. Corzine was there to make it work. Corzine wanted to create a new Goldman, and MF Global was his chance!

A dynamic, engaging, and inspirational leader, the avuncular Corzine was adored and almost worshiped by his traders and risk takers. He had commensurately wooed the board of directors into believing that he could simultaneously run a company while engaging in his passion of trading. They were overwhelmed by his pedigree and charisma, and they turned a corporate blind eye to the ever increasing scale of his trades. The only person who stood up to Corzine was the chief risk officer, Mike Roseman, who either somewhat tactfully resigned or was tactically replaced by a far less risk-averse risk manager, Mike Stockman.

In order to bolster MF Global's pitiful earnings, Corzine engaged in several gigantic matched-book repo trades, effectively buying bonds on leverage and then lending them to receive cash collateral. The trades were in government bonds in countries such as Italy, Ireland, Greece, Portugal, and Spain. His profit came from the difference between the interest which he received from the bonds he bought and what he paid in interest for the bonds he lent. The repo trade profit was booked at the inception of the trade and provided much needed profits for MF Global.

What Corzine hadn't factored into his trade was a potential government bond default in these countries, the likes of which hadn't been seen in Europe since 1998 with Russia. As it turned out, his $7 billion of positions all turned sour simultaneously, with a lack of confidence in all these euro-based countries, which in turn ramped up their interest rates and lowered the value of their bonds. As the value of his portfolio declined, Corzine was called for margin, which MF Global didn't have. There is an argument that MF Global committed the ultimate taboo by dipping into client funds to support the ailing positions, and there has been much debate over missing monies.

Either way, what did happen is that the market got spooked, MF Global's stock got pummeled, clients withdrew money, and it all ended badly soon after. Corzine's natural instincts got the better of him, and once again—as is the case for anyone who over-leverages, doubles down, or thinks he or she is smarter than the markets—the same lesson came to bear: the market is bigger than the individual!

SUMMARY

In bringing this chapter to a close, I reiterate what is written under the four main headings above. First of all, you need to do the work and come up with a compelling trading strategy, which you may very well need to test over multiple time frames. Second, it will be to your utmost advantage if you have a legitimate competitive advantage and make sure to keep that as secret as you can. Next, if this is the case, then you need to work out how scalable your trade is—in good times and bad. For example, what kind of noise does it make in the market, and how easy is it to get out in both a winning and a losing scenario? Lastly, risk management is directly proportional to scale. It's a must have! In almost every instance of trading across all markets, involving the most naturally gifted gutsy traders and mathematicians the markets have ever produced, there have been outsize blowups, and there will forever continue to be. If you apply strong discipline and risk management to your trading, you will survive.

With that said, I now delight in revealing the trading methods of some of the most successful currency traders to trade the FX market. Between them, their strategies involve global macro, option trading, technical trend following, market making, high-frequency trading, and arbitrage. The traders highlighted are all multimillionaires or billionaires, and many of them are still active participants in the market today. Their inspirational abilities and guile have made them all Currency Kings, and I hope these short trading biographies inspire any budding currency traders to think sensibly along winning lines before participating in the $5 trillion a day world of foreign exchange.

George Soros:
Global Macro King

It all begins with Soros, and Wednesday, September 16, 1992—a day that stands out as one of the United Kingdom's darkest trading days, ranking alongside Black Monday, the day the stock market crashed on October 19, 1987. This time it was currencies, and one single trader profited to such an extent that his name will be forever linked with Black Wednesday, as it is now called. On this day George Soros wrote his name into trading mythology when the Quantum Fund took the Bank of England for $1 billion. This was a trade that brought the world's attention to the foreign exchange markets and the might of Fleet Street's press to the front door of Soros's home in Onslow Gardens in South Kensington, London. From its stucco-fronted portico emerged a mild mannered hedge fund manager who spoke in broken English. He had just delivered a mighty blow to one of the grandest establishments in the world. Behind its Palladian exterior on Threadneedle Street, the aristocratic institution of the United Kingdom's sovereign bank had been laid bare by a humble Hungarian Jewish immigrant who had barely scraped through his economics course at the London School of Economics.

The day epitomized many contrasts and juxtapositions. David had slain Goliath. Calm hedge fund traders coolly executed a well-thought-out strategy while a provoked and panicked British government and central bank reacted to an untenable position. English FX traders guzzled bucketloads of champagne, having just participated in annihilating their own currency and driving the United Kingdom out of the exchange rate mechanism. Just as in cricket, the English took their hiding with grace. The world pondered whether perhaps Great Britain might wake up and start to compete—rather than assume her bygone Victorian right to free passage—in the financial markets. Soros, however, used his newfound fame and fortune to springboard himself into becoming one of the world's greatest living philanthropists, promoting and funding his belief in open societies and creating one man's unilateral foreign policy along the way.

THE EXCHANGE RATE MECHANISM SYSTEM

In 1992, the United Kingdom was just two years into its membership in the *exchange rate mechanism* (ERM), a system introduced into the European Economic Community (EEC) in 1979 aimed at achieving monetary stability among member countries. The exchange rate mechanism obliged its members to hold their currencies within certain bands relative to each other. The bands aimed to be flexible, but in fact they were rigid and constraining. Keeping inflation within preset parameters and currencies within their boundaries was proving difficult for some of the participating countries. In theory, keeping currencies within certain bands was good for stability and international trade within the pact. In practice, artificially strong or weak currencies were causing pressure on the whole mechanism, and the smart people with an objective view of affairs could sense that it was only a matter of time before there was a default. For many objective thinkers both outside and inside the financial institutions, the feeling was that the whole ERM system was doomed.

The trouble with the system was that the member countries were all at different points in their economic cycle. In freely moving markets, interest rates would necessarily need to rise and fall in order to stimulate growth or contain inflation. Interest rate hikes generally act like magnets for attracting foreign inflows of money. The money earns interest. This normally results in a strengthening of a currency. Lowering interest rates, however, sometimes leads to capital flight with a corresponding weakening of a currency. Depending on whether a country is trying to stimulate growth by reducing interest rates or contain inflation by raising interest rates, this naturally causes currencies to move against one another.

The first snap in the ERM occurred in Italy. Italy had already been given greater flexibility with its currency bands, but it still couldn't keep within them. On September 14, after joint efforts at intervention to support its currency had cost Italy, and Germany, billions of their reserves, the country devalued by 7 percent. The stage was set for an outright attack on the whole ERM. The United Kingdom was next up; the British pound was way too strong. Thatcher's economic miracle had fizzled out, and the United Kingdom was suffering from low growth and high inflation. Prior to joining the ERM, the chancellor of the exchequer, Norman Lamont, and his Treasury peers had been tracking the deutsche mark at an unofficial peg of about 3 deutsche marks to the pound. Britain had joined the ERM at GBP/DEM (sterling versus deutsche marks) 2.95, a rate that many considered unsustainably high, bearing in mind the delicate state of the U.K. economy. The ex-Chancellor Lawson's fiscal stimulated 1980s' boom was rapidly turning into the current incumbent Norman Lamont's bust.

After reunification in 1990, Germany had started to raise interest rates to contain inflation. That meant that the United Kingdom would have to follow suit in order to keep the pound within its band. In the United Kingdom, house price inflation was staggering, and many people had borrowed at exorbitant rates to get on the housing ladder. Raising interest rates would be political suicide, and the concomitant fallout in all sectors would drive unemployment back up—something the Conservative government at the time wished to avoid at all costs. The smart people in the room all knew that the pound had to devalue. The smart people were not in the government.

A THEORY OF SURVIVAL AND WINNING

At age 62, Soros was already a billionaire. Having set up the beginnings of the Quantum Fund in 1969, it had taken him only a brief 16 years to turn a little under $5 million into $1 billion, as shown in Table 2.1. Soros follows a global macro strategy, with the ability to trade markets in bonds, equities, currencies and commodities. He created his own theory for investing, which will be explained below.

Soros attributes much of his success to his teenage experiences in evading the Nazis and also to his "theory of reflexivity." He took great inspiration from both his father, Tivadar, in the war years and his philosophy professor, Karl Popper, who taught him at the London School of Economics.

In his book *The Alchemy of Finance*, Soros wrote, "If I had to sum up my qualifications, I would use one word: survival. When I was an adolescent, the Second World War gave me a lesson in survival I have never forgotten. I was fortunate enough to have a father who was a grand master in the art of survival, having lived through the Russian revolution as an escaped prisoner of war. Under his tutelage, the holocaust in Hungary served as an advanced course at a tender age. I have no doubt that my experiences as an adolescent played a major role in my subsequent success as a hedge fund manager. So did my conceptual framework."

TABLE 2.1

Quantum Fund Growth from 1969 to 1987

Date	Assets Under Management (AUM)	Net Asset Value (NAV) per Share	Percent Change
12/31/69	$6,187,701	$53.57	
12/31/70	$9,664,069	$62.71	17.5%
12/31/71	$12,547,644	$75.45	20.3%
12/31/72	$20,181,332	$107.26	42.2%
12/31/73	$15,290,922	$116.22	8.4%
12/31/74	$18,018,835	$136.57	17.5%
12/31/75	$24,156,284	$174.23	27.6%
12/31/76	$43,885,267	$282.07	61.9%
12/31/77	$61,652,385	$369.99	31.2%
12/31/78	$103,362,566	$573.94	55.1%
12/31/79	$178,503,226	$912.90	59.1%
12/31/80	$381,257,160	$1,849.17	102.6%
12/31/81	$193,323,019	$1,426.06	−22.9%
12/31/82	$302,854,274	$2,236.97	56.9%
12/31/83	$385,532,688	$2,795.05	24.9%
12/31/84	$448,998,187	$3,057.79	9.4%
12/31/85	$1,003,502,000	$6,760.59	121.1%
12/31/86	$1,567,109,000	$9,699.41	43.5%
12/31/87	$2,075,679,000	$12,554.16	29.4%

Soros applied the philosophical workings of Popper to challenge basic assumptions in economic theory. In pure science, hypotheses are tested, and it takes only one failed test to falsify a perceived truth, even if it has thousands of positive tests to support it. Nobody can reasonably know the ultimate truth.

Therefore, knowledge is imperfect. Some economic theory assumes perfect knowledge. Soros argues there is no such thing.

His conceptual framework, his theory of reflexivity, goes against conventional economic theory. Soros counters the prevailing wisdom that markets tend toward equilibrium as prescribed in Eugene Fama's "efficient market hypothesis" and says they do exactly the opposite. His view is that the financial markets have thinking participants whose investment objectives are to outperform the markets. These participants create a prevailing bias that affects the fundamentals that market prices are supposed to reflect. Market prices then tend to reflect and reinforce the prevailing bias, attracting additional speculators and participants, thus causing trends in the markets. Once the prevailing bias is considered flawed, the trends are altered and move in the opposite direction.

In a simplistic form, the diagram of a reflexive market movement is not too dissimilar to a marketing product life cycle. In the product life cycle curve in Figure 2.1, we see how the sales of a product grow over time from inception to maturity. These sales grow from the product launch and are then bolstered as early adopters come in. Next, the product starts to reach its peak in profitability, and then sales can fall away if, all things being equal, competition, price, and alternatives render the product inferior.

In the adapted example in Figure 2.2, Soros contends that the earnings per share (EPS) curve not only incorporates the underlying trend but also the influence of stock prices on that trend. The "fundamentals" that investors are interested in are reflected in the earnings per share. Here, the stock is identified as a stock with strong earnings potential. The stock price and EPS curves move together relatively harmoniously, and investors pile into the stock. The stock moves higher far more rapidly than the company earns profits. At this stage the move is overdone and recognized by the speculators, who exit the trade, leaving the followers

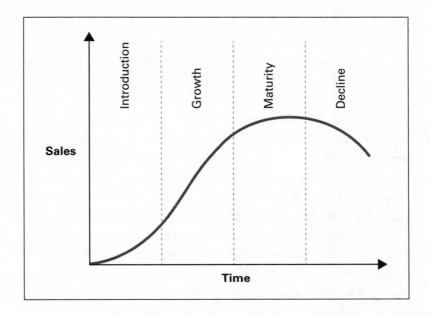

Figure 2.1 Product Life Cycle

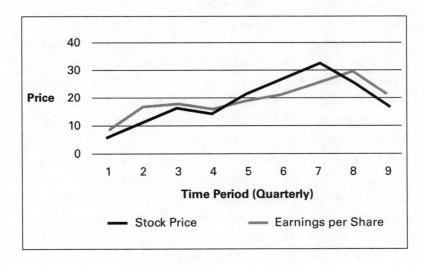

Figure 2.2 Reflexivity in Stock Prices

long in a stock in which earnings do not match perceptions of earnings. The stock moves lower!

Soros argues that markets are almost always wrong, and he looks to find the flaw. The greater the flaw, the larger the moneymaking opportunity when the prevailing bias reverses. This is not to say he will not go with the trend. Rather, he is constantly analyzing the prevailing bias and trying to determine when it has run its course.

In many ways, he considers this analysis strategy a competitive advantage. He has said, "Where I have something significant to add is in pointing out that it pays to look for the flaws. If we find them, we are ahead of the game because we can limit our losses when the market also discovers what we already know. It is when we are unaware of what could go wrong that we have to worry."[1] The added advantage of running a hedge fund is that he can also *go short*—that is, sell stocks, bonds, or currencies and therefore participate in both the movements up and down in a particular investment.

As much as Soros considers survival to be one of the key aspects of his success, another aspect is his uncanny ability to look for market opportunities. It is true to say that Soros has always had a vision. As he embarked on his financial career in the United States, his "five-year plan" was to make $500,000 and then pursue his philosophical studies. Some say you make your own luck, but in monetizing his vision, Soros, in his capacity as an arbitrage trader, was one of a few pioneers who took advantage of pricing anomalies of the same stock in two different markets, trading oil and gold shares in London and New York. He quickly made a name, and money, for himself and his firm F.M. Mayer when volatility in oil stocks erupted in tandem with the escalation of tensions in Egypt in what came to be known as the Suez Crisis.

As the crisis dissipated, Soros and a colleague discovered an incredibly profitable method of separating bonds from the warrants attached to them. They would sell the bonds to a reputable broker, who would in effect promise to deliver the warrants when they could be separated from the bonds. These delivery promises came to be known as "due bills," and they could be bought and sold in a secondary market. Once again there was an arbitrage between shares trading on exchange and those incubating in the warrants. And, once again, Soros gained riches and notoriety for himself in this market. At the same time, he networked with some of the big hitters at other much larger brokerages and investment houses.

As Soros outgrew Mayer, he quickly found a home for himself at Wertheim & Co. as a European equities analyst. Naturally, he was quite brilliant at spotting "hidden value" in stocks. He would take his findings to institutional investors and also trade stocks himself, therefore covering three functions—analysis, sales, and trading—while concurrently cultivating an impeccable apprenticeship for his future career as a hedge fund manager.

His time at Wertheim ended somewhat acrimoniously when he had to sweat out a trade that ultimately turned out well. He had to endure the ignominy of being "thrown under the bus" by a cowardly senior colleague who claimed he had no knowledge of, and certainly had not sanctioned, Soros's trading activity. So be it. Soros moved on to Arnhold and S. Bleichroeder, but not before taking a break to spend time working on his philosophical ambitions. It was at Arnhold that he would forge his partnership with Jim Rogers and from there set up probably the best-known and one of the most profitable hedge funds of all time.

The Birth of the Quantum Fund

It wasn't just luck that enabled Soros to find good trades. His stock analysis reports would often be written after visiting the companies he was following. It could be argued that in his triple role of analyst, salesperson, and trader, he was in fact doing the work of three people. And, like a magnet, he attracted others with similar appetites for hard work. In bringing Rogers to his team in 1968, he brought on a man who in his own words "did the work of six men." Rogers then, as now, could come across as prickly and opinionated, but casting his idiosyncrasies aside, the one thing he did "par excellence" was analyze stocks. An idea could quickly morph from analyzing a single stock to analyzing an entire sector. If the analysis fit into Soros's theory of reflexivity, then Soros and Rogers had a compelling reason to invest. Arnhold and S. Bleichroeder had already sanctioned setting up its First Eagle Fund in 1967 with Soros as manager. In 1969 Soros and Rogers set up a second fund, Double Eagle, a hedge fund with an initial capital of $4 million. Double Eagle had the additional advantage in that it could trade a wider range of investments and go both long and short.

The results of Double Eagle were staggering, and in four years it quadrupled in size. Because of certain conflicts of interest— namely, providing investment advice and simultaneously trading on that analysis in a fund owned by Arnhold and S. Bleichroeder— inevitably Soros and Rogers were better served going it alone. The Soros Fund launched in August 1973 with $18 million assets under management. In 1979, he changed the name to the Quantum Fund.

What differentiates Soros from Rogers is not their capacity for work or their remarkable track records for stock picking but their attitudes to scale. After 10 or so years of working together, their partnership finally ruptured over scaling up the fund and identifying, modeling, and nurturing additional personnel who could add value and help grow the fund to the next level. Here, the two men seemed to differ in their outlook. Rogers appears to have been satisfied with being intellectually superior to his peers and happy to keep the fund at about the $100 million mark. Soros wanted it to be bigger and better. Perhaps, after so much success, Rogers was keen to maintain their wealth and take smaller risks, aware that even intellectual men can suffer from hubris.

If this was the case, then Soros must be defended because it is clear in many articles about him that he is very much aware of human frailties, even his own. He cites survival as a competitive advantage, and, as would be witnessed later on in the life of the Quantum Fund, he was definitely not afraid of taking a loss if it meant that the fund would survive. In 1987, as Black Monday took hold of world stock markets, Soros stopped himself out of a huge stock portfolio at a massive loss. Just two weeks later he re-entered the markets, shorting the U.S. dollar. The fund returned 15 percent that year. The Dow Jones, a little over 2 percent.

After the departure of Rogers, apart from one down year, the fund grew massively. Once again, Soros chose an excellent partner, Victor Niederhoffer, who would remain at the fund until 1990, after which he handed over the reins to Stanley Druckenmiller. Niederhoffer was the original uber-quant, gaining a bachelor's degree in statistics and economics from Harvard and a PhD from Chicago. Niederhoffer joined Soros in 1982 from his own company, NCZ Commodities, and he would go on to put through all the fixed income and foreign exchange trades for the fund. Not only was Niederhoffer an outstanding academic and brilliant statistician but he was also a world-class hardball squash player and an accomplished chess player. His performance as a trader helped ratchet the value of the Quantum Fund into the billions. He himself claims to have taught or helped make many billionaires and multimillionaires.

Niederhoffer's skill set was to pick up nickels and dimes (in large amounts) in aimless meandering markets, a style of trading that was not so applicable to trending markets. Niederhoffer had the sound judgment to know when his particular trading style had run its course, and he retired gracefully while still ahead. As Soros admits, no one single approach to trading is correct. Sometimes markets trend, sometimes they stagnate, and arbitrages in time become efficient. With respect to Niederhoffer, Soros often remarked on Niederhoffer's integrity. The two men had different approaches to and styles of trading. Soros was open-minded enough and intuitive enough to allow for this and to follow what he considered as the right approach at the right time. His trick was, and still is, to constantly look for opportunities and to stay ahead of the curve.

At the time of the Bank of England trade, Stanley Drucken-miller was head of trading at the Quantum Fund. Although it was his idea to short sterling, it was Soros who obliged Druckenmiller to "go for the jugular" and short 10 billion pounds. In summing up Soros's competitive advantage, Druckenmiller has listed many qualities: "the ability to compartmentalize, intelligence, coolness under pressure, insight, and a critical and analytical mind."[2] Above all, though, he says it's Soros's ability to "pull the trigger!"— the sort of raw courage and intuition to upsize a big trade.

Not Just Intuition

While looking for the frailties or flaws he describes as his compet-itive advantage, Soros simultaneously looks to maximize oppor-tunities and, as he once wrote, "stay ahead of the curve." Whether as an arbitrage trader, a securities analyst and sales trader, or a currency speculator, Soros has always had the knack of making money and doing so on a scale that people can only read and dream about. Rigorous work is behind every trade, while envi-sioning the trade in a reflexive process. There is an appraisal of the risks and what could go wrong. Then there is sizing. How big depends on the situation, but if the situation requires it, Soros is not at all afraid to scale up. Criticism of self and others leads to fine-tuning of ideas and trades, and a keen sense of survival leads to modification of ideas and preservation of self and capital.

If it's all down to intuition, then Soros has lived on his wits for 70 years. It has to be more than that. He has proved beyond doubt that his theory of reflexivity works. Human behavior does manifest in trends, but beyond that it also manifests in greed, lazi-ness, and impatience. Humans like to make easy money without really understanding the dynamics of what they are investing in. Similarly, humans follow religious dogmas, political regimes, and other sets of rules without really challenging the rationale of what is behind them. Humans also panic and do illogical things. Reflexivity is the sum of these human characteristics. Intuition gauges to what extent there is a disconnect. Courage is the ability to reinforce intuition with risk taking.

THE LEAD-UP

At the beginning of 1992, the Quantum Fund was valued at about $3.1 billion, and Soros had plenty of ammunition to put together a very significant trade. From his offices on Seventh Avenue in New York, Stanley Druckenmiller would coordinate the trade, assisted by Scott Bessent and the Soros team in London.

Aside from all the banks and intermediaries in London, the key players in defending the pound were the prime minister, John Major; the chancellor of the exchequer, Norman Lamont; the home secretary, Kenneth Clarke; the foreign secretary, Douglas Hurd; and the president of the Board of Trade, Michael Heseltine. Armed with a transistor radio and working out of Admiralty House, these men were about as effective as their equipment. As will become clear, the weight of selling was colossal and ultimately overwhelming.

In truth, sterling and some of the other ERM currencies—notably the Italian lira—had been coming under pressure since mid-July, when the Bundesbank, following its monthly meeting, had raised interest rates. West Germany had to deal with the inflationary pressures of reunification with East Germany. When setting interest rates, the independent Bundesbank was mandated to look after domestic issues first.

John Major had pinned his leadership and effectively his government to a policy of keeping inflation low, thus mirroring the Bundesbank. When he had persuaded Margaret Thatcher to join the ERM and keep her premiership intact in October 1990, she almost unilaterally made the decision, despite her euro skepticism, to join the ERM at the then inflated rate of DEM 2.95 to the pound. Thatcher had been ousted in November of that year, and Major had taken on the mantel of a pro-Europe, strong pound, and low inflation policy. The trouble he faced, however, was that such a strong pound stifled exports and U.K. unemployment was on the rise. Thatcher's previous policy of promoting the United Kingdom as a nation of homeowners was beginning to look poisonous as pressure was mounting for the United Kingdom to raise its interest rates in tandem with Germany. The high interest rates meant that mortgage rates were becoming difficult for some households to repay. Worse still, some houses were losing value, putting their owners in the precarious position of having negative equity on their homes.

By mid-August there were calls for the United Kingdom to devalue the pound, but the inwardly Euro-skeptic, outwardly pro-Europe chancellor of the exchequer vigorously defended the United Kingdom's policy, stating that the government would not devalue and would do everything possible to maintain a strong pound and stay in the ERM. The Germans, while not unsympathetic to their sister nation's economic and political sufferings, had enough problems of their own. They proffered two solutions in fairly black-and-white terms. The first, devalue. The second, raise interest rates. The United Kingdom's Chancellor Lamont, however, had a third solution. He felt the Bundesbank should lower its interest rates and take some of the pressure off the struggling countries.

With this in mind, and somewhat buoyed by the fact that Chancellor Kohl had unofficially hinted that he would prefer lower German interest rates, Lamont saw the coming meeting of European finance ministers and bankers in Bath on September 4 as a chance to rectify the problem.

It was during this meeting that the salt-and-pepper-haired Norman Lamont, known as "Badger" among his peers, disposed of all cunning and political guile and came straight to the point. He virtually ordered the Bundesbank's Helmet Schlesinger to cut interest rates immediately. Schlesinger did his best to contain his fury at being treated as a subordinate, and he treated Lamont's approach with the opprobrium it deserved. He continued to play the political card that the Bundesbank address domestic issues first. He then abruptly left the meeting, metaphorically slamming the door in the U.K. chancellor's face.

The fact that there was no positive outcome from the Bath meeting was the next green light in a series of signals that would lead to the pound's demise. City traders started to accumulate German marks against weaker European currencies. First up was Italy. While the pound had a small breather and the Bank of England's traders monitored the price of the pound and intervened to keep it within its trading bands, Italy's number was by now nearly up, and in a matter of days the country would be the first to capitulate.

The Italian lira came under enormous pressure on Friday, September 11, with both the Bank of Italy and the German Bundesbank pumping in billions of dollars to defend the lira. Schlesinger had had enough and called the Italian prime minister, Giuliano Amato, to say the Germans would no longer support the lira. Essentially, Schlesinger told Amato, it was costing too much. After meeting Helmet Kohl, Schlesinger offered Italy a compromise. If Italy and some other countries devalued, Germany would cut rates simultaneously.

Amato rang John Major to relay the message. Major's positon was unambiguous. The United Kingdom would be keeping the pound in the ERM at its existing rate. He'd made this clear the night before in Glasgow at a Scottish CBI meeting. Despite Amato's pleas and assessment that the financial markets were aggressive and could well assault another currency, Major was adamant that the United Kingdom would not devalue.

Monday, September 14, was the day Italy devalued the lira by 7 percent and the Germans cut interest rates by a quarter of 1 percent. Pandemonium hit the dealing desks as those on the wrong side of the trade sought to cover their losses. They would be selling into the profit takers' bids. The contrast of delight versus disaster was plain to see. The peacocks preened their feathers. The ostriches buried their heads. The writing was on the wall for sterling, and it was just a matter of time.

If the quarter-point interest rate cut by the Bundesbank gave the United Kingdom a glimmer of hope, it would be short-lived. With Italy done, traders started to whack cable in immense quantities, with billions changing hands over the next two trading days. The Treasury convened a meeting for the evening of Tuesday, September 15, to agree to a support fund of a billion pounds to defend the pound against speculators. But just as they were about to close the meeting, they were sickened to learn that Schlesinger had made what he believed to be off-the-record comments in an interview with *Handelsblatt* journalist Werner Beckhoff, saying "that the Italian lira devaluation was not enough" and that what he wanted was a far more thorough and comprehensive devaluation from Italy and other countries.[3] This would be front-page news in the United Kingdom the next morning. The Treasury desperately called the Bundesbank and implored Schlesinger to retract his comments, but the comments remained "on the record." If he had slammed the door in Bath, he was now giving the British the proverbial stinkefinger. This was the final nail in the coffin. One billion pounds would not be enough.

WEDNESDAY, SEPTEMBER 16

The stage was set for a slaughter. Soros symbolizes the slaughterer, but there were many market players who encircled and disabled the U.K. currency with such bewildering ferocity that those in the

Bank of England must have felt like the 24th Regiment of Foot defending Rorke's Drift in the Zulu War in 1879. Wednesday, September 16, is likely to be a day none of them will ever forget. While the Bank of England's FX staff made for their desks for a dignified start at 8 a.m., the big guns were lining up from around the globe to start pulverizing "the Old Lady" from all angles.

In Singapore, as Asia started to transfer the trading books to London, a whiff of what was about to happen was evident in the money brokering market. The business of matching trades between intermediaries was the bread and butter of the Harlow Ueda Sassoon financial institution, and no one was more adept at this practice than Moorthy Sadasivam, who had multiple counterparties to go to for matching buys and sells in sterling. As he saw GBP/DEM trading lower, a wave of panic sellers lit up his dealer board. A high-pitched voice emanated from Manufacturers Hanover Trust Company. **Sell 5.** Sadasivam didn't even need to quote the bid/offer spread of the 10:20 market. "You sell 5 at 10!" he said.

"Who's my name?" came the reply at the other end of the phone.

"The Bank of England," Sadasivam replied.

"They're not on my list. Who are they?" came the anxious dealer's response.

"They are the U.K. central bank, my friend. We'll get back to you with the details. To recap, you sold 5 million pounds at 2.9510. Bye for now!"

In Switzerland, the Swiss banking desks had an hour head start on London. Beating up USD/CHF (dollars versus Swiss francs) usually kept these bankers entertained in the afternoons after lunching together, but this was a Wednesday morning, and these people were primed for bashing a different currency. They had already been shorting (selling) sterling before the Bank of England traders came in but in nothing like the scale they would be trading in over the rest of the trading day.

The people at the mighty Goldman Sachs were at their desks on London's Fleet Street well before 6.30 a.m. The enormous Fixed Income Currencies and Commodities dealing room on the second floor of Peterborough Court was always abuzz with activity, but today it would zone in on the FX department's small area of the floor. Goldman had two remarkable economists in Gavyn Davies and David Morrison on its team. Morrison had quite a following, and for a short time some argued that his utterances and conjectures actually moved markets. He had made a name for himself as somewhat of a sterling guru calling for a higher pound in previous years. Now, however, along with most of the City, he was calling it lower, and with Davies they had been calling sterling short in their morning meetings for weeks. Having correctly predicted Italy's devaluation and making a small fortune in doing so, the FX desk was brimming with confidence.

The Goldman dealing desk had made markets to some of the biggest hedge funds in the industry and was no stranger to taking huge risks on behalf of the house. Under the leadership of Mike O'Brien and fully sanctioned from the top down, Goldman's prop traders were good to go. Among them was Larry Becerra, a larger-than-life, boots and jeans–wearing, Harley-riding Chicagoan cowboy with a propensity for hitting home runs. And riding in tandem, Goldman's flow traders were deft and alert, ready to catch and mirror any unusually large orders. There would soon be an unusually large amount of sterling going through Goldman's desk.

Heading east along St. Paul's to 119 Cannon Street, there was a very junior Ross Donaghue, in his first weeks at U.K. money broker Godsell Astley and Pearce, who had just gotten the bacon sandwiches and coffees for his bleary eyed colleagues when he was called away from the USD/JPY (dollars versus yen) desk and asked to be an extra pair of hands on cable (sterling versus dollar, or GBP/USD) for the day. This would be a baptism of fire for the engaging and affable 17-year-old, something he admits he has never seen the like of since. Along with the U.K. entities of Harlow's and Marshall's, many money brokers would make their annual profit in just one day!

And continuing our journey to Devonshire Square, just off Liverpool Street, Barry Hannen had just finished writing the morning's currency rollover tickets at Prudential Bache, and he recalls the action starting at about a few seconds past 7 a.m. Prudential Bache serviced many hedge funds and commodity trading advisors, a lot of its clients being trend followers. It had the capacity to execute very large orders for very big names. But there was only one big name out there that day: Soros. In their darkened dealing room, Dimitri Nicolic was in charge of the GBP book. A cool cucumber with the nimble movements of a boxer, Nicolic dealt in cars in his quieter moments and raced Ferraris at Brands Hatch on the weekends. Pretty soon he would need all his dexterity and speed to keep pace with the free-falling pound!

In the London FX market in the 1990s, the go-to banks for sterling tended to be the U.K. commercial banks such as Midland, Lloyds, Barclays, NatWest, and RBS. Staffed with an eclectic mix of colorful, mainly British characters from all walks of life, these rooms tended to be a stew of cigarette smoke, last night's beer, and a chorus of cursing and profanities.

At NatWest, the cable desk of five was headed up by 30-year-old Nigel Mathews along with John Ramkin as his number 2. Ramkin, as the interbank dealer, was in for the busiest and most stressful day of his life. Already an 18-year veteran at NatWest, Ramkin had worked his way steadily up the FX ranks and felt privileged, alongside his colleagues, to be one of the bank's market makers in its premier currency.

They had all been out with Jim Trott and his Bank of England dealers only the night before. Trott and his team would regularly court the commercial bank dealers, gleaning information about who was trading cable. This generally took the form of a 9 p.m. call to the various clearing banks. When the Bank of England closed for the day, the commercial banks would still make markets in cable, both in London and then in the United States. The Bank of England dealers at this stage would normally be at home, armed with a Reuters pager that sent them price messages and a mobile phone the size and weight of a brick. If cable was getting close to touching one of its bands, then in the absence of placing the order through its own desk, the home-based Bank of England dealers would instruct the commercial banks to "sell" or "buy cable as noisily as possible." On the evening of September 15, the Bank of England dealers had a particular interest in where the big flows were coming from, perhaps sensing that the next day was going to be volatile. Trott and his team, having gone out for dinner with the NatWest dealers, unofficially briefed them to be on their guard.

It seems uncanny in this day and age that the flimsy defense of the U.K. currency was orchestrated from the homes of the Bank of England dealers whose days were spent doing a 10-hour shift and whose nights and sleep were interrupted by the buzz of a Reuters pager or a call from one of the clearing bank's overseas desks. And it's not as if the traders had much ammunition with which to defend sterling. The U.K. Treasury department's grasp of the situation was so naïve and out of touch that they had allocated a "war chest" of just GBP 1 billion to save the pound from falling out of the ERM. And this too just days after Italy had devalued.

So, over beer, wine, and steak, the dealers from NatWest and the Bank of England enjoyed their dinner, and with duty bound protocol, while they offered information about overall positioning, the dealers did not divulge names so as to protect the anonymity of their clients. The U.S. flow of information could be extremely useful in gauging the positioning of various funds, banks, and corporations. Overall, the Americans were positioned short sterling and had been steadily building an enormous position. It was becoming clear to Jim Trott that the Bank of England was the last line of defense, holding sterling from a dramatic collapse.

At the helm of Barclays was Humphrey Percy, an English aristocrat in charge of a barrow full of dealers. In other dealing rooms, the head trader might not even have passed an exam in basic mathematics, but somehow, simple mental arithmetic and a cool head had led to career advancement in probably the toughest of all banking departments. In the quieter moments, dealing rooms would be a laugh a minute, but when the markets moved or economic figures came out, there would be an intensity and a focus that are difficult to replicate in any walk of life. Almost instantaneously, banter and ribbing would be replaced with precision and concentration, and then just as soon as the chaos returned to order, the high jinks, laughter, and ribbing would start again. No place for the shy or half-hearted, dealing rooms could be cauldrons of frenzied activity with political correctness cast aside in many heated moments during the trading shift. For such a high-paced market, errors were typically very few, and as far as teamwork was concerned, FX teams could really be compared only to well-oiled machines, slipping effortlessly through the gears and speeding from zero to 60 and back again in the blink of an eye. As the day ended and the trading books were handed over to New York, the dealers could often be found unwinding in the pubs, still talking in overloud dealing speak, reliving the moments of the trading day as the adrenaline seeped away, replaced by beer and then the prospect of a far less exciting subway or train ride home.

Electronic platforms of the early 1990s were pretty much in their nascence, the only electronic communication network (ECN) of any repute being Reuters Dealing. Reuters also happened to be a favored tool of cable traders and was considered quite strong in the GBP/USD pair. Aside from that, it was all voice trading and paper ticket writing, with big back offices to input trades and act as a huge aids in making sure the books were balanced at the end of the day.

Other big players in the FX market were certainly Deutsche Bank, Bankers Trust, Merrill Lynch, J.P. Morgan, Morgan Stanley, Bear Stearns, Chemical Bank, Salomon Brothers, and Citibank. Although only mentioned here in name, these banks would all play their part and participate in one of FX trading's most infamous days.

The day started off muggy; there was thunder in the air. As London's bankers and traders made their way into the City, there was a tension that matched the weather outside, a heaviness that something wasn't quite right and in many a gut feeling that something big was about to happen.

John Ramkin arose as usual at 5:20 a.m. The process that got him from his bed to the office was mechanical now, and he soon found himself at Romford Station boarding the 6:10 a.m. train for the 29-minute journey to Liverpool Street. His office was just around the corner from the exit, at 135 Bishopsgate. The feeling of being a bit jaded from the night before was countered with the adrenaline of expectation of another busy day in the foreign exchange markets. The people at NatWest were nervous. For the last few days, since the Italian gasket had blown, they had been intervening on behalf of the Bank of England, buying cable in both London and New York hours.

In a normal week, trading FX in the 1990s was a hectic flurry of barking orders, filling trades, and writing reams of trading tickets. By Tuesday night, FX traders had already done the equivalent of a week's work. By the end of Wednesday evening, many desks would make the equivalent of a year's profit. To put it bluntly, there was a one-way trade that the whole world was on, and only the Bank of England, with 19 billion pounds of foreign currency reserves, was standing between the traders and a massive payday.

As Ramkin recalls, "So on Wednesday we all got in the office for 7 a.m., a bit tired from the night before, a few customers trading, but interbank did not start 'til 8 a.m. There were a few prices from the brokers to support the market in a couple of quid [GBP 2 million]. Sometimes that gives you a feel for the direction of the market. There was lots of activity on the GBP/DEM desk, as calls came in. Good two-way trades were going on. At 8 a.m. the calls started coming in on the cable desk from the usual suspects: Bankers Trust, Chemical Bank, Midland, Barclays, and a few others. All most probably asking each other and getting calls to cover. The Bankers' trader was a big player in the market, and he would often try to spoof the market and get calls out to change the direction of the pricing. But in the current market conditions, it was not a practice to carry on with. It started to get very busy very quickly, and the direction became obvious. It was soon a question of covering any sell orders as quickly as possible. My own short positions were also quickly covered because I had to buy from the market."[4]

The headlines in the tabloids could not have made worse reading. The *Daily Mail* led with "Sabotage by the Germans!" Banks, investment funds, pension funds, and hedge funds were all in the queue to sell pounds. Their willingness was unrelenting because some were still smarting from Italy's devaluation. The Bank of England started to intervene.

At Godsell's, things were starting to heat up. "We had the Bank of England on the bid and loads of names offering it," Donaghue explained. "It started off in 5s and 10s. The Old Lady just bought it all up, paying everything. Everything got filled, and then almost instantly loads more offers came in, and it went back to the floor. I'm not saying it was chaos from the outset, but man, we were busy!"[5]

At Prudential Bache there was a similar phenomenon. With its network of branch offices and large CTA client base, the dealer boards were lighting up with inquiries as to what was going on, and decent volumes were going through the trading desk. With every Reuters inquiry, there would be a shout across the desk for someone to pick it up. Usually this would be Hannen.

As near to a six-handed human supercomputer as you could get, Hannen was keeping his cool despite the escalating tension. A call came in for a price in 200 million. "Figure: 50," cried Nicolic. "Yours!" cried Hannen. "Get me calls in 20s!" cried Nicolic. The whole room immediately hit the dealer boards. "Price in 20, please." "16 bid." "Yours!" "10 bid." "Yours!" "12 bid." "Sell!" "8 bid." "Sell!" "6 bid." "Sell!" "9 bid." "Sell!" "4 bid." "Sell!" "How many have I done?" "140 here!" "That's enough." Nicolic had gotten 60 away elsewhere. With an average of 8 pips profit on his sells, he was up $160,000 on the trade.

There were also large orders going through the desks at the Swiss banks and Goldman Sachs. Typically with very large orders, a hedge fund or CTA would ask the dealers to work the order quietly in the market. Today's market was very different. With the Bank of England intervening and holding the lower band of its ERM peg, it was quite easy to off-load a billion without the rest of the market pushing the price lower. However, the Bank of England's slush fund of a billion pounds of cash was running out, and it wasn't quite 9 o'clock!

At the helm of the Bank of England, Governor Robin Leigh Pemberton, an old Etonian and Oxford graduate, was marshaling his troops. In at the dirty end was Jim Trott and his dealing team. Trading was frenetic. Paying up cable and holding the bid, the team was getting buried from all sides. Trott spoke with Eddie George, the deputy governor. They were running out of ammunition. The bank had two options to try to raise the price of sterling. It was clear that intervention wasn't working. Leigh Pemberton and his deputy, Eddie George, felt it was time to elect option 2 and put a call in to the Treasury proposing that interest rates needed to be raised.

The chancellor, Norman Lamont, was in accord and put a call into the prime minister. John Major then rapidly convened a meeting with a quorum of his senior ministers: Home Secretary Kenneth Clarke; Board of Trade President Michael Heseltine;

and Foreign Secretary Douglas Hurd. What dawned on them was the stark realization that in order to protect their ERM membership, they were effectively going to commit political hara-kari by issuing a startlingly aggressive interest hike to an economy that couldn't support it. The four men gravely sanctioned the rise, and it was communicated to the City. At 11 a.m., U.K. interest rates were raised to 12 percent.

Druckenmiller and Soros had already accumulated a net short position of about 4 billion pounds before the rate increase. With respect to the newspaper reports on Schlesinger's comments, Soros recalled, "The Bundesbank was basically egging on the speculators to speculate against the weaker currencies. And we took our cue from the Bundesbank."[6]

As the United Kingdom raised rates, he couldn't believe his luck. He pushed Druckenmiller to "go for the jugular," and the Quantum Fund started to sell sterling with alacrity. Soros continued, "We had a fairly strong sense we were on to the kill. It [the interest rate hike] indicated to us that we were in at the end game, that this was an act of desperation. So instead of restraining us, it was really an invitation to double up. To try and sell as much as possible!"[7]

Jim Trott and his beleaguered team now experienced a renewed barrage of selling. Far from bolstering the price of sterling, the City took Soros's cue. U.K. interest rates at 12 percent were unsustainable. The rate hike was a sign of weakness. It was as if the whole City took its chance to pulverize sterling. Things were heating up all over the market.

After four hours of relentless selling without pause, the atmosphere at Prudential Bache was reaching electric proportions. "Price in 10, price in 50, price in 30." It was all one way with never ending requests on Reuters, and the dealer boards all lit up red. One of the senior salespeople, normally a bastion of self-control, momentarily let off steam at a slacking junior. "I'm on two phones, four Reuters conversations, give me a broom, and

I'll sweep the floor as well. Now pick up the phone, you idiot!"[8] It was just what the room needed. Raucous laughter and ribbing soon put the smile back on his face, and on it continued to go.

At Godsell's, Donaghue was also feeling the pressure. "The orders were in 50s now, and we were just giving them and giving them [the Bank of England], and they just held the bid. It was amazing!"[9] At the Bank of England, Trott and his team were intervening at the rate of 2 billion pounds per hour. At this rate, the bank would start to run out of reserves!

It very rapidly became clear to the prime minister and his senior team that the 2 percent increase in interest rates had not done the job. He reconvened the meeting with his senior ministers. Both the chancellor of the exchequer and the deputy governor of the Bank of England were of the opinion that the United Kingdom should suspend membership inthe ERM. This was proposed to the four ministers seated around the table at Admiralty House, and they rejected it. In their minds they had one last chance, and that was to raise interest rates a second time. At 2:15 p.m., interest rates were raised to 15 percent.

The City correctly assumed this was a panic move and took its cue to sell in far greater volumes. It's astounding that Trott and his small team held up for so long. Soros has described the scene as a "veritable avalanche of selling."[10] A momentary respite occurred as a very thin rumor that the Bundesbank was going to cut its interest rate circulated on the market. But it wasn't true. On and on the pounding went, and on and on the Bank of England kept on intervening.

Trott described the scene as follows: "The cavalry were the Bundesbank. We kept on looking over the hill, but there was no dust, and there were no hats and no sabers. And then later at the conference call, they suddenly didn't speak English, which was extraordinary. So we were kind of stretched on that day."[11] "Stretched" is an understatement! Trott and his team had bought about 15 billion pounds, nearly using up the whole of the Bank of England's reserves. On every trade they had lost money. And the losses were about to get worse.

Sensing that squandering the remaining 4 billion of reserves was pointless and futile, the top executives at the Bank of England via the Treasury urgently requested that ERM membership be suspended. Finally, the government acceded, and the decision was made to temporarily suspend membership of the ERM. The Bank of England pulled its bid and stopped supporting the pound.

To describe the scene thereafter would be to liken it to the noise of a fireworks display's crescendo. If it had been noisy before, the markets reacted to the bank's decision to stop supporting the pound by smashing sterling in a ferocious, chaotic, frenzied, and violently destructive final phase.

As John Ramkin recalled, "With no buyers in the market, both cable and sterling-mark went into free fall with cable (GBP/USD) dropping from roughly 1.90 to 1.60 and GBP/DEM dropping from roughly 2.90 to 2.40 in just a few minutes. The fall was only halted by profit taking." Ramkin continued, "As a bank, we were short of GBP, so the day was very profitable."[12]

It was the same across the City with banks, mutual funds, pension funds, corporations, and hedge funds all desperately scrambling to sell sterling as it came crashing down. "The amounts were now 50s, 100s, and 200s," commented Donaghue, "but there were no bids, so it was very difficult to get stuff away. Whatever bids were there just got steamrollered."[13]

The noise in the dealing room at Prudential Bache was such that the desks and personnel adjacent to the traders just stopped working and watched in awe as the focus zoomed in on about 20 people screaming and shouting at the top of their voices with phones pinned to both ears and gesturing with anything they possibly could to sell sterling. Customers were held in a queue to even get a price, desperately waiting and mentally calculating their losses with every downtick in the market. But the downticks were not downticks. They were "big figure" downticks, where every figure in a million pounds equated to a $10,000 loss. In 50 million, a big figure was worth $500,000. And the market was dropping by several big figures per minute.

For the prop traders at Goldman and all the other traders who were already short, it was a few moments of unbounded joy. The only difficult choice was where to take profits. If Italy had devalued 7 percent and Schlesinger thought that wasn't enough, then well, maybe 10 percent would do, or 15 percent? Ten percent on a billion-pound position would be $100 million. On a profit and loss, $100 million would equate to a $10 million bonus in just a few months' time. Not bad for a day's work!

The traders at NatWest had in fact made in excess of $10 million, a theme that was echoed across the City. At Godsell and Prudential Bache, the profits were in the millions; at Goldman Sachs, in the tens of millions. It capped a remarkable week for Goldman Sachs in a highly profitable era. Along with the earlier successes in deutsche marks against the lira, the Goldman Sachs FX desk made a fortune. Goldman CEO Stephen Friedman, described the trading opportunity as "the best" he'd ever seen.

The biggest loser of course was the Bank of England, and for his efforts in defending the pound, Jim Trott deserves a medal. Of course he got nothing, while the governor, Robin Leigh Pemberton, received a life peerage. Trott describes the day as "stunningly expensive" with the bank losing in excess of 3 billion pounds and using up 15 billion in reserves. Despite cries for their resignation, all the government ministers kept their jobs and ultimately received life peerages.

The biggest winner by far, though, was George Soros. Quantum made in excess of $1 billion that day—more than 10 percent on a 10 billion pound position. If Stanley Druckenmiller takes the credit for coming up with the trade, then it is Soros who takes the credit for managing the trade and sensing he could outgun the Bank of England. Without Soros's more than doubling the trade from 4 to 10 billion, the Bank of England might well have survived the day. His incessant selling put pressure on the U.K. government to raise interest rates, and his selling post that decision, the one-way traffic through the broker-dealers and the contagious effect of his selling, created its own reflexive process. Soros had the capacity to trade 15 billion, which was precisely the scale of the intervention: just about enough to take on the bank single-handedly. But big trades create noise in the market, and "institutional herding" is what ultimately caused the Bank of England's defense to buckle. What was just as remarkable about Soros's trade was that he managed to take profit and buy 10 billion pounds as the market sold into his bid. It was a truly remarkable trade, of enormous scale, brilliantly executed on what has now become the foreign exchange market's most infamous trading day.

SOROS'S IMPACT

To say it all begins with Soros is no understatement. Soros energized a generation of traders into living the trading dream. He made "hedge fund" a recognized household term, and he made a billion dollars in one afternoon when making a million dollars a year was considered an enormous amount of money. But what can we learn from him, and is it likely that any of us can replicate his success?

There are a lot of positive aspects of Soros's life and career that can inspire any budding trader. Here is a man who started out his career without any significant assistance, who did not graduate from college with any exceptional honors, who struggled initially to get into the financial markets, and who started his fund at almost 40 years old with limited capital—only about $4 million. Remember, he managed to turn this into $1 billion in only 16 years.

What he did have was a vision, albeit not a vision to become a billionaire. Rather, he had a vision to make enough money to follow his passion to become a philosopher. His philosophical concept evolved into a work in progress, proven by astounding financial gains and put to good use in creating open societies—that is, societies that have democratically elected governments, uphold the rule of law, and respect human rights, minorities, and diversity of opinion.

Soros often alludes to his true mentor, his father, and his perceived mentor, Professor Karl Popper. His World War II experiences, his father's leadership in adversity, and his survival taught him many lessons, among them how irrational human behavior can be and how humans can flock or herd like less intelligent species. Having seen death in its most vicious and nasty form, Soros learned the value of life. And he has used his life in the most positive of ways. His philanthropic donations have certainly aided in making the world a better place, having donated in excess of $8 billion to philanthropic causes since 1979. Thank God for George Soros!

In the context of his fund, he fundamentally understands the notion of preserving capital, constantly assessing the risks, and critically analyzing his trades in real time. He also demonstrates tremendous intuition and raw courage. Nobody more aptly extols the virtues of the consummate trader. From brilliant and intuitive strategist to bold and ruthless investor. While he is resolute and cutthroat in his pursuit of profit, particularly if he senses weakness, he also shows humility and a lack of arrogance. He is aware that while he may have some influence on the market, ultimately the market is bigger than he is, and not all of his trades will be winners. Soros senses when the prevailing bias is about to change, keeps aware of his situation, and adjusts his position accordingly.

If Soros has donated to us a trading gift, it is his theory of reflexivity. If we were to apply this to our trades, we could create a new era of thinking traders. Survival is about staying in the game, and you can make money only if you are in the game. Foreign exchange is a high-stakes market that can involve considerable amounts of leverage. Soros demonstrated in 1992 how to use leverage correctly.

There are constant reflexive processes in the market, and they will continue to occur. Since September 2012, we have seen the U.S. dollar appreciate nearly 60 percent against the Japanese yen, and since mid-2014, we have seen the U.S. dollar appreciate more than 20 percent against a broad spectrum of currencies. In December 2014, the Russian ruble had its own Black Tuesday and lost nearly 25 percent of its value against the U.S. dollar in just one day. How long will the U.S. dollar continue to appreciate?

The fact is that there will always be opportunities in the FX market. For example, in January 2015, the Swiss National Bank ceased to support an artificially weak Swiss franc with USD/CHF free-falling nearly 40 percent in as many minutes, bankrupting many FX clients and brokerages alike and reinforcing the point that it pays to be prudent when entering fail-safe trades.

At age 85, Soros has accumulated a staggering net worth of nearly $25 billion. And while he may wish to be remembered for his philanthropic causes, he will almost certainly be remembered for one spectacular day, Wednesday, September 16, 1992. On that day he became a trading legend and the original, and greatest, Currency King.

John Henry: Technical Trading Genius

3

If there's one man in the FX world who oozes "cool," it is Joh
W. Henry. With his custom foot-long Cuban Havana cig
Henry appears to be Clint Eastwood's character "the man w
no name's" elder and richer brother. While "no name" fough
"a fistful of dollars," Henry has buckets full. He is one of t
following's greatest, and he is a giant in the financial market
30-year reign as a commodity trading advisor (CTA) and
cial futures trading genius puts him at the forefront of tr
lowing superstars. A thousand dollars invested in his f
and metals program in 1984 would have compounded
$160,000 by 2004. Ironically one of only 3 losing ye
20-year period was in 1992 when Soros and others v
billions off the Bank of England. Otherwise, in a rem
riod of success the program ratcheted up average an
in excess of 30 percent with a bonanza year in 1987
exceeded 252 percent.

After a sequence of drawdowns, Henry retire
ing other people's money in 2012, and he now de
pursuing his sporting interests. He owns the Bost
ball team in the United States and the Liverp
in the United Kingdom—which, incidentally,
the color red for its first team strip. As Henr

successes in the eighties, so too was Liverpool Football Club—
they won the European Cup (now known as the Champions
League) in the 1983 to 1984 season, and during Henry's most
stellar year, they won the Football League First Division, now
known as the Premier League, in 1987 to 1988. Henry and his
company the Fenway Sports Group acquired the Liverpool Football Club in October 2010. In the few seasons prior, Liverpool
had not been at their best, but with Henry's undoubted sporting enthusiasm, new management, and an exciting and energized
squad including the Uruguayan scoring phenomenon Luis Su-
arez, Liverpool was extremely unlucky not to win the Premier
League title in the 2013 to 2014 season, narrowly missing out to
Manchester City. If, as Henry believes, the trend is your friend,
with continued investment and the same winning attitude, Liverpool will once again become champions.

If John Henry has become a household name in the city of
Liverpool, he is already a legend in Boston. When he and his partners acquired the Boston Red Sox in 2002, the team had not won
the coveted World Series since 1918. Some people of a superstitious nature called this failure the "curse of the Bambino" and
attributed it largely to the sale of (ultimately) the Hall of Fame
player Babe Ruth. Ruth was sold in the 1919 to 1920 off-season
the New York Yankees. The form of the Red Sox—who until then had been one of the world's most successful baseball
—plummeted, while that of the Yankees somewhat propor-
tionally skyrocketed. Henry and his coinvestors set out to break
the curse, which they achieved two years later in 2004, again in
and once again in 2013.

A LUCKY COLOR

is as passionate about sports as he is about the mar-
seems to be a color that brings him luck. And why not?

Red in Chinese culture corresponds with fire and symbolizes joy and good fortune. It is powerful, energizing, and motivating. It signifies a pioneering spirit and leadership qualities, promoting ambition and determination. Henry carries many of these attributes and qualities and deserves his luck. After all, having waited for 86 years, he put a smile on the faces of many Bostonians!

Henry is not the only trader appearing to be superstitious about something. George Soros has his New York office at 888 Seventh Avenue in New York. The number 888 means money, balance, and abundance, which sums up Soros perfectly. There's nothing wrong with these men believing in luck. The famous probability guru Nassim Nicholas Taleb would argue that almost all trading performance is about luck. Good performance: lucky: poor performance: unlucky. He might also admit to having worn the same tie and using the same entrance door to his office the day after a particularly successful trading day.

It takes a good dose of humility to admit you're lucky. And normally luck doesn't continue forever. John Paulson who famously made $15 billion in 2007 with one of his funds—Advantage Plus, which boasted returns of 158 percent in that year, 38 percent in 2008, 21 percent in 2009, and 17 percent in 2010—was rather unlucky in both 2011 and 2012 with the fund losing 52 and 19 percent, respectively. Maybe Paulson believes he was unlucky in those two years. Does he admit to luck having a hand in his returns for the previous four years?

HENRY'S TREND FOLLOWING MODEL

In his university days, it was not obvious that Henry would become a trading giant. The late 1960s and early 1970s had a different allure, and Henry paid considerable attention to playing guitar for two rock 'n' roll bands. A philosophy major at the University of California, he failed to graduate. He had somewhat of a safety valve in that his father owned several farms, and when he left the university, Henry joined the family business. It was there, in the mid-1970s, that Henry started to trade on the commodity exchanges, hedging soybeans, corn, and wheat: an apprenticeship that would lead him to understand the market dynamics and set him up for much greater things.

It was while on holiday in Norway in the summer of 1980 that Henry had his eureka moment. He mentally and conceptually devised a trend following model to systematically enter long and short positions in the commodities futures markets. As Henry explained to Michael Peltz in an August 1996 interview for *Institutional Investor Magazine,* "I didn't speak the language, so I was bored quite a bit, and I started working on some ideas I'd had for a more mechanical approach to trading." On his return from a vacation to California, he spent the next nine months back-testing his system on every conceivable bit of data he could get his hands on. He continued, "I was so excited about what I had discovered, that you could have a fairly simple philosophy of trends, and trend following, and that it worked so well!"

Not only did the system work on agricultural futures, its performance also showed similar if not better results for financial products. Henry had followed up his brilliant idea by doing the work. In an era when computers lacked the power and performance that they have today, Henry had painstakingly tested reams of data that could be considered his competitive advantage. The question would be whether he could scale it up, risk manage it properly, and crucially, whether future price movements would conform to his model.

HENRY'S RETAIL COMPANY

John W. Henry & Company, Inc., was established in 1981, and it started trading money for retail clients in 1982. The firm's management methods, according to its literature, make "mechanical, nondiscretionary trading decisions in response to systematic determinations of reversals in each market's direction, with the explicit intention of precluding not only human emotion but also any subjective evaluation of such things as the so-called fundamentals, to trigger each decision to be long or short each market, or not." In a nutshell, Henry created an automated trend reversal trading model. The only human element was in trade execution.

The system was either long or short different markets, with trade initiation points close to reversal levels. In markets that exhibited infrequent reversals followed by long-term trends, the system was incredibly potent, avoiding the natural human emotion to take quick profits. In whipsawing markets with frequent trend reversals, the system could be vulnerable. The other point to note is that in some instances the first move might be negative, which over time might become positive. By trusting the "black box" or "algorithm" to position size and risk manage the position, once again the need for a courageous trader to wait out large drawdowns was eliminated.

What better place to trade for the King of Cool but the Windy City? While Chicago is famous for its architecture, museums, and food, it is also home to the CME Group, a giant futures exchange that encompasses the Chicago Mercantile Exchange (CME), the Chicago Board of Trade (CBOT), and the New York Mercantile (NYMEX) and Commodities (COMEX) exchanges. It is here that Henry executed trades for many of his stellar programs.

THE FUTURES MARKETS

The origins of trading futures in the United States came about in the nineteenth century as many farmers wished to hedge the price received for corn and other commodities. Chicago, with its proximity to Lake Michigan and to millions of acres of farmland, evolved as the main center for trading futures in the United States. In 1848 the Chicago Board of Trade was formed. It started life as a centralized meeting place for trading forward contracts. The first contract (on corn) was written on March 13, 1851. In 1865 standardized futures contracts were introduced.

The Chicago Mercantile Exchange was established in 1919. It can find its origins from the Chicago Butter and Egg Board (itself a spin off from the CBOT). In 1972 the CME formed a division called the International Monetary Market (IMM) to offer futures contracts in seven foreign currencies. The International Monetary Market was largely the brainchild of Leo Melamed, who became chairman of the CME in 1969. In 1987 Melamed was also hugely influential in creating CME Globex, the world's first electronic trading platform. The CBOT and CME merged in 2007.

Futures are derived from assets such as commodities, currencies, metals, or financial instruments. As such, they are classified as derivatives. The characteristics of futures contracts are that they are standardized agreements between buyers and sellers to exchange an amount and grade of an item at a specific price and future date.

Futures are traded on exchanges all over the world, and the trades are settled at clearing houses. Clearing houses settle trades for members at centralized locations, and they act as a counterparty to both sides of a trade. Trading members buy seats on the exchanges and may execute trades at discounted rates. Investors who are not trading members can access the exchanges through *futures commission merchants*. (They pay a commission to the merchant to execute the trade on their behalf.)

Proponents of exchange-traded products often cite the transparency of trading on the exchanges as well as the efficacy of the counterparty risk mitigation of settling through a centralized counterparty as compelling features in making the decision to trade futures on exchanges as opposed to over the counter (off exchange). Other useful properties of exchange trading are volume and open interest. *Volume* represents the total amount of trading activity or contracts that have changed hands in a given commodity market for a single trading day. *Open interest* is the total number of outstanding contracts that are held by market participants at the end of each day. So, for example, if a buyer (and seller) open a contract in a March dated future, the open interest is one contract. This may accumulate to many thousands of contracts before the future is settled in March. On a particular day there may be a huge volume traded in this contract. Some technical analysts look at volume, open interest, and price action to try to determine the next direction of the commodity.

As futures markets have evolved, settlement dates have become more frequent and contract sizes have become smaller to allow greater flexibility and reach to investors. Traditionally there were four trading dates: March, June, September, and December, denoted as symbols H, M, U, and Z on futures markets. Nowadays, futures in certain currency pairs, particularly from emerging markets, can be traded monthly on the various exchanges worldwide. *E-mini futures* in equity indexes are readily accessible to many, as are mini-currency contracts.

HENRY'S FIRST SUCCESS AS A TREND FOLLOWING CTA

John Henry's Financial and Metals program was launched in 1984. The results were phenomenal and launched Henry to becoming one of the greatest ever trend following CTAs (Table 3.1).

While it is clear that the program was massively positive, and there were some sizable monthly gains, there were also some huge drawdowns. As his success grew, he quickly multiplied his assets under management. In an industry where it is common to demonstrate a three-year track record before managing

TABLE 3.1

John W. Henry & Company, Inc., Financial and Metals Program

Year	Return	Drawdown	Assets
2006	−0.07%	−12.13%	$258,000,000
2005	−17.34%	−24.12%	$318,000,000
2004	6.01%	−33.33%	$498,000,000
2003	19.41%	−11.35%	$357,000,000
2002	45.05%	−14.27%	$256,000,000
2001	7.15%	−17.83%	$251,000,000
2000	13.04%	−25.88%	$366,000,000
1999	−18.69%	−23.90%	$713,900,000
1998	7.21%	−18.30%	$1,119,300,000
1997	15.26%	−13.53%	$1,324,700,000
1996	29.67%	−5.53%	$1,182,700,000
1995	38.52%	−4.04%	$842,600,000
1994	−5.32%	−14.31%	$657,100,000
1993	46.85%	−1.98%	$709,500,000
1992	−10.89%	−39.53%	$457,400,000
1991	61.88%	−15.45%	$619,200,000
1990	83.60%	−22.73%	$274,600,000
1989	34.62%	−37.17%	$69,200,000
1988	4.02%	−20.31%	$36,800,000
1987	252.42%	−27.59%	$15,200,000
1986	61.55%	−19.88%	$1,200,000
1985	20.66%	−34.68%	$200,000
1984	9.93%	−3.16%	$100,000

Year-by-Year Analysis

Total number of years	23
Average year	30.63%
Largest year	252.42%
Smallest year	(–18.69%)
Standard dev. of year returns	55.10%
Average win/average lose	4.02

Month-by-Month Analysis

Total number of months	260
Average month	2.51%
Largest month	44.19%
Smallest month	(–27.32%)
Standard dev. of monthly returns	11.11%
Average win/average lose	1.69

Month-by-Month Returns

Year	Jan	Feb	Mar	Apr	May	Jun	Jul	Aug	Sep	Oct	Nov	Dec
1984	—	—	—	—	—	—	—	—	—	1.61	–3.16	11.72
1985	6.62	17.71	–9.28	–7.77	–7.69	–1.75	41.26	–10.12	–27.32	6.37	26.63	1.93
1986	4.79	21.87	–6.30	3.67	–17.52	17.57	24.95	9.42	–0.23	2.56	–3.56	–0.46
1987	33.01	12.10	34.24	18.23	–7.16	–10.69	12.25	–14.61	–8.89	28.02	32.54	21.21
1988	–12.56	9.77	–2.30	–15.02	0.28	44.19	5.47	6.89	–8.09	2.50	5.18	–19.19
1989	31.69	–8.66	8.51	3.17	37.03	–6.63	4.43	–8.17	–14.92	–17.53	21.63	–4.53
1990	27.98	19.50	11.40	2.41	–22.73	6.91	12.16	11.16	8.32	–5.01	3.09	–3.68
1991	–2.28	3.80	4.46	–0.79	–0.32	–1.29	–13.39	4.78	25.80	–7.74	6.62	39.37
1992	–18.03	–13.53	2.98	–12.17	–5.68	21.90	25.46	10.18	–5.23	–4.50	–0.80	–2.59
1993	3.34	13.89	–0.30	9.34	3.35	0.12	9.69	–0.78	0.22	–1.10	–0.33	2.88
1994	–2.93	–0.55	7.21	0.89	1.29	4.47	–6.11	–4.12	1.49	1.65	–4.38	–3.51
1995	–3.76	15.67	15.35	6.10	1.24	–1.66	–2.33	2.08	–2.13	0.31	2.64	1.65
1996	5.99	–5.53	0.66	2.28	–1.74	2.25	–1.13	–0.76	3.22	14.33	10.95	–2.55
1997	4.41	–2.23	–0.69	–2.85	–8.33	4.15	15.75	–3.65	2.20	2.02	2.48	2.86
1998	–3.50	–3.98	–1.56	–7.93	3.18	–4.84	–0.92	17.50	15.26	–3.78	–7.50	8.87
1999	–4.84	0.90	–2.56	1.63	5.89	6.12	–2.30	–3.15	–7.01	–8.12	–3.18	–2.78
2000	–3.59	–6.20	–2.28	2.51	–2.06	–8.97	–1.74	–0.43	–6.20	9.39	13.33	23.02
2001	3.34	2.53	12.84	–8.30	1.01	–4.14	–4.44	8.47	5.41	4.64	–17.83	7.44
2002	–0.81	–6.00	–5.45	–1.04	11.01	28.33	11.25	3.59	7.39	–8.53	–6.28	10.01
2003	11.38	4.51	–3.48	1.85	9.11	–4.96	–3.36	2.52	–3.86	0.65	–2.71	7.89
2004	1.66	6.53	–6.50	–10.73	–5.52	–5.45	–10.59	5.08	0.51	14.07	18.72	2.66
2005	–9.48	–6.74	–5.90	–1.70	8.67	9.34	–3.78	–12.82	–2.51	4.45	9.36	–4.63
2006	–2.47	–8.51	11.20	13.04	1.39							

significant assets, Henry's assets snowballed in his first three years, but it was after making nearly 100 percent in the first three months of 1987 and creating a positive track record for eight consecutive years that his assets under management ballooned from $15 million to well over $500 million. He topped $1 billion in 1996.

However, the program had a very poor period from mid-1999 to September 2000 when it posted 14 monthly losses in 15 months. Assets under management took a hammering from their peak of $1.325 billion in 1997 to just over $250 million in 2001. Ironically the program posted excellent returns for three years thereafter. But the roller coaster ride was too much for many investors, and the P&L swings were too volatile for some of a more conservative nature.

TECHNICAL ANALYSIS

Those who wish to pursue a technical trading strategy must be acutely aware that losses are part of the game. If monthly standard deviations of returns in this program are in the region of 11 percent, those who embark on trading with leverage can expect to win or lose this amount and more with regularity. Trend following is not for the faint hearted, and therefore it is advisable to back-test a strategy (as Henry did) and, once the trading parameters have been set, to follow them with rigorous discipline. Henry took the human element out of his trading. It might be advisable to do just the same.

Technical analysis has been in the ascendency since Charles Dow created his stock averages in the late nineteenth century. What came to be known as *Dow theory* was an accumulation of trading principles based on the Dow Jones averages of railroad and industrial stocks and how they interacted with one another. As the relationship between the two indexes developed, various tradable patterns became apparent, whether they were highly correlated simultaneous movements in one direction, reversions of one or another indicator to the underlying market direction from a period of nonconformity, or simply leading and lagging movements in the same or an opposite direction. The price movements could be charted, and predictable patterns could be traded. Dow theory was born and accumulated a tremendous following.

In the much revered and almost textbook of technical analysis, *Technical Analysis of Stock Trends* by Edwards and Magee, the late John Magee states his three principles that are equally applicable to stocks, commodities, and currencies—namely, prices tend to move in trends, volume goes with the trend, and a trend, once established, tends to continue in force. Furthermore, he was known by his peers to advocate following a major trend instead of trying to pick tops and bottoms. That said, much of the book is devoted to picking tops and bottoms and the various patterns and shapes that denote potential turning points.

ENTRIES AND EXITS

It is almost universally agreed that if you ride a trend, you will make money. Millions of hours of traders' time have been spent working on entry points. It is generally easier to trade entry points because at the inception of any trading strategy, there is normally a pool of capital to invest. Once in a trade, it would appear that the majority of traders take profits too early, and so the exit strategy, which arguably should be the converse of the entry strategy, is somewhat more of a difficult conundrum. Emotions get in the way. People pick tops too early and veer away from their trading rules. Panic sets in when some profits are eroded during small market corrections. The trading playing field therefore skews heavily in favor of bookmakers who cater to multiple small accounts. If thousands of clients emotionally and psychologically are incapable of trading with discipline and exit profitable trades early, then statistically the edge is with somebody who can absorb that collective risk on his or her books and ride all client positions to the point of attrition. This, in essence, is what some retail brokers do.

John Henry did not fall for this trap. His back-tested system eliminated the human emotion and the gut-wrenching aspect of watching short-term profits disappear. His was the pursuit of much greater profits, and his preprogrammed black box decided the trade, the size of the trade, when to scale in and when to scale out, when to elect stops, and when to take profits. The system was almost always in the market, whatever the direction, catching rising trends and falling trends. Humans were employed purely to control trade execution and to monitor slippage.

For the layperson, the most distressing part of trading is losing. Winning is far more fun. Drawdowns can be sickening. Watching money go down the drain is stressful. But not all trades are successful. The same discipline that is involved in executing stop-losses is exactly the same discipline required to run winners, however severe the drawdowns. John Henry's system had some enormous drawdowns, but over a 20-year period he clocked up 17 successful years and immense returns. He believed in his system and put his own money behind it. He did not try to intervene or interfere. He played out his strategy with impeccable discipline.

Magee is quoted as saying, "When you enter the stock market, you are going into a competitive field in which your evaluations and opinions will be matched against some of the sharpest and toughest minds in the business. You are in a highly specialized industry in which there are many different sectors, all of which are under intense study by men whose economic survival depends on their best judgment. You will certainly be exposed to advice, suggestions, offers of help from all sides. Unless you are able to develop some market philosophy of your own, you will not be able to tell the good from the bad, the sound from the unsound."[1]

Robert Edwards, the coauthor, has stated, "Technical guides to trading stocks are by no means infallible. The more experience one gains in their use, the more alive he becomes in their pitfalls and their failures. There is no such thing as a surefire method of beating the market; the authors have no hesitancy in saying there never will be!"[2]

Way too often, by falling victim to superlative marketing, gullible investors become victims of fail-safe trading systems that are just hyperbole. In order to trade with any modicum of a successful outcome, people need to do their own work, develop their own philosophy or system, and trade with discipline. Magee and Edwards propose just that. It's what Soros did with his theory of reflexivity, and it's what Henry did with his technical trading reversal system. Other traders in this book also applied their trading philosophies with scale to achieve phenomenal results. That's why they are billionaires. This is a key point behind trading successfully. People must understand this before they trade!

If one of the most brilliant technical trading authors simplifies his approach into three simple principles and provides a warning that technical trading is by no means a surefire way to success, then it is worth taking heed.

To reiterate Magee's principles:

1. Prices tend to move in trends.

2. Volume goes with the trend.

3. A trend, once established, tends to continue in force.

Of these, it would appear that principle 3 would be the most compelling to follow. If traders can consistently follow a trend in force, then they will make money. The challenge is how to latch on to that trend.

Fortunately, we have one area of technical analysis that purports to have identified elements of a trend that seem to be of a longer duration than others.

AN ELLIOTT WAVE CYCLE

Ralph Nelson Elliott, a professional accountant by trade, wrote the 1938 blockbuster *The Wave Principle*, which was subsequently summarized in a series of articles in *Financial World* magazine in 1939. His view was that market prices move in rhythmical patterns because human behavioral characteristics repeat themselves. In short, he suggested that in a typical phase, there are upward and downward movements in prices (Figure 3.1). An *impulsive wave* moves upward, followed by a small *retracement* (points 1 and 2 on the chart). It happens again (points 3 and 4). The fifth wave is up, followed by a larger retracement (points 5 and A). To complete the cycle, there is a small impulsive wave followed by a larger *corrective wave* (points B and C).

What is beautiful about this sequence is that it can apply to any time scale. But a caveat for any budding Elliott wave disciple is to allow for large drawdowns as the parameters of percentage corrective reversals are quite broad. For those who are looking for the biggest reward to risk, Elliott argued that wave 3 was the longest impulsive wave. Some in the commodities market have contended that wave 5 is the longest. So maybe, and I'm sure millions have tried, there is a way to capture this period of the cycle.

Elliott wave cycles have been categorized this way:

- *Grand supercycle:* Multicentury

- *Supercycle:* Multidecade (about 40 to 70 years)

- *Cycle:* One year to several years (or even several decades under an Elliott extension)

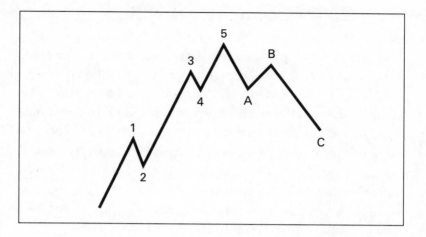

Figure 3.1 An Elliott wave cycle.

- *Primary:* A few months to a couple of years

- *Intermediate:* Weeks to months

- *Minor:* Weeks

- *Minute:* Days

- *Minuette:* Hours

- *Subminuette:* Minutes

Caveat number 1 is that in some instances, what appears to be a bone-fide cycle can suddenly exhibit characteristics that don't quite fit the pattern.

Caveat number 2 is that the shorter the time frame, the greater the erosion of capital due to spreads and slippage. And then the questions arise of how much capital to commit to trading and where to leave stop-losses. If the analysis is wrong and the trade goes in the opposite way to the way it should, there must be a stop in place to preserve capital. Remember, technical trading is by no means a surefire way to success.

FIBONACCI NUMBERS

It is in the area of predicting the magnitude of waves that some have resorted to Fibonacci numbers as a tool. Fibonacci, who lived in the twelfth and thirteenth centuries, was an Italian and is considered one of the outstanding mathematicians of the Middle Ages. In 1202 he completed the *Liber Abaci* (*Book of Abacus* or *Book of Calculation*), which popularized Hindu-Arabic numerals in Europe. The book, a classic of its time, posed and solved a problem involving the growth of a population of rabbits. The solution, generation by generation, was a sequence of numbers later known as *Fibonacci numbers*.

The sequence is as follows: 0, 1, 1, 2, 3, 5, 8, 13, 21, 34, 55, 89, 144, 233, 377, 610, 987, . . . , and it extends to infinity. The relationships of pairs of numbers exhibit some very interesting characteristics, and it is from here that many technical support and resistance levels are derived:

- After 0 and 1, each number is the sum of the two prior numbers (for example, 8 + 13 = 21).

- A number divided by the previous number approximates 1.618 (for example, 13/8 = 1.625).

- A number divided by the next highest number approximates 0.6180 (for example, 8/13 = 0.615).

- A number divided by another number that is two places higher approximates 0.3820 (for example, 8/21 = 0.381).

- A number divided by another number that is three places higher approximates 0.2360 (for example, 8/34 = 0.235).

The numbers above are linked with the *golden ratio*, or 1.618. The number 1 divided by 1.618 is 0.618. The number 1 minus 0.618 is 0.382. The numbers 0.618, 0.382, and 0.2360 are often used to predict support (or resistance) levels from charts of financial instruments. Fibonacci analysts will predict resistance for a currency after a period of retracement that may be 23.6 percent, 38.2 percent, or even 61.8 percent of the move from the lows.

An example is AUD/NZD. AUD/NZD peaked at 1.3757 in March 2011. It then steadily declined to 1.0034, which was reached in April 2015. The decline was therefore 37.23 big figures. The currency abruptly rebounded and found resistance at 1.1258 in June 2015. This was a 32.8 percent rebound, somewhat larger than 23.6 percent but smaller than 38.2 percent. It would be considered a success in Fibonacci terms because the levels are really just guides and the parameters are quite broad. Essentially, while the predictive capacity of these numbers is more or less accurate, there are now so many participants trading that the actual retracements generally are never quite spot on. Indeed, as in arbitrage, if there are inefficiencies in the market, arbitrage irons them out. Similarly, if the majority of the market uses Fibonacci levels, there will be many that put their orders in before these significant levels, therefore impinging on the predictive accuracy of the absolute levels.

Support and resistance levels can be so subjective that it is almost impossible to accurately forecast where they will be. Round numbers such as 1.00 or 1.1 or 1.2 are considered emotional levels and are often well protected whether it be by spot orders or option barriers. Around these numbers for a few pips on either side, there is often a lot of congestion. Once these levels are taken out fully, it can mean a significant move through the level, or if successfully protected, a large rebound in the opposite direction. Take AUD/NZD trading near parity, for example (1.0034). Having trended lower for several years from the high 1.30s, it rallied sharply from a level near parity.

In the 1990s on spot trading desks, traders would often state that support was at "80" or resistance was at "20" around a big figure. So, for example, in GBP/USD, support might be at 1.5080 and resistance at 1.5120. The traders would base their opinions on their order books. The advice as to whether these levels would hold was somewhat spurious. Sometimes they did. Sometimes they did not! Clients at the other end of the line could take or leave the commentary. There were many contrarians to oppose the trend followers. Another fact was that computers were less sophisticated and charts harder to come by for the individual. Then as now, there were so many players in the market and so many orders that nobody could really consistently predict where these levels were. Everyone will have a golden period and then, well, they won't. Hubris has humbled many traders big and small.

TRADING FOR THE LONG TERM

If John Henry has taught us something, it is that he traded for the long term. His system picked markets to follow, often for years. He was looking for long-term trends, not trading levels. Once his system had established that he was following a trend, his system would hold on to it for as long as possible. All the 80s and 20s, big figures, 23.6 percent, 38.2 percent, 61.8 percent, and any other parameters were just noise! Sure, he would have levels, and he could monitor his execution prices from broker to broker. But his system had more to it than buying zigs and selling zags. He designed a system that predicted reversals and then held on until the reversals reversed.

By now, readers should have realized that trend following is not day trading. If people want to throw away money, day trading technical signals will quickly eat into their capital by paying away spread. Victor Niederhoffer called it paying the VIG, or the "vigorish." It is that nasty little tax that is charged in the difference between the bid and offer. It's also known as the "juice" or the "cut." It is the broker's fee for making a market. Something he or she will be happy to do all day long. The VIG is worse on stops. Then there's financing VIG, which could be akin to loan sharking. Even the most successful day traders will pay astronomical amounts in spreads or markups.

John W. Henry & Company's modus operandi was to make "mechanical, nondiscretionary trading decisions in response to systematic determinations of reversals in each market's direction."[3] Magee and Edwards have devoted a lot of their time to explaining entry strategy. The geometrists among us can spend hours analyzing triangles and rectangles, flags and pennants, and drawing retracements from heads and shoulders. We can even add clouds, shooting stars, dojis, hammers, and hangmen. There are so many ways to get into the market.

TIMING STRATEGIES

Henry chose to keep it simple: "I was so excited about what I had discovered, that you could have a fairly simple philosophy of trends, and trend following, and that it worked so well!"[4] Simple means it's not rocket science. For all the time that graduates have spent learning about math and business, the truth is that trading can be as simple or as complicated as you make it. A simple philosophy cuts out the noise. A simple set of rules is easier to follow. Henry discovered a way to catch hold of a reversal and then follow a trend. His model worked for the best part of 20 years.

There are several "simple" ways to get into the market. Simple *moving averages* are used by many. The principle is that when a shorter-term mean of prices crosses a longer-term mean of prices, then the implication is to go with the shorter-term average. The shorter-term average is considered more relevant. A step further is to give more weight to recent prices and less weight to further out prices in the averages, thus creating *exponential moving averages*. The point is that the crossover implies a reversal of direction: an entry level. The hope is by catching it early, the trend can be followed for greater profits.

A very useful indicator that may assist in trying to identify a reversal pattern is the *relative strength index* (RSI), especially when it is used in conjunction with moving averages or some other momentum indicator. The RSI is a technical momentum indicator that compares the magnitude of recent gains to recent losses in an attempt to determine overbought and oversold conditions of an asset. It is calculated using the following formula:

$$RSI = 100 - 100/(1 + RS*)*$$

where RS = average of x days' up closes / average of x days' down closes

The indicator oscillates between 0 and 100 without ever quite touching 0 and 100. A currency pair is considered overbought when the RSI exceeds 70 and oversold at below 30. The levels of 30 and 70 are really alert levels.

In the example shown in Figure 3.2, the EUR/USD breached 70 on the RSI in February 2008. The currency continued its route higher until late April. At the beginning of April, however, the RSI diverged from the price action and started to fall. The 3-day moving average then crossed the 10-day moving average, and the currency pair started to move lower.

There is no surefire way of picking tops and bottoms. There are some fairly amusing traders' adages to warn against going counter to the trend. For example, "Every bottom has a hole" or "He who picks bottom gets a dirty hand." It's definitely a risky business to try to time the market. But if you can catch and then follow a trend, ride the downturns and hold on, and manage your risk and leverage, outsize returns are possible.

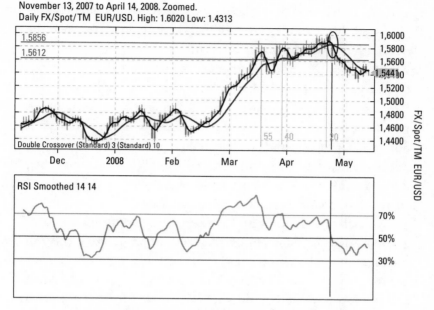

November 13, 2007 to April 14, 2008. Zoomed.
Daily FX/Spot/TM EUR/USD. High: 1.6020 Low: 1.4313

Figure 3.2 A relative strength index (RSI) chart.
Source: Copyright © 1985 to 2016 Tradermade Systems Ltd.

HENRY'S TRADING DISCIPLINE

This is exactly what John Henry did. Professional discussions about his positive trading traits nail three recurring characteristics:

1. His discipline

2. His ability to ride trends for significant periods

3. His risk management

Henry was not afraid of accepting drawdowns as part of the business of trading. This is primarily because he believed in his system and philosophy. He therefore had confidence to ride out the difficult phases of holding on in losing periods when following a trend. These tend to be the periods when others might capitulate and throw in the towel, only to kick themselves when the trend resurges and advances forward.

On discipline and confidence, Henry said the following: "You create discipline by having a strategy you really believe in. If you really believe in a strategy, that brings about discipline. If you don't believe in it, in other words, if you haven't done your homework properly and you haven't made assumptions that you can really live with when you're faced with difficult periods, then it won't work. It really doesn't take much discipline if you have a tremendous confidence in what you are doing."[5]

Mark Rzepczynski, who for a period ran the firm's daily operations, once commented on the firm's approach to trend following: "Once a trend is identified, they ride it, sometimes for months or years, until they are convinced it has peaked." Henry, in his 1996 interview with Michael Peltz added, "If we get a profit of 5 to 10 percent, we are willing to give that up in a calculated attempt to earn a much larger profit. Our basic philosophy is that real money is made by holding on to successful trades for the very long term."[6]

There have been many comments on Henry's risk management skills, from scaling in and out of trades to eliminating losers with predetermined stop levels. In the CTA industry, Henry was renowned for being an excellent risk manager. He needed to be, as only 38 to 40 percent of his trades were actually winners. While Henry is credited for his discipline and tenacity and risk management, in reality it was the system that called the shots.

THE TURTLE TRADERS

One of the greatest tutorials one can ever read is by Curtis Faith, who was one of the original "Turtle traders." The knowledge one can gain from reading his 34-page epic *The Original Turtle*

Trading Rules is second to none. The reason that it is such a compelling read is that the trading Turtles was a cohort of individuals with practically no trading experience who had been handpicked by Richard Dennis—himself a trading wizard—to take part in a trading experiment.

Richard Dennis was born in Chicago and has trading in his veins. He entered the Chicago Mercantile Exchange as a runner at age 17. After graduating with a degree in philosophy from DePaul University, he accepted and then rejected a scholarship to further his studies in philosophy at Tulane University, preferring instead to trade on the Mid-America Commodity Exchange. Here, he quickly turned his starting stake of $400 into over $1 million by the time he was 25. Moving on to the Chicago Board of Trade, Dennis profited immensely from a trend following philosophy in a period of high inflation, making in the order of $200 million in the process.

Dennis had a bet with his friend and fellow trading giant Bill Eckhardt that trading could be taught to novices. The Turtles got their famous name from Richard Dennis's likening them to turtles reared in special farms in Singapore. Dennis contended that he could "grow" his turtles in the same fashion. He mentored his cohort to follow a simple set of trading rules and follow a mechanical trend following system that he created. He then let them loose to trade the futures markets in currencies and commodities with his own capital. His Turtles returned him more than $100 million. He proved his point, and in doing so, he has provided hope and motivation to anyone who is really serious about making money trading.

What is remarkable about Faith's tutorial is that it not only presents the basics of the mechanical trading system but also covers all aspects of trading from philosophy to psychology. The similarities to John Henry's philosophy and system are uncanny, and the characteristics of what makes a good trader are equally well explained. Faith's tutorial is a must read. Below are some principles that worked for both John Henry and the Turtles. And there are some warnings about bogus system sellers.

"There are far more people out there making money selling others' systems and ways to make money trading than there are making money trading."[7] It's true. He's right. There's no easy way. You have to develop your own philosophy, test it, and stick to it. John Henry gives the same advice.

Faith wrote, "Trading rules are only a small part of successful trading. The most important aspects of successful trading are confidence, consistency, and discipline."[8] It's no coincidence that John Henry has said exactly the same. He had utmost confidence in his system, and it was the system that created the discipline that he is famous for. Discipline in the down periods is doubly important. Richard Dennis, the godfather of the Turtles, has echoed this: "The key is consistency and discipline. Almost anybody can make up a list of rules that are 80 percent as good as what we taught our people. What they couldn't do is give them the confidence to stick to those rules even when things were going bad."[9] How many people can stick to their New Year's resolutions or diet successfully or give up drinking or smoking, or take more exercise? Trading a system for days, months, or years requires precisely the sort of discipline intended in the original rules.

Faith wrote, "A good mechanical system automates the entire process of trading. The mechanics of trading are not left up to the judgment of the trader. If you are relying on your own judgment, you may find that you are fearful when you should be bold, and courageous when you should be cautious."[10] John Henry could not put this better himself. His system made "mechanical, nondiscretionary trading decisions in response to systematic determinations of reversals in each market's direction, with the explicit intention of precluding not only human emotion but also any subjective evaluation of such things as the so-called fundamentals."[11] The philosophy is almost exactly the same in the Turtle trading system: "Its rules covered every aspect of trading and left no decisions to the subjective whims of the trader."

Without going into the whole details of the system, it did cover what to buy (or sell), when to buy, how much, how often (scaling in), how to trade in spiking markets, where and when to elect stops, and also how to take profits. Suffice to say the system was a reversal system (like Henry's), position sizing was volatility adjusted, and trends were followed for weeks, months, or years.

Two other similarities are quite striking. As with John Henry, most trades resulted in losses! The positive returns were made on fewer big winners. And consistent with Henry's philosophy, taking profits too early was not an option. As Faith said, "It is necessary to let prices go against you if you are going to ride a trend. Early in a trend this can often mean watching decent profits of 10 to 30 percent fade to a small loss. In the middle of a trend, it might mean watching a profit of 80 to 100 percent drop by 30 to 40 percent. The temptation to lighten the position to lock in profits can be very great." The profitable Turtles followed the system's rules. "The ability to maintain discipline and stick to the rules during large winning trades is the hallmark of a successful trader."

SLIPPAGE

John Henry's returns might have been even greater but for slippage. As with most trend following models, it doesn't take much for brokers to guess the direction of the trade, particularly if a currency pair has been trending for several days. For Dennis and his Turtles, it would mean adding positions; for Henry, the same. In fact, for the vast majority of professional trend followers, it would mean holding on to or adding to positions.

Slippage, it must be said, is an occupational hazard with brokers. It can take percentage points off performance. Illiquid pairs and predictable trading times are an invitation for brokers to wreak havoc. The paradox of this moneymaking stream for the broker is that it shortens the life cycle of the moneymaking opportunity. Dealer myopia is the bane of every salesperson trying to protect a decent account. Gouging by so-called FX dealers is so counterproductive, it's pitiful. And yet for many years gouging was considered risk taking by senior managers at some brokerages and banks, and their best gougers were rewarded according to the profits they generated rather than punished for the accounts they helped destroy!

Henry used an innovative product to try to avoid slippage. He would trade on the over-the-counter (OTC) market—that is, the spot market—and give the trade up to the exchange where he held his account for settlement. This product is known as an *exchange for physical* (EFP) *trade*. The OTC trade would be converted into futures contracts—a EUR/USD contract on the Chicago Mercantile Exchange is the equivalent of EUR 125,000 on the spot market—by taking the spot price and adding or subtracting the currency swap price to the nearest future's settlement date. It would then be posted to the exchange, therefore leaving the books of the OTC broker. In theory, the broker would not know how large Henry's open position was because he had given up the trade. In practice, the spot price could still be slipped because Henry was a trend follower and brokers could guess the direction of his trade with relative certainty.

As unfortunate as it was for Henry to suffer from slippage, the quid pro quo of dealing with many of the brokers was that they allocated some of their own funds and those of their clients to the CTA to manage. After negotiation of acceptable slippage rates, a compromise could be reached where everybody was happy. Henry also used the tactic of calling early in trading sessions, such as the London open or New York open, perhaps to trade in periods of greater liquidity and with several counterparties. If you were lucky and your slippage rates were acceptable, he would trade more and trade first with your broker. If he had a large amount to trade and you were the last broker on his list, it could be very painful to make a market. By this stage, the voice broker boxes would have alerted the whole market that there was a big CTA buying or selling currency. Liquidity would suddenly become scarce, and counterparties fewer.

Henry's staff was meticulous and disciplined, polite and correct, never excited and never stressed. It was as if they were part of the system. In a word, they were professional. In quiet markets they would ask brokers to work their orders without trying to disturb the market. In more volatile markets they would always show their side. Generally, for brokers, you could not wish to have a better account to deal with. Henry tended to trade in clips of $40 million to $100 million. John Henry was a CTA for whom everybody in the business had a phenomenal amount of respect.

CLOSING UP SHOP

They say, "All good things must come to an end," and for Henry, the end came in 2012 when assets fell below $100 million. In truth, assets had been tumbling since 2007 when Merrill Lynch withdrew roughly $600 million. A combination of trendless markets and low volatility contributed to a lack of performance commensurate with investors' expectations. With some of his programs suffering losses for the previous three years and client redemptions eating into management fees, the firm became too small to sustain itself. Henry returned the remaining assets to investors and closed the shop.

There were many autopsies about the reason why the trading behemoth imploded. Some said that Henry's diversification of interests away from running John W. Henry & Company to owning sports teams led him to take his eye off the ball. Some argued it was senior management turnover. Others, that the system didn't adapt to the times, or that he was running too many programs—up to 17 at one stage. Two things are certain: one, the volatility of his programs would not permit many successive downward years, and two, people don't like investing in losing systems.

In its heyday, the Financial and Metals program seldom lost money. In fact, in its first 20 years, it did not have any consecutive years of negative performance. In his last 7 years of trading, Henry's returns were consistent with flipping a coin. No one knew if he would win or lose. Perhaps the feeling of backing a certain winner disappeared, and the risk of heavy losses was too much. The painful fact was that on a 2 and 20 management and performance structure, 2 percent fees on $100 million doesn't feed many mouths, particularly if there is zero to negative performance. "The trend is your friend until it bends at the end."

In investment banking, traders either get promoted or move to other banks depending on how successful they are. In money management, it is very difficult to recover from significant downturns. Lose 20 percent, and you have to make 25 percent to get back to even. Lose 50 percent, and it takes 100 percent to get back to par. For hedge funds and CTAs, the incentive is to participate in performance fees. The management fee is really imposed to cover operational costs. The ability to recover performance to self-imposed "high-watermark levels" can be a long process after consecutive negative years. A question that no doubt crossed Henry's mind. In rosy times, companies can expand and hire rising stars. In times of difficulty everybody suddenly becomes more accountable. Vulnerabilities can quickly become exposed. Henry had nothing to prove to anybody. In fact, by closing down John W. Henry, he showed great tactical awareness. For many years he had been at the top of his game, and he had made millions from the market, he had made millions for other people, and he had provided jobs for a stack of people in his firm and for many at brokerages and banks who covered his account. Now quite simply he has transferred his skill set and business acumen to following another passion: sports. Hats off to John Henry!

So should we take trend following and technical trading with a large pinch of salt? The answer is yes and no. On the one hand, it can be a very risky strategy, and drawdowns can be large. On the other hand, returns can be magnificent. Trend following is not for the faint hearted or the lily livered. It requires patience, tenacity, and discipline.

HENRY'S SUCCESSES

While you cannot say Henry has a maxim per se, he did reveal his philosophy to *Profit & Loss* magazine in March 2005. He follows this philosophy across all his interests whether they be financial, sporting, or personal:

- One must have a valid personal philosophy.

- There is no Holy Grail to trading.

- Discipline is more important than genius.

- Persistence is more important than talent.

- Performance is more important than capability.

- Ability to create value is more important than ability or creativity in any realm.

- Continue to look for ways and to think about how you can create value.[12]

It is interesting that while many call him a genius, he puts a lot of his success down to philosophy and discipline. He also says there is no Holy Grail to trading. Richard Dennis and his Turtles proved that trading could be taught and that the quality of discipline, coupled with consistency, creates confidence.

On the subject of performance, it is remarkable, in both individual cases and at a more institutional level, how positive performance can attract attention and capital backing, however fortunate the reasons behind it. A good solid track record with the right voice finds wealth to back it. An individual can have positive accolades showered upon him or her. Small companies suddenly become large companies. As Henry said, "Performance is more important than capability." Henry is certainly no journeyman. He is a man of exceptional capability, and for many years his performance was second to none. His words have the wisdom and humility of a guru.

At the other end of the scale, sometimes the most talented traders in the world may suffer downward spirals and end up dispirited and possibly outcast. Luck certainly plays a role in things. It's amazing how quickly wealth can be destroyed and support retracted. Everybody likes to back a winner. It takes a special person to nurture losers, and yet ironically, some of the greatest gains in trend following happen shortly after huge drawdowns. To reiterate Curtis Faith's remarks, "It is necessary to let prices go against you if you are going to ride a trend. In the middle of a trend, it might mean watching a profit of 80 to 100 percent drop by 30 to 40 percent."[13] It takes tremendous courage to take these kinds of hits in the middle of a winning run. In a trend following system, investors should not bat an eyelid if it drops 10 percent in a year.

It's his final two points which may ultimately be the reason why Henry moved on:

- The ability to create value is more important than ability or creativity in any realm.

- Continue to look for ways and to think about how you can create value.[14]

At some stage, Henry realized he was no longer creating value in the financial markets. Whatever the reason, his Midas touch was no longer there. There comes a time when everybody must move on. Henry created something truly fantastic that worked incredibly well for two decades. He transitioned gracefully from running other people's money to using his undoubted genius to follow his sports passion. He almost instantly added value to the Boston Red Sox, and without doubt, with Henry at the helm, the Liverpool Football Club will rise again to English and European footballing greatness.

Henry is a superb role model on how to approach trading from both a philosophical and a psychological standpoint. From a well-researched and tested approach, he had an outstanding start to his managed futures program, ratcheting up 8 consecutive years of positive returns and increasing assets to well over $600 million. For a 20-year period, his programs were phenomenally successful, and his gains averaged over 30 percent. He ended up managing billions of dollars and making millions for himself and others. He had guts, determination, and above all discipline—qualities that, coupled with his mechanical approach to trading, allowed him to follow it with complete confidence. With respect to currencies, he took a very long term approach to trading. His stubbornness and willingness to follow a trend to its limits contributed to his outperforming his peer group and his becoming the number one trend following superstar. We can learn many lessons from Henry and indeed other trend following legends. It seems to be black and white. Follow your system with rigid discipline, manage your risk, and believe in the trend. Henry did it better than most. That is why he is a Currency King.

Urs Schwarzenbach: Writing FX Option Strangles

The *Sunday Times Rich List* is a peculiar publication. The annual compendium of the United Kingdom's richest is akin to the Forbes 500 list of American billionaires, but the *Sunday Times* focuses uniquely on those who reside in Great Britain and Northern Ireland (at least for part of the year). For some it comes (at least partially) as an intrusion on their privacy; for others of a more arriviste nature, it is the pinnacle of recognition of their achievements. Here, old-money aristocrats jostle for position with property tycoons and grocery parvenus, dandy football players and other athletes, beer-bellied brewers, and the like.

For a country of multiple social classes, it must be as ghastly for some blue bloods (who tend not to talk about money) to be ranked alongside the hoi polloi as it is joyous for some nouveau riche types to be seen mixing with the toffs. At the end of the day, it's all a bit of fun, which pops up a few surprises. And mixed in there with all the media moguls, industry barons, shipping magnates, or just plain inheritors, there are of course one or two characters from the world of hedge funds and financial markets.

One man who consistently makes the grade is the secretive Swiss billionaire Urs Schwarzenbach. The *Sunday Times* says he made his fortune trading currencies!

Urs Schwarzenbach is a very interesting man. He is perhaps the king of options trading. It takes tremendous courage to write options, and that is exactly what his Zurich-based foreign exchange dealership, Intex Exchange, does. Schwarzenbach is not afraid to take risk, neither in his vocation nor in his private life. If writing options is not a hazardous enough pastime, he until recently used to hurtle down St. Moritz's Cresta run—the one-man skeleton bobsleigh—until he broke his neck! He then concentrated on his other high-risk passion: polo, a high-paced amalgam of field hockey and flat-out horse riding. He owns his team, of course: the Black Bears. (*Urs* sounds like "ours" in French, which means "bear." *Schwartz* in German means "black.")

Schwarzenbach is a man of humble beginnings. He was born the son of a print shop owner on September 17, 1948, in Thalwil and raised in Küsnacht, both in Switzerland. Schwarzenbach graduated from the Commercial College of Zurich, after which he took a job at the Swiss Bank Corporation in 1968, making it onto the currency trading desk before being transferred to London in 1972, the same year that the Chicago Mercantile Exchange introduced currency futures. He successfully traded some money for his father, and by the mid-seventies he was already a millionaire. In 1976 he set up his own company, Intex Exchange, speculating in currencies with his own capital. It is here where he ultimately became one of the world's great options traders.

In terms of timing, Schwarzenbach joined the currency desk at Swiss Bank Corporation at precisely the right time. Until 1971, dealing in currencies was about as interesting as watching paint dry. But after the collapse of the Bretton Woods accord, trading currencies became an infinitely more exciting proposition and a source of profitability to many market making banks. Dealing in currency transformed from a tedious back-office function to an electrifying front-office market. As trading evolved, so too did those individuals who were in at the beginning. These were the innovators and dealers of the many new products that gained traction as worldwide FX volumes exploded exponentially.

BRETTON WOODS

Bretton Woods is the name of a town in northern New Hampshire in the White Mountains. It is here that as World War II was eking out its end game, 730 delegates from 44 allied countries met in July 1944. At this meeting in the Mount Washington Hotel, both the International Monetary Fund (IMF) and the International Bank for Reconstruction and Development (IBRD) were created as well as a system of rules and procedures to regulate the international monetary system and help refinance and rebuild the world after the many years of war.

Part of this set of rules was that member countries would fix their currencies to the U.S. dollar. The dollar in turn could be converted into gold at a price of $35 for 1 ounce of gold. In 1944, the United States held about two-thirds of the world's gold reserves, and the U.S. dollar was a robust reserve currency backed by a tremendous amount of gold. The gold depository was at Fort Knox in Kentucky, an impregnable fortress in the middle of a vast military camp.

NIXON AND THE GOLD STANDARD

The Bretton Woods Agreement held fairly solidly until the late sixties and early seventies. During this time there were significant outflows of gold, and U.S. reserves of the precious metal dwindled. President Richard Nixon felt impelled to sever the link between the U.S. dollar and gold because the United States simply did not have enough gold to cover the dollars held in foreign hands. He therefore prevented a "run" on Fort Knox. By 1973 Japan and the European Economic Community had allowed their currencies to float freely, therefore abandoning the era of fixed exchange rates.

THE BLACK-SCHOLES MODEL

The year 1973 can be remembered for another reason. It was the year that the Black-Scholes model for calculating the premium of an option was first introduced in a paper titled "The Pricing of Options and Corporate Liabilities," published in the *Journal of Political Economy*. The paper, written by three economists—Fischer Black, Myron Scholes, and Robert Merton—formed the basis of options pricing as we know it today. Scholes and Merton were awarded the 1997 Nobel Prize in Economics for their work in finding a new method to determine the value of derivatives. Fischer Black passed away in 1995, and he was not eligible for the award although his role in devising the model was acknowledged by the committee.

From the year 1984 until his untimely death in 1995 from throat cancer, Black worked at Goldman Sachs. Merton and Scholes, perhaps bizarrely, found infamy with Long-Term Capital Management, a hedge fund they cofounded in 1994. As Roger Lowenstein's aptly named book *When Genius Failed: The Rise and Fall of Long-Term Capital Management* describes, even the biggest, boldest, and best traders, backed up by the smartest quants of their era, could not defeat "Mr. Market." When their secret was out, their game was up! Having made spectacular returns for its first three years, LTCM blew up in 1998, losing $4.8 billion in just over four months—just one year after the Nobel Laureates had received their prize.

THE PHILADELPHIA STOCK EXCHANGE

Back in 1973, options trading was in its nascence. The newly created Chicago Board Options Exchange (CBOE) traded its first stock option on April 26, 1973, in a celebration of the 125th birthday of the Chicago Board of Trade (CBOT). Nowadays, the CBOE offers options on over 2,200 companies, 22 stock indexes, and 140 exchange-traded funds (ETFs), and it trades about 1 billion contracts annually.

Over on the East Coast, Philadelphia, which housed the oldest stock exchange in the United States, was looking for a new product. Chicago had currency futures, and Chicago had stock options. For some reason Chicago was not trading currency options. It took a lot of work, determination, and patience, and of course time, for currency options to be introduced on an exchange, but it was in Philadelphia and not in Chicago that they were first traded. And the credit for fighting through tiers of bureaucracy and regulation and getting options on the exchange goes to Arnie Staloff, by then a 10-year veteran of the exchange who was tasked with handling automation and new product development. The Philadelphia Stock Exchange traded its first currency options contracts on December 10, 1982.

THE EVOLUTION OF
FOREIGN EXCHANGE MARKETS

There is a perpetual argument on where it is better to trade: on exchange or over the counter? Proponents of exchange-traded contracts cite transparency and centralized clearing (therefore negating counterparty risk) as two of the most compelling reasons to trade on exchange. Those who support over-the-counter (OTC) trading explain that contract sizes are more bespoke and flexible, that liquidity and pricing are better, that more currency pairs can be traded, and that counterparties can remain anonymous. It's horses for courses. The market overall is ultimately more efficient because of these two trading media. About the same time as the Philadelphia Stock Exchange was launching its exchange-traded options, some investment banks started to launch options products of their own.

Schwarzenbach was by now a seasoned proprietary FX trader at Intex Exchange. The late 1970s and early 1980s were fruitful times. A combination of loose U.S. monetary policy and high global inflation pushed both the Swiss franc and the German mark up appreciably against a weakening dollar. Gold rose in an almost exponential fashion, moving from a low of about $100 per ounce in mid-1976 to just shy of $900 per ounce in January 1980. Schwarzenbach made a fortune during this time. Having watched how stock options had evolved, he saw the potential of FX options trading. He had experience and capital behind him. His destiny was set.

———

To say that the foreign exchange markets have evolved over the last 30 years is an understatement. In the 1980s spreads in the spot market were so wide you could drive a bus through them. Derivatives in foreign exchange—that is, products derived from, in this case, the spot market—were a license to print money. Every new complexity added a way to extract more profit. Those who devised these products or who had the balance sheet to assume the risk of writing options were in for bonanza profits. Naturally, it was clients who would suffer. In his book *F.I.A.S.C.O.*, Frank Partnoy describes how some clients in the fixed income derivatives markets had their "faces ripped off" or were just so gullible that they paid huge fees to buy products they didn't understand. In FX, it was a similar story. Buying protection (or hedging) against currency moves was expensive business. Options allowed investors to buy protection. The banks and market makers sold options and so held all the aces.

Suppose that spreads in the 1980s were 10 pips in, say, a liquid currency pair such as U.S. dollars against German marks. It could be more, it could be less. (Nowadays this pair would be euros versus dollars, and some brokers may offer 0.3 pip or even *choice*—that is, no spread.) The quote might look like this: 1.4320/1.4330. An inter-dealer broker would sell dollars at 1.4330, and he might be able to buy them at 1.4320. If the notional amount traded was $1 million, then the broker's profit would be 1,000 marks, or nearly $700 (1,000 marks divided by 1.4330, or $697.84 marked to market). The point to remember here is that there is a spread—quite a wide one—and a dealer, by being very neutral, could capture the spread all day long. USD/DEM was the busiest market, and dealers would make two-way prices as well as watch client orders. Sometimes they would cover their position; sometimes they would keep it on their books. Life was hectic, but there was a good deal of money to be made.

Take now a future. Not only is there a spread, possibly a wide one, but the currency is traded sometime in the future. This involves an interest rate—or two actually, as two currencies are involved. Say the interest rate differential between dollars and marks was 2 percent. There would be a spread on that too. A future is a slightly more complex instrument, and complexity means more ways to make profit—better for a dealer, worse for a client.

MONEYMAKING OPPORTUNITIES IN OPTIONS TRADING

When we move into the world of options, a whole plethora of moneymaking opportunities opens up for the market maker. I will explain these as simply as I can, but suffice it to say, the price of an option is made up of several components. If a client buys with a bank or dealer on the OTC market, then if she sells to the same dealer, she will pay the spread on top of that too. Perhaps here an options exchange is a better place to trade because there's nothing worse than being slipped on a profit or, worse still, getting skinned on a stop-loss by somebody who already knows your position and can make whatever market he wishes.

In the 1980s there was plenty of latitude for profit making in options. First, prices in the spot market were wide; second, there were many aspects to pricing an option that dealers could use to their advantage; third, there were few market makers; and fourth, the level of client sophistication and access to information and knowledge were inferior to what they are today. Buying options was a very expensive business indeed!

When you trade spot, the normal settlement date is two days later. So if you trade on January 18, you would expect your trade to settle on January 20, which is the spot date. In most brokerages, unless you desire physical delivery of currency into your account, the position will be rolled over. So on January 19, your positions will be rolled over "tom-next" from January 20 to January 21 (from tomorrow to the next day). You will be paid interest minus a spread (of course), or you will pay interest (plus a spread) for this service. So, for example, if you buy New Zealand dollars against U.S. dollars and the New Zealand interest rate is 2.75 percent and the U.S. rate is 0.25 percent, you would expect to receive interest on your New Zealand dollars. If you buy New Zealand dollars in the future, it will cost fewer U.S. dollars to buy New Zealand dollars because the interest differential is favorable to the kiwi. The logic is as follows. If NZD/USD is trading at 0.6740 for spot (two-day settlement), why would you pay more to buy NZD in the future if you receive interest for owning NZD?

Options allow you to buy or sell an amount of currency at a guaranteed price at some time in the future. This might be above or below the current spot price. Just as in actuarial science, used for calculating the likelihood of future events for insurance purposes, the rules of probability are applied. In the case of options, the Black-Scholes model for pricing options provides the basis for obtaining the correct price. The Black-Scholes model was originally derived to calculate the price of "European-style options"—that is, options that can be exercised only on a set date in the future. "American-style options" allow you to exercise them at any time after a deal is struck. This added flexibility of course increases the price you pay to buy an option. It is one of the many components that need to be taken into account. The main components of an options price are the *current market price*, *strike price*, *volatility*, and *time*. Other variables such as interest rates can affect an options price. Some of the characteristics of pricing are attributable to "the Greeks," which include delta, gamma, and vega, in addition to the already mentioned rho (interest) and theta (time). Below is an explanation of how they all work together to determine an option's price.

There are two basic types of options: calls and puts.

A *currency call option* is a contract in which the holder (buyer) has the right (*but not the obligation*) to buy a specified quantity of a currency *A* versus another currency *B* at a specified price (*strike price*) within a fixed period of time (until its expiration).

For the writer (seller) of a call option, it represents an obligation to sell the quantity of currency *A* versus currency *B* at the strike price if the option is exercised. The call option writer is paid a premium for taking on the risk associated with the obligation.

A *currency put option* is an option contract in which the holder (buyer) has the right (*but not the obligation*) to sell a specified quantity of a currency *A* versus another currency *B* at a specified price (*strike price*) within a fixed period of time (until its expiration).

For the writer (seller) of a put option, it represents an obligation to buy the quantity of currency *A* versus currency *B* at the strike price if the option is exercised. The put option writer is paid a premium for taking on the risk associated with the obligation.

An example would be if you were to buy a euro call option against U.S. dollars. The option would be priced as a euro call (dollar put) in, say, 1 million euros at a strike price 1.10 for one month. If EUR/USD were currently trading at 1.10, then this would be *at-the-money* (ATM). If EUR/USD were trading at 1.12, then the option would be *in-the-money* (ITM). You could exercise the option at 1.10 and sell euros at 1.12. If EUR/USD were trading at 1.08, the option would be *out-of-the-money* (OTM).

Option pricing is based on a *normal distribution*—an arrangement of a data set in which most values cluster in the middle of the range and the rest taper off symmetrically toward either extreme (Figure 4.1). Most of the data values can be found within 3 standard deviations of the mean. A standard deviation of 1 on either side of the mean covers 68.2 percent of values; 2 standard deviations, 95.4 percent; and 3 standard deviations, 99.7 percent.

Annual volatility is equal to the expected 1 year, 1 standard deviation price change. If this is 10 percent, then in our EUR/USD option example with the euro trading at-the-money at 1.10 versus the U.S. dollar, we would expect with 99 percent confidence (3 standard deviations) that the euro will trade between 0.77 and 1.43 against the U.S. dollar in the next year: $1.10 \pm 3 \times 0.11$.

Volatility is proportional to the square root of time. To calculate one month's volatility, we divide the annual volatility by the square root of 12, which equals 3.464. Weekly volatility can be found by dividing the annual volatility by the square root of 52, which equals 7.211. To work out our one-month 1.10 ATM call, we calculate 10 percent annual volatility in monthly terms: 10 percent of 1.10 is 0.11. Therefore, we calculate 1 month, 1 standard deviation as 0.11/3.464, or 0.03176. We would expect with 99

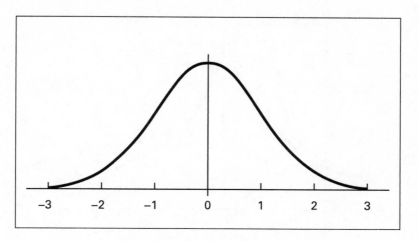

Figure 4.1 A normal distribution.

percent confidence that the euro would trade within a range of 1.10 ± 3(0.03176), or between 1.0047 and 1.1953 during that month.

OPTIONS RISKS

Options buying and selling may seem pretty straightforward, but in fact, it is not. There are two things we must know.

First, in times of stress, markets do not follow a normal distribution. Tails get fatter (Figure 4.2). Extremes in price movements happen. We cannot be 99 percent sure that our currency will trade in the range that volatility predicts. While currency markets appear to be far more liquid nowadays, this in some cases is a mirage because there are many high-frequency algorithms that trade billions and billions of dollars per day. These algorithms are programmed to seek out value in all manner of ways. When panic sets in, algorithms panic faster and can drill markets far beyond 3 standard deviations of volatility. The Swiss franc

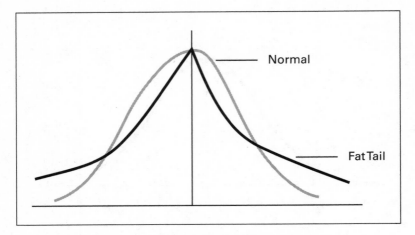

Normal

Fat Tail

Figure 4.2 A *fat tail* means a distribution of prices much greater than 3 standard deviations from the mean. There are far more prices at the extremes of the distribution. It could be 5, 6, or more standard deviations.

movement in January 2015 was a good example of this. The Swiss franc gained nearly 40 percent in a matter of minutes.

Second, in currency markets, as in other markets, we have something called a *volatility smile* (Figure 4.3). This causes ITM and OTM calls and puts of the same expiry to trade with increasing rates of implied volatility—something that was not lost on Schwarzenbach and something we should all remember! With respect to the possibility of a fat-tail events, people pay for the right to buy deep out-of-the-money calls and puts in the case of just such an event. This pushes up the volatility of the OTM options. People are paying more for the less likely event.

Why is this worth remembering? Because in rosy times when prices conform to the Black-Scholes model, at least 30 percent of options expire worthless. There are some who argue that 80 to 90 percent of options lose money! If volatility is overpriced in the first place, the options writer has a better chance of collecting her premium, again and again. Others' options are closed out before expiry and may not cover the premium paid. The writer of

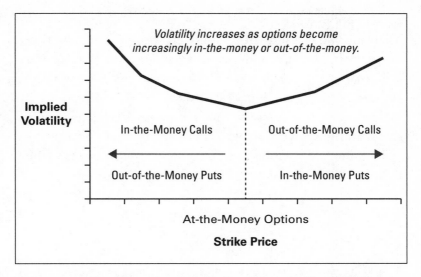

Figure 4.3 The *volatility smile* depicts the volatility of ITM and OTM calls of the same expiry increasing compared to ATM calls.

the option always collects premium. If the purchaser of an option does not exercise, the writer collects the whole premium. The purchaser of the option will normally exercise on or before expiry if the option is in-the-money. Failing that, he may close out the option at a loss before expiry to collect what little time value is left on the table.

Should we all therefore write options? Not necessarily. First, it is highly unlikely you will ever be paid the correct premium. Remember, you are dealing with market makers who hold all the aces. Second, extreme events can happen that can ratchet up the volatility and hence the price of an option. If you are on the wrong side of a big move in volatility and the underlying currency pair, your losses can be considerable. The fallout of the Swiss franc in January 2015 was a good example of this. The flash move undoubtedly humbled many, as did the rapid collapse of the Russian ruble in December 2014. In fact, there have been several fat-tail events in the last 20 years. Writing options is risky business because losses are potentially unlimited.

In options, volatility is a key component of an option's price. There are two measures of volatility that people should be aware of—namely, historical and implied volatility. Historical volatility is derived from actual prices and is known as *statistical volatility*. *Implied volatility* is a gauge of market traders' expectations. By and large, implied volatility trades at higher levels than historical volatility. It is worthwhile comparing the two measures, especially if implied volatility is trading higher. When one is writing options, this is a source of extra profit in stable markets.

THE GREEKS

The measure of an option's sensitivity to changes in volatility is known as *vega*. The price of an option may change despite the spot price not moving. Longer-term options are more sensitive to changes in volatility and therefore have a higher vega. Say you are long a six-week euro call. There may be news that some hitherto unexpected announcement has been tabled to be released in the coming few days regarding the eurozone. Volatility may increase. That increase is due to vega. The option call may become more expensive.

A better-known Greek is *delta*. The definition of delta is the amount that an option price will change given a small change in price of the underlying currency. So, for example, if a euro call is trading with a delta of 50, for every pip the euro trades higher, the option will gain half a pip in value. As the option moves more into-the-money, the delta increases. Deep in-the-money options have deltas near 100.

The rate of change of delta is known as *gamma*. If you know what gamma is and you have an original level of delta, you can calculate the new delta. Just below the option strike price, when delta is at 50 percent, gamma is usually at its highest and then will start to tail off. At this point the rate of change of delta will start to decelerate. It is important to remember that delta is valid for only a narrow range of currency prices. If you have a call option with a 50 delta, you cannot assume that if your currency rises by 200 pips, your option will rise by 100 pips.

Rho, or rate of interest, has less of an effect on an option's price, but any rate increase or decrease in either of the currencies involved in the option will affect the price. An increase in the interest rate differential will increase call values and decrease put values with options, sensitivity to interest rates increasing with longer expiry dates.

The other great moneymaking mechanism in writing options is time, or *theta* (Figure 4.4). The atrophying effect of the value of an option in its last few weeks if all other factors remain constant is certainly due to time decay. The theory behind this is that an option with four months until expiry has a much greater chance of ending up in-the-money than one with four weeks until expiry.

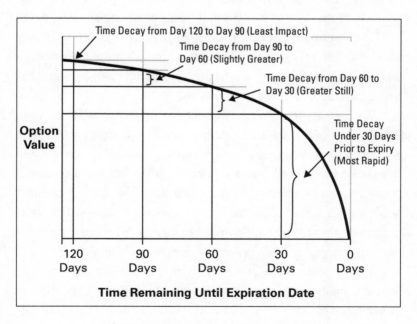

Figure 4.4 Time decay for options.

As can be seen from the diagram, the last month before an option expires sees the greatest decay in an option's value due to time.

There are many great textbooks for learning about the Greeks, and indeed how they interact with each other. One of the best practical workbooks is *The Option Trader's Workbook* by Jeff Augen. It works through progressively more complex problems involving the Greeks, and it is well worth reading for a more thorough understanding of option pricing dynamics. There are also several option calculators that you can use online to give you an idea of how option prices move with different input values for the option variables.

STRADDLES AND STRANGLES

But what we have now, and what Urs Schwarzenbach had right at the inception of option market making, are two of the key ingredients to success in an option writing strategy. Sell short dated out-of-the-money options and benefit from mispriced volatility and time decay. How could he do this and minimize his risk even further? The answer is found in combining puts and calls in what are known as *straddles* and *strangles*.

With a *long straddle*, the purchaser simultaneously buys both a call and a put at the same strike price. It is a strategy in which the buyer expects a breakout of a particular price range (around his strike price) and looks to benefit from both a directional move and an increase in implied volatility. This is a "precision" trade, and it is best executed at times of low volatility. The trade suffers doubly from time erosion because the effect of time is felt on both the put and the call as the options near maturity.

The opposite, of course, is a *short straddle* (Figure 4.5). The writer benefits from earning premium on both the call and the put. If implied volatility is at elevated levels and is higher than historical volatility, then provided that the market stays relatively

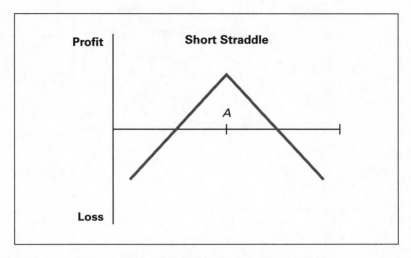

Figure 4.5 Profit and loss for a short straddle
(the maximum profit is at point *A*).

range bound, the option loses its value at an ever increasing rate as time eats into the trade. The writer of this option hopes to benefit from the volatility dropping and the time value diminishing to zero.

With a long strangle, the purchaser simultaneously buys both a call and a put at different strike prices. It is a strategy in which the buyer expects a breakout of a particular price range (outside of the strike prices) and looks to benefit from both a directional move and an increase in implied volatility. This is also a precision trade, and it is best executed at times of low volatility. It is less expensive and more conservative than a straddle. The trade suffers doubly from time erosion as the effect of time is felt on both the put and the call as the options near maturity. Because of the different strike prices, the trade has to at least breach one of the strikes in order for it to make any money.

And now to the *short strangle* (Figure 4.6). The writer benefits from earning premium on both the call and the put. As both the call and put strike are out-of-the-money, if we take into consideration

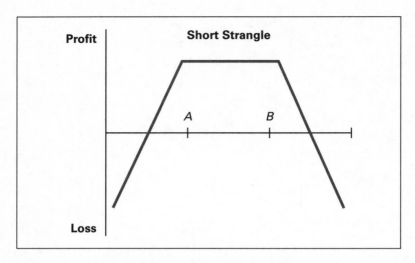

Figure 4.6 Profit and loss for a short strangle.
(Maximum profit is between points *A* and *B*.)

"the volatility smile," we know that the option seller benefits from higher implied volatility than is attributable to the at-the-money strikes of the straddle. If implied volatility is at elevated levels and is higher than historical volatility, then provided that the market stays relatively range bound, the option loses its value at an ever increasing rate as time eats into the trade. The writer of this option hopes to benefit from the volatility dropping and the time value diminishing to zero.

Et voilà! For a market maker, selling strangles of short duration in the high-spread, high-commission markets of the eighties was almost a no-brainer. In most cases the option would expire worthless. In a few cases, with one side of the strangle in-the-money, the out-of-the-money element of the strategy would mitigate some of the losses. If the in-the-money part of the option was exercised, the market maker could make money on the spread and charge commissions. Finally, if the option was moving well into-the-money, the market maker could buy or sell spot currency or options to hedge her risk.

This was the basis of Schwarzenbach's strategy. It was immensely profitable. There are a few non-bank market makers in the FX world. Schwarzenbach became the biggest and best in the FX options market. He was young and dynamic and respected, and he had already made millions for himself. He had the capital to support a product where he had an excellent chance of winning every time he wrote an option. He turned his knowledge into his competitive advantage and became a market maker at the earliest stage of FX options.

SCHWARZENBACH'S NONBUSINESS ACTIVITIES

Tracking down Urs Schwarzenbach is no easy task! Information about his business activities is about as sparse as that of the chief of the Secret Intelligence Service. Intex Exchange has no website although it is often labeled as the biggest foreign exchange dealership in Switzerland. Checking out Schwarzenbach on Bloomberg reveals very little aside from the odd business investment in Mongolia.

But the social pages run riot with seemingly his every activity. In the United Kingdom he has settled down on a large estate, Culham Court, near the River Thames in Henley, Oxfordshire. He has acquired several other neighboring estates and river frontage, and he has paid over the odds for many of them. His accumulation of land is also an accumulation of privacy. He is rumored to police his estate with former Special Forces soldiers. In every essence he lives the life of an English aristocrat. Culham Court comes replete with a deer park, walled garden, maze, and mile-long drive. It is a stone's throw from Henley, famed for its rowing regattas. He sponsors the rowing gallery, and the River and Rowing Museum is named after him.

Then of course he has his polo ponies—a passion that leads him to compete at all the great polo playing venues, such as the Guards Polo Club grounds in Windsor, Cirencester Park in Gloucestershire, and Cowdray Park in Sussex. He is coincidentally CEO of the St. Moritz Polo Corporation, which organizes the famous Polo on Ice on Lake St. Moritz, the exclusive Swiss ski resort. Through polo, of course, there are links to the British Royal Family. Schwarzenbach is a friend of Prince Charles. His wife, Francesca, is the godmother of the daughter of Prince Edward. Prince Harry stayed at one of the Schwarzenbachs' properties in Australia during his year off.

Collecting property and collecting art are two of Schwarzenbach's extravagances. And it is here that we can understand a little more about his character. Apart from being incredibly shrewd and secretive in his business life, he indulges passionately in things he considers beautiful and in need of nurturing.

With respect to architecture, he owns some wonderful examples of buildings in many different countries, and he has lavished millions of dollars in renovating and improving them. Culham Court in the United Kingdom is a fine example of a Georgian country home. Schwarzenbach paid millions over the asking price to acquire the property, and it has a budget of many more millions for the extensive upgrading of the house and grounds. In Scotland, Schwarzenbach bought the Ben Alder estate on Loch Ericht with grounds of 26,000 acres. In Australia he has land and houses and farms and polo fields encompassing 123,000 acres. In Marrakesh, Morocco, he owns Palais Layadi, a ruin of some 4,000 square meters that took him 18 months and millions of dollars to restore to its original glory. Schwarzenbach admits, "I have a passion for building! For the last 30 years, I have been doing up houses from Australia to Scotland."[1] In the United Kingdom, he also owns an estate in the Isle of Wight, home of many famous sailing events.

Perhaps his greatest personal investment in terms of time, money, and attention to detail is the Dolder Grand Hotel in Zurich, Switzerland. Schwarzenbach is a 90 percent shareholder of the property, and he is rumored to have spent nearly half a billion dollars renovating it. It was a project that took 10 years. Of this iconic Swiss hotel and the finished product, he remarked, "The result is spectacular—and even more beautiful than I had hoped."[2]

What better place, then, to house his art collection? If he made a fortune trading currencies, then he has certainly made another fortune by astutely buying priceless works of art. The contemporary art market has spiraled in the last 30 years, and Schwarzenbach's fortune has benefited from it. In July 2015, Schwarzenbach was fingered as being the anonymous seller of a collection of Andy Warhol silk-screen paintings of dollar bills at Sotheby's in London. Those that did sell netted tens of millions of dollars.

However, it is at the Dolder Grand, Schwarzenbach's showpiece hotel, where he exhibits many of his finer pieces. *Centurion Magazine* has described the hotel thus: "A picture-perfect retreat on the outskirts of Switzerland's buzzy financial hub, Zurich, this immaculate property, well over 100 years old, is considered one of Europe's finest, not least for its magnificent collection of artwork, which includes pieces by Dalí, Miró, Haring, and Andy Warhol. Eclectic, yet subtle decor makes for an elegant milieu in each of its 176 rooms and suites."[3] Here, in addition to the masterpiece paintings, you will find sculptures from Man Ray, Enzo Cucchi, and Miquel Barceló. In the private dining room, there is an entire series by Danish French Impressionist Camille Pissaro. Outside on the terraces, pieces by Henry Moore and Fernando Botero. The collection ratchets up Schwarzenbach's net worth by many more millions. Perhaps fittingly he displays the vast trappings of his wealth in the city where he made it.

BUYING FROM SCHWARZENBACH

Meeting Schwarzenbach outside of high-end social events is also a difficult task. As a foreign exchange sales team, a colleague of mine and I met with Schwarzenbach in early 2000 at his villa in St. Moritz. To get that far involved a series of other meetings with intermediaries in what could be described only as a discreet vetting process. Prior to the meeting in St. Moritz, we had a meeting at Intex Exchange in Zurich. Our purpose was to provide foreign exchange pricing to one of the biggest hitters in the market. We were confident that he would need our liquidity. It turned out that we were mistaken.

Schwarzenbach was exceedingly polite and courteous, and after the perfunctory offer of tea or coffee, we got down to business. We explained who we were and why we were there, and we gave the usual sales pitch of how we could add value, how superior our pricing was, and how this was so obviously a "win" opportunity. Schwarzenbach's retort was unequivocally cutting. "But you are not market makers!" He was right, of course. We were "agency brokers," and while we could make a market to anybody, in general, we would have to get calls out to cover most of that risk. He was taking far bigger positions than we could reasonably take onto our books. And our pricing would not be good enough for him.

It was then that we talked about options in a little more detail. We had a successful options dealing desk, and we really thought we could make him a market. "Of course you can make me a market, but I am a seller of options." By definition, therefore, he was a collector of premium. We would be buying from him, which in turn meant that we therefore either wanted to create a long position in either a put or call or we had somebody else we could sell it on to, at a profit. He was a bigger market maker than we were, and we would have to pay his price to buy the options that he wished to sell. He would sell us strangles in quite sizable amounts, in, say, $50 million or $100 million. We knew that strangles suffered from both time decay and mispriced volatility. Unless we really wanted the position for a speculative punt, our only resort was to sell it on to the market. It would be very difficult for us to find the other side of the trade. If we sold to a bank, we would be selling at a loss. In reality, Schwarzenbach was already selling to the banks.

This launched us into a discussion about strangles and straddles and the evolution of options trading. Schwarzenbach was an expert on his subject. We sat there in awe as he explained that in the beginning of options trading, the level of sophistication was poor. He had worked out very quickly the attritional value of time on an options price. In the early days he sold very short dated options with one day's or two days' or a week's duration. As the banks got into the game, he had to sell longer duration options, one to two weeks to one month and then finally one month and longer. He was helped by the volatility smile, the fact that in-the-money or out-the-money puts and calls of the same expiry have higher volatility compared to at-the-money puts and calls, and how this and selling strangles allowed him to profit.

RISK MANAGEMENT

Clearly this man was an early adopter of a strategy. He had done the work and built himself a reputation first at a high-pedigree bank and then as a courageous and successful trader with his own company. Lack of product knowledge and sophistication by the market had allowed him to milk his competitive advantage in options market making, and he benefited from having the capital to scale up his trades. As the banks became more adept at pricing themselves, they ate into his profit making abilities but still allowed him to make a sizable living. His investments had been thorough and wise. He'd kept his business under the radar and not trumpeted from the turrets about the source of his wealth. He'd successfully built up a large property and art portfolio, and it was only the trappings of wealth and his property investments that had really brought him into the limelight. We had indeed found his name in the *Sunday Times Rich List*, which is how our journey to meet him had come about.

But what about risk management, the key definer of winning big or blowing up? Ninety-nine percent of people lose money in FX by either overleveraging or overtrading. How on earth could a strategy of writing options stand up to the big fat-tail potential of unlimited losses should the market go crazy? The events of 1998—the events that humbled Myron Scholes and Robert Merton, the great option theorists and Nobel Prize winners of 1997; that leveled Long-Term Capital Management; and that scarred the careers of the successful bond traders who had been plucked from Salomon Brothers to run the original super quant fund—would also affect Intex Exchange. If 1992 and Soros's attack on the Bank of England had given us a sample of how quickly FX markets could implode, then there were several very jittery days in 1998 and one in particular when USD/JPY fell out of bed.

The events of the summer of 1998, in particular in Russia, triggered a very violent phase in the foreign exchange markets. Russia defaulted on its domestic debt and devalued the ruble on August 17, 1998. Prior to this, the Russian Central Bank had maintained a "floating peg" currency band of USD/RUB 5.3 to 7.1, and either side of the band, it would intervene to preserve currency stability by either selling or buying rubles. Russia is one of the BRIC economies composed of Brazil, Russia, India, and China. In 1997, the world had suffered from the Asia financial crisis, and the fallout from this "contagion" had spread west throughout 1998.

Russia's foreign exchange reserves evaporated as the demand for oil and commodities deteriorated as a consequence of the Asian financial crisis. Foreign investment into Russia reversed as money was repatriated and left the country. In June, Russia raised short-term interest rates on zero-coupon Russian Government Treasury Bills (GKOs) to 150 percent in order to stem capital outflows while maintaining the currency peg. But still capital moved out of Russian investments. On July 13, 1998, in a bid to rescue the situation, a financial package was approved with the International Monetary Fund and the World Bank to swap GKOs into Eurobonds to the tune of $22.6 billion. By this stage confidence in the Russian capital markets had all but disappeared. The final nail in the coffin for the Russian treasury was that it could not service its debt repayments because its fiscal deficit was in a mess. On the August 13, the Russian ruble came under severe pressure, and stock and bond markets got hammered. The stock market even closed for 35 minutes to catch its breath. Something had to give, and on August 17 the world got the shock that it had in some ways been prepared for.

On August 17, 1998, the Russian government announced a set of emergency measures aimed at stemming the crisis. These included devaluing the ruble to a band of 6.0 to 9.5, defaulting on its short-term bond debt, and establishing a 90-day debt moratorium on payments by commercial banks to foreign creditors.

The lower boundary on the ruble was soon put under pressure, and ultimately the government abandoned the peg and allowed the ruble to float freely. It found its lowest measure at about 21 rubles to the dollar in September—a massive devaluation. The ructions of this almost unspeakable phenomenon—a central bank defaulting on its debt—reverberated around the world, and the flying money sought safety in, among other things, newly minted, liquid Treasury bonds. As the demand for these increased, so too did the price. Long-Term Capital Management happened to be short vast quantities of on-the-run liquid bonds as part of a convergence arbitrage strategy against less liquid off-the-run bonds of the same maturity. It capped a disastrous few months for the fund, which started to implode, causing wide-spread panic among its counterparties, eventually leading to a New York Fed and investment bank consortium bailout and a quarter-point interest rate cut in the United States, on September 29, to stabilize matters.

Russia, on the other hand, quickly emerged from its crisis due in part to the weak ruble and a recovery in the price of oil. It would become one of the stalwarts in the BRIC quartet of emerging countries that would offer excellent investment opportunities for the next 15 years for those of a less risk-averse nature.

The whole episode in Russia, the collapse of LTCM, and the U.S. interest rate cut added increased uncertainty in the markets and caused many fraught and tense days in the London time zone as Asian desks passed their books to London and the dealers not only had to cope with Asian jitters but also had to look forward to the day ahead with gold, USD/DEM, and USD/CHF all bouncing around on rumors, counterrumors, feints, and counterfeints. In a word, the markets were choppy, and traders were irritable as good trades suddenly went sour and poor trades would seemingly cost more to exit from. "It was just one of those periods you had to work through as best you could!" said Mark O'Niell, who traded EFPs at Prudential Bache at the time. "The best strategy was neutrality and to quote and cover, because the markets would just suddenly spike up or down and even small positions could end up hurting."[4]

One of Prudential's bolder traders, Mark Davison, was looking after the USD/JPY book. Prudential, with its network of Asian branches and metals business in Tokyo, had some big accounts in the Far East, and Davison was kept busy with this and also quoting some sizable hedge funds and commodity trading advisors. Along with USD/DEM, USD/JPY was probably the most active currency pair that the brokerage made markets in.

OCTOBER 7, 1998

Davison was a very sharp operator and a cool head under pressure. In busy times, as others in the room started to flap and their voices became more shrill, Davison was the complete opposite. He seemed to thrive under pressure, and his voice if anything became deeper. His calmness was somehow inversely proportional to the chaos going on around him. He was the perfect man to control the USD/JPY book. Thankfully he was there when it all booted off! October 7, 1998, was one of those days. In contrast to the heavy pressured relentless assault on sterling in September 1992, the USD/JPY collapse on the afternoon of October 7 was short, sharp, and brutal. The intensity of the collapse was incredible as was the sudden recovery. As dollar-yen got hammered from all sides, Davison kept his cool and booked his annual P&L in the space of about 75 minutes.

Hindsight analysis of those tumultuous moments pins the finger on carry trade unwinding and institutional deleveraging although Mintao Fan and Richard Lyons, in their piece "Customer Trades and Extreme Events in Foreign Exchange," have suggested that non-leveraged institutions such as pension funds, mutual funds, and insurance companies had a hand in selling dollars before and during the collapse that was taking place.[5] One thing is for certain: as the yen rapidly increased in value, it was definitely leveraged players trading through Prudential Bache. And for the most part, they were all sellers of dollars!

It's not as if it started off gracefully. One large order in the market ruptured whatever support there was, and dollar-yen nosedived. Rumors through the broker boxes were that Tiger, a fund run by fabled FX hero Julian Robertson, was off-loading. As the rout got more and more intense, salespeople all over the City were clambering over each other to get prices out. But prices were scarce to come by. "There was a lot of noise, and the best gauge was the Marshalls and Tullets boxes," said Davison. "There was nothing tradable on the electronic platforms, and the banks were quoting one to two big figures wide." Davison continued, "Any buyer of dollars just got bull-dozered, and I held on to those positions to set off against all the dollars I was being given!"[6]

"The screaming and noise were just extraordinary," commented a back-office observer, "as a frenzied group of about 16 men just seemed to yell at each other."

No time for swearing now. This thing was as slick as it gets, and in just over an hour it was done. Dollar-yen had collapsed from the high 120s down to 112 and then back to about 116. Calm was restored, and the process of writing out tickets and checking blotters to see that all trades matched occupied the rest of the afternoon.

If traders like Davison had enjoyed a profitable afternoon, those who had been distressed sellers and those who had been writers of options did not fare as well. As dollar-yen came tumbling down, volatility ramped up, and long straddles and strangles moved into the money. The volatility smile only added pain, and Schwarzenbach's strategy at least partially backfired. He is estimated to have lost in the hundreds of millions of dollars that afternoon. Robertson is believed to have lost $2 billion.

In nominal terms, these amounts might sound extraordinary, but if you compare them to some of John Henry's intra-month profit-and-loss swings, then they are not. In 1998, Schwarzenbach was arguably valued at over a billion dollars. A $100 million or $200 million loss, while painful, was not the end of the world. Similarly, Robertson was running a fund with assets of the order of $20 billion at the time. In both cases, given the severity of the move, a 10 percent loss seems acceptable. John Henry, by contrast, had 14 monthly drawdowns of more than 10 percent in the years from 1984 to 1998 at an average of 1 per year, and yet it hardly raises comment.

MANAGING LOSS EXPECTATIONS

There's a lesson for all of us here. A 10 percent loss, however unpalatable, should be the kind of acceptable risk we are prepared to take in order to make longer-term gains in the foreign exchange markets. In the dollar-yen move of 1998, there were no doubt multiple wipeouts. The move was roughly 10 percent. Multiply this by the degree of leverage to work out the potential for losses. Ten times leverage for the whole move would compute to a total wipeout.

Retail FX was in its early stages in 1998 with Saxo Bank and CMC Markets in their infant years and FXCM not yet formed, and so fortunately, the 400-to-1 leverage that some retail brokers now offer was not available. There were also plenty of opportunities to get out of a long USD/JPY trade. There were prices—albeit wide ones—the whole way down. In 1998, voice dealers ruled the market. In later years, as computer technology advanced, with 2008 and 2015 as two good examples, a new word entered the FX vernacular. *Collapse* was replaced by *flash crash*! And getting out of poor trades would become infinitely more difficult.

OPTIONS-BASED PRODUCTS

Schwarzenbach would continue to trade options after 1998 and look to monetize his competitive advantage, although the banks by now were more than competent at making markets in strangles and straddles. He diversified in some part by investing in properties and in their renovation and pursuing his other passion as an art collector. Intex Exchange survives, but nowadays Schwarzenbach is more likely to be considered an investor. Among other things, he owns a stake in Mongolian Bank, Golomt, through his company Swiss-Mo Investment Ag.

As we draw this chapter to a close, it seems that there is a whole range of new options products being offered to, shall we say, less sophisticated investors. Binary options with win/lose payouts attached to them are available on very small time framed trades. "Where will EUR/USD trade at the end of the next minute?" seems to make a mockery of serious trading! Longer dated call or put options on stocks (known as *warrants*) are very popular in Asia. I'm not sure either of these two products has sufficient information explaining them or options properly to the hungry investor induced to trade by the potential of quick short-term profits in the case of binaries, or in the case of warrants, longer-term unlimited gains.

Many structured products, such as capital-protected products, are based around zero-couponed bonds coupled with option calls and puts. It can be quite a complex process to decompose a structured product into its components to find the true cost of the product and the hidden fees and charges. Too difficult, perhaps, for the layman buyers of these products to understand? But for the longest time, that's how the sellers of these products wanted to keep it!

SCHWARZENBACH'S SUCCESSES

Nothing, however, should be taken away from Urs Schwarzenbach, and he deserves full credit for being a market maker for many years to the banks, using his own capital and nous to offer products that the banks wanted and putting his cash on the line for his just rewards. For a trader to survive for 40 years in the market and incrementally increase his wealth shows that whatever formula he used is correct.

In the previous chapter, we learned how discipline seemed to be the standout prerequisite for trading the trend. In the chapters about Soros and Henry, we learned that trusting a philosophy was also a key ingredient in mastering the trading game. And in times of hardship, two other key qualities are courage and tenacity.

Schwarzenbach possesses all of these skills and attributes. Schwarzenbach epitomizes the Swiss propensity to maintain secrecy about business dealings. This in itself requires the utmost discipline. He would keep the limelight off himself entirely if the trappings of his wealth weren't so eagerly reported by glamour magazines. Soros divulged his trading philosophy in his book *The Alchemy of Finance*. Long-term trend following is well documented in, among other places, books about Turtle trading. Schwarzenbach has kept absolutely tight lipped about his trading methodology and profits. Why on earth would he wish others to share in his winning formula or have others encroach on his privacy?

In his private sporting activities, both riding the Cresta run and playing polo require immense courage, nerve, and skill. Trading big is a different skill, and very few traders have the stamina or mental courage to cope with the pressure of running huge positions. Scaling up and riding through tough times is a skill set all its own. And it is this that separates the truly great traders from the also-rans. Schwarzenbach once again shows he has this skill set. He brushed off his losses in 1998 as part of the hazards of trading. He was still writing options in the years after the dollar-yen collapse.

Perhaps one quality that some might miss but that is so apparent in Schwarzenbach is passion. Artists are considered passionate, but foreign exchange traders seldom are. To master an instrument requires passion, but to master a market? Schwarzenbach exudes passion in everything he does. Renovating the Dolder Grand in Zurich is perhaps his masterpiece, a showpiece he built up to by spending years renovating other beautiful buildings. He has only the very best horses. He is passionate about the countryside and landscapes. A trip to Loch Ericht in Scotland or to the skiing town of St. Moritz and you will quickly understand the allure. He is passionate about art and sculpture. He is also passionate about currency trading, for which he is a grand master.

A legitimate competitive advantage is so difficult to find and yet so crucial to winning in any field. Maybe Schwarzenbach was in at the right time, but he found his competitive advantage, and it was in writing currency options. He had a solid grounding in FX as an interbank dealer with one of Switzerland's top banks. He knew his product inside out and where he could extract maximum profit. When it came to executing his trading strategy, he had the capital to support his business, and his risk management systems were robust enough to take a hit in 1998. For me, he ticks all the boxes and covers the "four basic principles" set out in Chapter 1. He has personally made billions from the markets. Urs Schwarzenbach is one of the greats of options trading in the FX market, which is why he stands out as a Currency King.

Online Currency Entrepreneurs: How the Early FX Market Makers Grew from Pioneers to Billionaires

PETER CRUDDAS

"Monaco to Prescot Street, how the mighty have fallen!" These were my welcoming words to CMC Markets from Peter Cruddas, the billionaire owner who had hired me to set up his Hong Kong office. I had indeed met Cruddas in Monaco, where we both lived, and his enthusiasm and vision for his company were irrepressible. He had spotted, very early in the game, that the market for retail FX was stratospheric, and he was intent on building CMC's footprint far and wide.

After meeting his senior management team, I was to spend a few weeks in London, learning the systems, meeting with key individuals, and embracing the CMC culture. I would then depart for Asia. Here, of course, there was an "outstanding opportunity!" Evidence from his Australian office had proved this.

Hong Kong, he considered, was the gateway to China and potentially millions of clients—regulators and authorities permitting. Simultaneously, CMC was embarking on expanding its reach into Canada and Germany. If Cruddas had a vision, he was certainly implementing it. The year was 2004. Cruddas's welcome, albeit caustic and representing his own inimitable humor, was at the same time inspiring. Here was a man who just 15 years earlier had started his company with GBP 10,000. Since then, he had taken it and himself to the doorstep of billionaire status. And his story was just beginning.

Cruddas is all the more remarkable because of his humble beginnings. The son of a Smithfield Market meat porter, Cruddas was brought up in London's East End, and he left Shoreditch Comprehensive School at age 15 without any qualifications. His first job was at Western Union in the City of London, where he worked as a telex operator. Over the next few years he worked at various banks as a foreign exchange dealer, including Marine Midland and the Bank of Iran, before heading up foreign exchange at the London branch of the Jordanian-based Petra Bank. He left Petra Bank in 1989 and set up CMC, becoming an inter-dealer broker, which is the business of matching foreign exchange trades for banks in the interbank market. His Middle Eastern contacts would come in handy. In the summer and fall of 1990, it would become increasingly apparent that the West would go to war with Iraq. Cruddas had all the connections to match Middle Eastern counterparties with liquidity providers as times got tougher and money sought safety in Swiss francs, gold, and deutsche marks.

CMC'S FIRST ONLINE TRADING PLATFORM

Cruddas was quick to spot the potential of the Internet, and he transitioned himself from inter-dealer voice broker to online market maker. He said, "As soon as I saw the Internet, I couldn't believe how good it would be for the business. I saw it instantly!"[1] In 1996, he launched his first online trading platform, and with it he became one of the pioneers of retail foreign exchange. The system he developed was a complete front-to-back package, where customers could trade at the click of a mouse and instantly understand their positions and profit and loss.

The beauty of trading online from the point of view of CMC as provider was that it skipped many manual processes, from front-office voice brokering to back-office trade input. The efficiencies in staffing were considerable, making many dealing and settlement functions redundant. Fewer costs meant more profits, and as Cruddas and others found to their immense advantage, retail foreign exchange clients had a habit of losing. If Cruddas and others could monetize client losses for their gain, it would far exceed the profits from cutting headcount.

KIM FOURNAIS AND LARS CHRISTENSEN AND SAXO BANK'S ONLINE PLATFORM

About the same time as Cruddas was making a fortune brokering deals during the first Gulf War, two Danish traders, Kim Fournais and Lars Seier Christensen, were putting the finishing touches on creating their own brokerage. Fournais, an engineering graduate from the Technical University of Denmark, was at Lannung Bank, and Christensen was heading up the Scandinavian FX desk at American brokerage Gerald Metals.

Together they would form Midas Fondsmæglerselskab in 1992 with Fournais as CEO. Christensen joined as co-CEO in 1995, and the success story that is now known as Saxo Bank accelerated its good fortune and race to launch an online platform. In 1997 Midas launched its first FX platform, MITS, and alongside CMC, online retail FX trading became a reality.

U.S. ONLINE PLATFORMS

The European companies CMC and Midas had a small business time advantage, but it was not too long before competition came from America. In 1999 some of the biggest names in U.S. domiciled retail FX platforms were founded, among them GAIN Capital and FXCM. Glenn Stevens was chief dealer at Merrill Lynch and head of FX North American sales and trading at NatWest Bank prior to founding GAIN. Dror (Drew) Niv served in the U.S. Army and worked at MG Financial before setting up FXCM. If making money from retail clients was objective 1, then, in line with dreams about the wonders of leverage, objective 2 was a golden three-letter acronym: IPO, or initial public offering.

In 1999, Internet stocks were booming, and the Nasdaq was on fire. Price-to-earnings multiples were in the hundreds, and seemingly every good idea had a value. Retail FX was the way forward. A savvy marketing campaign, a decent website, client hits, client trades, client numbers, and above all income could lead to an incredible valuation. With perhaps the exception of Midas, all of the above companies had visions of trading publicly. And with it the dream of untold riches!

EDUCATING CONSUMERS IN ONLINE TRADING

The dot-com bubble soon turned to bust, just as online FX companies were gaining traction. For now, any Nasdaq inspired IPOs were put off as many Internet companies crumbled back into the sand they were built on. Retail FX, on the other hand, was on the up. And was taking off across the world. The trouble was that a great many customers had lost money trading it. Retail FX shops had to think smart. How do you continue to fill a leaking bucket? The answer was clear: give customers what they needed to convince them that they could make money trading FX.

Education was required and in the form of educational seminars, booklets, CD-ROMs, chatrooms, and websites replete with news, views, information, and data. In addition, the brokers needed to put forward the notion that FX was an asset class of its own, comparable with equities and bonds, and essential in any portfolio. The third solution to the challenge was to take FX trading to countries with clients of a less risk-averse nature. These countries would be found in Australasia. Many companies sought to infiltrate China and Japan, as well as countries, such as Australia and New Zealand, with large Asian populations. With superlative marketing and ease of account opening, FX could be readily accessible for all. People just had to know about it—the positives anyway.

CONTRACTS FOR DIFFERENCE (CFDs) AND FINANCIAL SPREAD BETTING (FSB)

Along with marketing came the ever present need for advances in technology and product offerings as well as being able to cope with scaling up the business and to cope with the transactions. Cruddas regularly told his staff that CMC was a "half marketing and half technology company." And true to his word, he delivered spectacularly on some new innovations. In this field, CMC was among the leaders of the pack, and in 2000 and 2001 following Gerard and National Intercommodities (GNI), he launched two prolific moneymaking products: contracts for difference (CFDs) and Financial Spread Betting (FSB).

In many ways CFDs and FSB are one and the same. In the United Kingdom and some other European countries, spread betting on financial instruments is considered gambling and not investing, despite being a regulated product covered by the Financial Conduct Authority. In the United Kingdom, therefore, despite the investor (gambler) trading spreads on financial instruments, the investor's winnings are not subject to capital gains tax or stamp duty (which is paid on stock or equity transactions). Cruddas had had a scoop popularizing punting on equity spreads as an alternative to holding physical stock and paying transaction charges and taxes. In Australia, the contract for difference would take off in some style. As Australia entered a bull market in equities, CFDs would provide a win-win formula for both client and broker. Leveraged bets on rising equities could only magnify gains. Even retail punters could win on this! The trick for brokers was to monetize the flow.

A CFD is a highly potent investment product. As its name suggests, it is a contract for difference, the difference being the sell price minus the buy price multiplied by the size of the position. CFDs can be traded on equities, indexes, commodities, bonds, and currencies. The reason they are so potent is that among other things, they are leveraged bets on the underlying instrument. Margin requirements on equity CFDs range between 3 and 20 percent depending on the liquidity (not volatility) of the stock, which means a client may gear up her trade between 5 and 33.33 times compared to buying the stock on an exchange.

So far so good. Most people understand the concept of leverage. But not as many people understand that stocks in general are far more volatile than currencies. Even stalwart stocks such as Vodafone move on average more than 1 percent per day. Stable bank stocks such as Citigroup can easily move upward or downward in the region of 3 to 4 percent. A 4 percent move in currencies is considered extreme. Not so for stocks, however. There are many more stocks that can move by 5 or 10 percent per day, and many of these can be found in major indexes! Leverage works nicely when you are winning. A 3 percent move multiplied by 33 times leverage equates to a 99 percent gain on the initial margin. Superb if you get it right. But it's a 99 percent wipeout if you get wrong!

At the outset of CFD trading, brokers or market makers such as CMC would often take the other side of customer trades. The trades would be put into the B Book, or "bucket" or "broker's book." Effectively the broker was betting against the customer in whatever CFD the customer was trading. In FX, this concept worked well because there was a smaller number of currency pairs and FX flows would concentrate around "major" currencies such as the euro, yen, sterling, Swiss franc, and U.S., Aussie, and kiwi dollars. There would be natural hedges as trades offset one another and stops canceled out limits.

On CFDs in single stocks, trading against customers, while offering profitable opportunities in volatile markets, was a riskier affair, especially in times of rising stocks. The retail customer propensity is always to be long stocks. The domain of shorting stocks is more consistent with hedge fund trading strategies. Outside of running a book, hedging single stocks or index sectors, and making money on spreads, there was a far safer way to earn money on CFDs. When brokers started charging commissions on CFD trading, their profits really took off. The other cash cow for the provider was charging overnight interest on long positions at LIBOR (or whatever central bank interest rate) plus a spread in the order of +2 or +3 percent and, conversely, paying LIBOR minus a spread of 2 or 3 percent on short positions. If CFD stocks could be crossed up—that is, a buy and sell matching off—the overnight interest on that position could be at an annual rate of 4 to 6 percent. Essentially earning money for nothing!

It is worthwhile going through a couple of examples to show how CFDs can be excellent short-term investments in rising (or falling) markets, but they should not be relied upon as a long-term strategy.

An example of buying a CFD is as follows:

Buy 100 Citibank CFDs at the offer price of $55.10.
Therefore, the cost is 100 × $55.10, or $5,510.00.

Initial margin at 5 percent is $5,510 × 5/100 = $275.50.

Commission at 0.1 percent = $5.51.

Hold the position overnight. Assume the LIBOR is
1 percent. Financing at LIBOR + 3 percent = $5,510
(0.01 + 0.03)/365, or $0.60.

Sell position at $56.00. Proceeds equate to 100 × $56.00,
or $5,600 – initial cost of $5,510 for a profit of $90.00.

Commission on sell trade at 0.1 percent = $5.60.

Total commissions and overnight financing equals
$5.51 + $5.60 + $0.60 = $11.71.

Net profit is $90.00 – $11.71, or $78.29.

As a percentage of initial margin, the net profit =
$78.29/$275.50, or +28.42 percent. A fantastic one-day
return.

But say you hold this trade for two months and you sell at
$56.00 as before:

Overnight interest at $0.60 × 60 = $36.00.

Profits now are $90.00 – $5.51 – $5.60 – $36.00,
or $42.89.

$42.89/$275.5 is still 15.57 percent. A fabulous
two-month return!

At six months, or 180 days, the interest component is 0.6 × 180,
or $108.00. The trade has now lost money:

Profits are now $90.00 – $5.51 – $5.60 – $108.00,
or –$29.11.

This is –$29.11/$275.50, or –10.57 percent. Oops.
Not so good!

If you bought and sold Citigroup at the same price after one
year, you would get a big surprise on your costs:

Buy 100 Citibank CFDs at the offer price of $55.10. Therefore, the cost is 100 × $55.10, or $5,510.

Initial margin at 5 percent = $5,510 × 5/100 = $275.50.

Commission at 0.1 percent = $5.51.

Sell 100 Citibank CFDs at the bid price of $55.10. Therefore, the cost is 100 × $55.10, or $5,510.

Commission at 0.1 percent = $5.51.

Financing at the LIBOR + 3 percent for 365 days is $5,510 (0.01 + 0.03) = $220.40.

Add commissions buy and sell = $5.51 × 2, or $11.02 for a total cost of $231.42.

Or a total loss in percentage terms of $231.42/$275.50 × 100 percent = −84 percent. Ouch! Of which interest is $220.40/$275.50, or 80 percent. Staggering, isn't it!

A quick rule of thumb is to multiply the rate of interest you pay on financing by the amount of leverage you use. So if the total annual interest is 2 percent and you are leveraged by 25 times, your annual interest cost if you hold a position open is 50 percent. There is no other word for it than usury!

Still, CFDs were marketed as the ultimate retail investments with advertisements reflecting super cool male golfers practicing their perfect swings and being self-satisfied trading CFDs. Even now, in some advertisements the vision of the athletic trader, with rowing machine and trading station both at hand, seems to be the metaphor for success. You see, equity CFDs work brilliantly when people are long and markets go up. CFDs work brilliantly too for brokers!

SAXO BANK

While Cruddas was working on launching new products, Midas was also busy, but in a different area. Midas had been working on significantly upgrading its platform and improving its brand and status. In 1999 and 2000, Kim Fournais concurrently acted as managing director of CL Markets.com, a joint venture between Midas and Credit Lyonnais aimed at developing Internet-based trading systems and websites. At the beginning of 2001, Midas effectively took over all shares of CL Markets.com from Credit Lyonnais and merged the main activities with those of Midas. In 2001, Midas also obtained a Danish banking license, changed its name to Saxo Bank, and moved to new headquarters in Gentofte.

It also launched its first "white label," with a Portuguese securities dealer—that is, it entered into a relationship with another party in which that party would effectively use Saxo's platform under its own name and branding. Saxo would provide the trading, back-office, settlement, and reporting services in return for an undisclosed fee and/or profit share. Kim Fournais and Lars Christensen could quite clearly see the potential scale of distributing Saxo's software and trading expertise through partnerships in multiple countries, and to its great credit, Saxo continued with that vision.

CURRENEX, FXALL, AND HOTSPOT

The years 1999 and 2000 saw the launch of three of the great institutional platforms. Currenex was founded in 1999 and quickly became a favorite of brokers with its fantastic functionality and its "intelligent pricing server." It gave brokers the flexibility to manage clients and flow simultaneously and to offer an online trading venue for brokers' clients as an alternative to voice-brokered dealing.

FXall, or FX Alliance, which started business in 2000, like Currenex was another *aggregator platform* originally created as a dealing venue for 16 banking institutions. In essence, it was not too dissimilar from Electronic Broking Services (EBS), by then a 10-year veteran, insofar as its owners were banks in the FX sector. EBS and Reuters Dealing had long vied for currency supremacy in the interbank market, but ultimately they had somehow both ended up being the go-to platforms for differing currency pairs. Reuters was strong in Commonwealth currencies such as sterling, Aussie, kiwi, and Canada, whereas EBS was strong in euros, yen, Swiss francs, and their crosses.

Hotspot also launched in 2000 with Howard Silverman as cofounder and trading legend Joe Lewis as investor. Lewis is a formidable businessman and arguably is a Currency King himself. Some say he netted more than George Soros in the 1992 sterling devaluation and similarly made a fortune speculating against the Mexican peso in 1994 and 1995. An East End boy, who left school at 15, he developed his family's catering business before selling out and moving to the Bahamas. Hotspot teamed up with Bear Stearns in 2003 with Bear Stearns acting as market maker and prime broker, effectively giving online FX access to Bear Stearns' many institutional clients and at once making the Hotspot platform a formidable brand.

REFCO AND FXCM

During this time FXCM focused on building its Introducing broker network and client base. In 2003, it embarked on expanding its footprint and established offices in London and Hong Kong, the Hong Kong office being run by Drew Niv's sister, Ornit. FXCM also entered into a relationship with Refco LLC, a leading futures and FX broker that acquired 35 percent of FXCM. Refco, with some 17,000 FX clients, would add 40 percent to FXCM's profits by 2005.

Refco had huge plans for FX, and its subsidiary in London, Refco Overseas Limited (ROL), teamed up with Saxo Bank in a white label deal that would again add to volumes and profits in Denmark. "For ROL, the decision to partner with Saxo signals another phase of expansion into online trading. We like the real-time prices and execution capabilities, the multi-product platform, and the access to Saxo Capital Markets analysis as well as the ability to provide our own," explained Nigel Watts, the then head of investor services at ROL. "For our clients, the added selection of instruments and the relative ease of use is a key addition to our current offering."[2]

FX MARKETS IN ASIA

By 2004, western retail FX brokerages were queuing up along the Chinese border to access millions of potential clients. The Chinese border in this case was Hong Kong with a well-respected regulatory body—the Securities and Futures Commission (SFC)—and legal system. Hong Kong had had its own trouble with FX brokerages in the past, and there were detailed requirements for brokers, not least of which was that initial margin requirements in FX for Hong Kong clients were to be 5 percent with a maintenance margin at 3 percent. FXCM at this stage had already received its license, paying up capital of HK$30 million (roughly US$4 million).

CMC received the first Introducing broker license with a paid-up capital requirement of HK$5 million. It would introduce clients to its Australia entity. Both CMC Markets Asia Pacific Pty Ltd. and FXCM LLC in New York could offer leverage of 100 times, and the SFC made it clear that the 5 percent initial margin requirement for Hong Kong clients introduced overseas was to be upheld. By the same token, the Internet allows users free access to roam and open accounts wherever they so wish, whether it be in Greece, Cyprus, Macau, New Zealand, Australia, London, New York, or anywhere else. *Regulatory arbitrage*—that is, getting around the regulator's rules—is almost impossible to enforce without effective cooperation from all regulators. CFDs were even more difficult to offer in Hong Kong. But not in Singapore, where many retail brokerages ultimately headed.

China offered a whole different set of problems, not the least of which was how Chinese clients could trade offshore and how clients funded their accounts! But first, it was important to alert Chinese clients to the magnificent moneymaking opportunities of trading currencies and CFDs through offshore retail brokers. There were many who argued that this activity was prohibited, but one only had to step into Shenzhen—home to over 10 million people—to one of the many "retail FX seminars" to realize that procuring clients from China to trade offshore was a very big business indeed.

Shenzhen borders Hong Kong and is a short car or train ride away. Chinese clients from Shenzhen could open bank accounts in Hong Kong. Hong Kong banks issue debit and credit cards. It became a relatively simple process to open an FX account and fund it with a debit or credit card. In addition, some brokerages accepted transfers from Western Union. Many introducing brokers lived in Shenzhen and Guangzhou, and they seemed to pop up from just about anywhere. These people knew their stuff (that is, what they could receive from brokers), and many of them traded with limited power of attorney for their hapless clients, often demanding wider spreads to receive greater kickbacks from brokers.

If this was the modus operandi of some brokers, then others, among them CMC, sought to pacify regulators and open "representative offices" in some of the larger Chinese cities. CMC opened its Beijing representative office in 2004 after having received the permission of the China Banking and Regulatory Commission (CBRC)—the primary banking regulator in China, which supervises banks and non-bank institutions and their business operations within the country. A representative office allows an offshore company to build relationships within the Chinese financial community. It is not meant to be a conduit to market offshore services and products to Chinese clients because soliciting clients to trade is not permitted under such a license. There's no rule against interested parties registering their contact details with rep offices. There does not appear to be a rule against those clients receiving calls from offices outside of China. Another form of regulatory arbitrage, perhaps?

Many other brokers similarly opened representative offices in China, among them IFX in 2005. In August 2007, Saxo Bank opened its representative office in Beijing. "Our Chinese office will be used to facilitate active interaction and representation of Saxo Bank's business and services to the increasingly international financial community within China and will be responsible for establishing and building a strong business network to support our future development plans for China," Shailendra Robin Patel, Saxo Bank's then senior executive director for global business development commented.[3] CMC also opened a "wholly owned foreign enterprise" that would offer "training seminars" to Chinese people interested in learning about foreign exchange and CFD trading.

In 2008 several Chinese banks launched retail FX products. The rationale was simple. Why shouldn't well-capitalized local entities offer a product in China with full transparency and oversight from their own regulators? Among the banks to offer retail FX were China Minsheng Bank and Bank of China, Shanghai Branch. China Minsheng Bank offered a very creditable spot foreign exchange and bullion business on an MT4 system. It supported the venture with some excellent training seminars. Client enthusiasm was strong. It was a product that local people wanted, and they were more than happy to trade with an entity they trusted. The clients were well briefed on the dangers of using excessive leverage. Strangely, the venture was suspended a few months later, just prior to the 2008 Olympics.

Some other brokers actually openly solicited Chinese clients through Chinese language websites. Chinese FX trading clients meant for big profits for offshore brokerages, as GAIN Capital's Form S-1 on August 31, 2009, to the Inland Revenue shows:

> For the year ended December 31, 2007, net revenue associated with customers residing in China was $20.6 million, compared to $8.7 million for the year ended December 31, 2006. For the year ended December 31, 2007, customers residing in China represented $103.4 billion of our customer trading volume, $26.0 million of our net deposits, and 11,561 of our traded accounts, compared to $50.8 billion of our customer trading volume, $10.5 million of our net deposits, and 5,533 of our traded accounts for the year ended December 31, 2006.

In May 2008, the CBRC informed GAIN that it had breached rules that prohibit forex trading firms from providing retail forex trading services through direct solicitation to Chinese residents through the Internet without a permit. GAIN stopped taking Chinese clients from that year and closed down its relationships with existing Chinese introducing brokers. However, by May 2011, GAIN Capital had joined the band of brokers with legitimate representative offices in China, opening up in Beijing. CEO Glenn Stevens said the following: "We believe the Beijing representative office will assist us in building strong relationships in China's growing financial community and help provide a strong foundation for our future strategic plans in that country."[4]

For the moment anyway, it seems that the CBRC is amenable to allowing representative offices of foreign brokerages to set up in China, and it monitors their conduct and enforces its rule of law. But why are foreign brokers so keen to tap into China? Perhaps it's because of a ridiculous stereotype that Chinese clients gamble more than others!? Trading in China with a well-capitalized local bank and lower levels of leverage would perhaps be a great deal safer for clients than sending money offshore to trade at 400 times leverage.

GLOBAL CFD MARKETS IN THE MID-2000s

The period of 2003 to 2008 was to become the halcyon era for retail brokerages as equity indexes across the world literally took off and with them the demand for CFDs (Figure 5.1). In this period the Hong Kong Hang Seng Index jumped nearly 200 percent and the Australian ASX over 100 percent, fueled in part by demand for commodity stocks. Commodity companies saw their shares skyrocket as prices for products such as iron ore and copper advanced due to China's seemingly insatiable demand.

The *carry trade*—that is, borrowing a currency that costs little in interest to fund and then investing in a country or currency that pays a greater interest rate (or has an exploding equity market)—simultaneously took off in Australia and New Zealand. All things were good in Australasia. Similarly, in Japan, carry trading reached frenzied proportions. Japanese households could sell the yen and buy Aussie or kiwi dollars, sterling, or euros and get paid much more interest than on their yen (Figure 5.2). They could do this with huge amounts of leverage at the many Japanese retail FX brokerages. It was all so simple. Not only did they get paid the carry—the interest rate differential—but the currency of which they were long was appreciating. Currency trading was easy!

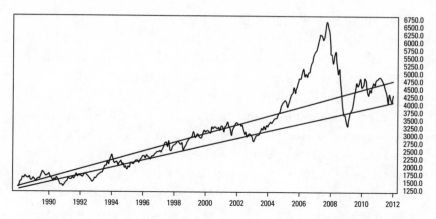

Figure 5.1 Australian Securities Exchange Index, 1988 through 2012.
Source: Copyright © 1985 to 2016 Tradermade Systems Ltd.

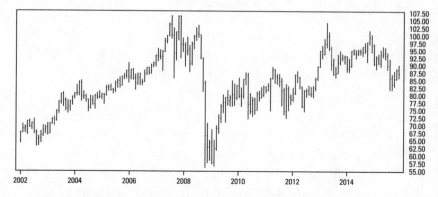

Figure 5.2 AUD/JPY monthly chart for 2002 through 2015.
Source: Copyright © 1985 to 2016 Tradermade Systems Ltd.

INITIAL PUBLIC OFFERINGS

By 2005, the race for IPOs was truly on, and first up was Refco on August 11, 2005. That morning, Refco offered 26.5 million shares to the public out of 127.5 million outstanding at an offer price of $22 per share. By close of play, they had added 25 percent, valuing Refco at $3.5 billion. Refco was now favorably positioned in the race to expand, and its fortunes, as well as those of FXCM, of which it owned 35 percent, were intertwined.

Sadly for all, the Refco story had a sorry end as shortly afterward, some hidden debts to the tune of $430 million were uncovered. The stock plummeted, and on October 17, 2005, it was announced that the firm and certain subsidiaries had filed for Chapter 11 bankruptcy protection. Refco's stock was subsequently suspended from being traded on the New York Stock Exchange. And its 35 percent of FXCM would be put up for sale. While this was an unnecessary setback for FXCM, its brand was still proving to be a winner in Asia, and fairly soon, it would add additional platforms to its product suite.

MT4, SOCIAL TRADING, AND EXPERT ADVISORS

MetaTrader MT4, developed by MetaQuotes and released in July 2005, very rapidly became the platform of choice for smaller brokerages. The reason was that it could be easily set up for an affordable flat fee and a recurring monthly maintenance charge. In a swoop, it gathered momentum as many iterations of MT4 sprung up as the platform offering of small brokers, normally in jurisdictions with low capital requirements. Brokers using MetaTrader would often offer leverage of up to 400 to 1. Clients liked it for its ease of use and charting. MetaQuotes would later develop MetaQuotes Language 4 (MQL4), an integrated coding language that would permit the development of trading algorithms and technical market indicators.

With robotic trading and technical indicators at hand, the volumes traded on MT4 would explode. MT4 would become the platform used extensively for a phenomenon known as "social trading," and software would be developed to allow people to follow "Expert Advisors" (trading robots)—effectively handing over trade management of their funds to algorithms—or to subscribe to technical analysis indicator packages and self-manage their trading. Either way, the indicators or robots could trade on very small time scales, with very high leverage, somehow going against the logic of long-term trend following with prudent risk management systems.

CURRENEX

Currenex was also proving to be a fabulous platform in terms of both functionality and trade execution. Currenex was essentially an aggregator that allowed brokers to amalgamate the best bids and offers of liquidity providers. The banks could stream their prices to Currenex, which would then show the best bid price of its participating providers and the best offer to the market. The aggregated spread was incredible!

All of a sudden EUR/USD spreads compressed from, say, 3 pips to 1 pip. The real price in the market had become transparent to all. Brokers were overjoyed because they could offer tighter spreads and charge more commission to clients. Clients were satisfied because they could trade larger amounts with very fine pricing. Market making banks in theory were happy to collect flow that they could monetize. In an age when volume was a key metric, banks scrabbled over one another to provide the best pricing and collect the trades. The best price won the trade, and the race to what is now called "fractions" or "decimals" began.

Currenex was among the first platforms to offer pricing to the fifth decimal. Known as *fractions*, every tenth of a pip in 1 million EUR/USD adds up to $10. Brokers did not necessarily need to pass this on to clients because the Currenex intelligent pricing server allowed brokers to maintain a fourth decimal price to their clients and keep the difference between the fourth and fifth decimal for themselves. The fifth decimal spread capture could add up to many thousands of dollars in broker profits.

CMC'S FIRST ATTEMPT AT ISSUING AN INITIAL PUBLIC OFFERING

By 2006, having posted excellent profits in Australia, CMC was on the cusp of its own IPO. However, after months of preparation, and a jittery stock market, Cruddas unexpectedly pulled out, citing market conditions. The reality was that the price wasn't right. Some analysts valued CMC at somewhat less than the sought-after GBP 800 million.

Cruddas was right! In just 18 months, he would sell 10 percent of his company to Goldman Sachs for GBP 140 million. With Cruddas and family retaining more than 85 percent of the company, Peter Cruddas, at least on paper, was worth well over GBP 1 billion.

THE SALES OF HOTSPOT TO KNIGHT CAPITAL GROUP AND CURRENEX TO STATE STREET

Timing as usual means everything. In early 2006 Joe Lewis and his partners sold Hotspot for $77.5 million to Knight Capital Group (KCG). In a press release announcing the sale, KCG remarked, "Hotspot's platform has experienced remarkable monthly growth since its inception in 2000, and it now supports 24 currency pairs and executes 5,000 to 10,000 FX spot trades per day." As FX evolved and a new brand of high-frequency traders joined the market, these volumes could be surpassed in one hour. HFTs now have the capacity to send millions of orders per hour! Buying Hotspot turned out to be a steal for KGS.

Just one year later, in January 2007, Currenex sold out to State Street for $564 million. Cruddas made the headlines with his 10 percent sale to Goldman Sachs in November 2007, and in the same week, Lehman Brothers took a 9.9 percent stake in FXCM, the other 25.1 percent going to Long Ridge Equity Partners, therefore accounting for the 35 percent stake of FXCM that was auctioned off from the Refco estate.

SAXO BANK IN SINGAPORE, SWITZERLAND, AND FRANCE

Meanwhile, Saxo Bank had been extending its reach in all directions, opening its flagship Asia Pacific office, Saxo Bank Capital Markets, in Singapore, in November 2006, as well as acquiring small FX businesses in Switzerland and France in 2007. Saxo Bank had also been significantly developing its platform. In November 2007, Saxo Bank sensationally announced it would white-label its platform to Citigroup under the brand name CitiFXpro.

Lars Christensen summed up the alliance nicely: "The combination of Citi's world-class product infrastructure, global brand, and size with Saxo's best-of-class facilitation and technology will change the way global capital market products are being distributed and serviced worldwide."[5] The three household name FX brands of Saxo Bank, CMC Markets, and FXCM had all teamed up with major banks in the same week. A truly remarkable achievement for them all.

GAIN CAPITAL'S FAST GROWTH

Not to be outdone, GAIN Capital had been growing organically with impressive results. In the period 2002 to 2006, GAIN Capital Group's revenues increased 829 percent, and it achieved a ranking of 14 in Deloitte's Technology Fast 50 Program for New Jersey, a gauge of the region's 50 fastest-growing technology, media, telecommunications, and life sciences companies.

In early 2008, GAIN would announce a joint venture with Rosenthal Collins Group, LLC, a Chicago-based futures brokerage, to establish operations in the United Kingdom. It would also secure $117 million in investment finance with $97 million from the 3i Group and $20 million from VantagePoint Venture Partners.

THE GLOBAL FINANCIAL CRISIS OF 2007 AND 2008

While 2007 and the beginning of 2008 were seeing impressive landmarks for online FX and CFD brokerages, a storm of monumental proportions was brewing in the financial markets. Mid-2007 marked the starting point of what is now known as the "global financial crisis" (GFC)—a meltdown of such immensity that it almost crippled the financial system as we know it today. In its 2011 report, the U.S. Financial Crisis Inquiry Commission concluded that the events that unfolded were "an explosive mix of excessive borrowing and risk by households and Wall Street that put the financial system on a collision course with crisis."[6]

This time, the source of the boom and bust was the U.S. housing market. As house prices rose and more and more investors wished to join the market, the facilitation of credit somehow became easier, and loans were made to individuals, some of whom were considered more likely to default on their mortgages than others. These "subprime" mortgages in turn could be bundled into *mortgage-backed securities* (MBSs), which could in turn form part of *collateralized debt obligations* (CDOs). A CDO typically was cut into slices, or *tranches*, and the different tranches paid varying amounts of interest depending on whether the tranche was considered higher or lower risk. The tranches were rated by rating agencies such as Standard & Poor's, Moody's Investors Service, and Fitch Group. They were bought by institutional investors, such as hedge funds, pension funds, and insurance companies and traded heavily in the financial markets.

As momentum in the housing bubble turned to torpor, housing prices started to fall, debt exceeded equity on some houses, defaults on mortgages increased, and some tranches of CDOs very quickly lost their value. In a rush to off-load CDOs, liquidity dried up, and there were no bids to be found. Stage 2 of the GFC had begun! It soon became evident that one or two investment banks were long large amounts of CDOs whose marked-to-market value was a great deal less than what they had paid for them. Bear Stearns was the first to come under pressure, being heavily exposed to CDOs in two of its in-house hedge funds. Its stock price nose-dived, and in March 2008, the 85-year-old investment bank and brokerage was sold at the "fire sale" price of $10 per share to J. P. Morgan, a 92 percent discount to its previous 52-week high of $133.2. Worse was in store, and the eye of the storm hit New York in September!

A common factor of markets going into defensive mode is that smart money moves from riskier, less liquid investments to safer, more liquid investments. Some may call it a flight to quality. In some instances, safety is sought in Swiss francs and in gold. U.S. Treasuries are also considered a safe, liquid investment. Another common factor is that leverage works its way out of the system. When a ship "battens down the hatches," it means it is sailing into trouble, and only a fool would be at the top of a mast in such a scenario. Similarly, when something is amiss in the markets, wise money seeks safety, and when a lot of wise money seeks safety at the same time, a rapid sell-off in riskier assets can quickly ensue. The waters suddenly become a lot more turbulent.

Such was the scenario in September 2008. If "risk on" meant borrowing huge quantities of yen and exchanging it for currency to invest in either higher-paying currencies or stock or bond markets outside of Japan, then "risk off" meant the converse. The carry trade that had worked so well for the previous four years started to evaporate as riskier assets were sold and the yen was repatriated. USD/JPY and yen crosses had not quite had their free-fall moment as in 1998, but USD/JPY and its crosses had all been sold since August 2007, and the pace of the carry trade unwind was increasing as stock markets across the world started to tumble.

THE STOCK MARKET'S SEPTEMBER 2008 MELTDOWN AND TARP

On September 14, 15, and 16, 2008, the terror of a financial markets meltdown materialized. On Sunday, September 14, the Bank of America agreed to buy investment banking power house Merrill Lynch for a pittance. Early on Monday morning, Lehman Brothers filed for Chapter 11 bankruptcy protection. On Tuesday, September 16, AIG, an insurance giant, was rescued by the Federal Reserve Bank of New York, which created a secured credit facility of up to $85 billion for AIG to meet its obligations. The Dow Jones roller-coastered between acute sell-off on Monday, to marginal optimism on Tuesday (on the back of the NY Fed bailout), to acute sell-off on Wednesday, to a whipsawing Thursday as rumors of a government rescue package spread, to a spike on Friday as President George W. Bush announced an unprecedented financial aid package for companies caught out in the mortgage crisis. The Dow actually closed the week out higher than Monday's open, but the financial markets were still a very dangerous place to be.

As LTCM found out to its detriment in 1998, when Mr. Market sniffs a kill, there is little hope for his prey. Lehman Brothers' demise in a way was similar to that of Bear Stearns.

Clients pulled their money. The stock got pulverized. Credit rating agencies stuck the boot in. The spoils this time were bought by Barclays and Nomura. FXCM was again the victim of an unfortunate alliance. It had been only three years since Refco had blown up! Fortunately the Lehman stake in FXCM was 9.9 percent. The failure of Lehman was enough to be irritating but not catastrophic to FXCM. The downside for FXCM was that it traded a lot through its shareholder, and its open FX positions would have to be novated to whoever took on Lehman's FX book.

Market nervousness continued into October. On Friday, October 3, 2008, President Bush signed a bill into law that would create the Troubled Asset Relief Program (TARP) to purchase failing bank assets. The Dow, S&P, and Nasdaq indexes of stocks all closed the week down heavily.

MOUNTING GLOBAL LOSSES
IN MID-OCTOBER

By October 6, the contagion had spread. Japan, London, and Russia all posted huge losses, and the Dow and S&P continued to plummet. Across the world from Indonesia to Iceland, world markets went into a free fall. On October 10, the Australian ASX dropped 8.3 percent, ending down nearly 16 percent for the week. The U.S. indexes had a terrible week, with the Dow Jones Industrial Average (DJIA) falling 18 percent and the S&P 500 more than 20 percent.

Carry trades were not faring much better, and euros, pounds, and Australian, U.S., and New Zealand dollars all took a beating as clients sold equities in these countries and paid back their yen loans. In more simplistic terms, the yen increased in value, and just as in 1998, the move was rapid. This time perhaps less so, but still the currency moves were extreme. On October 24, as sterling tumbled 7 percent against the dollar, the yen strengthened, magnifying the move in GBP/JPY to around 10 percent. The USD/JPY implied volatility went off the scale, touching 35 percent at one stage. Talk of a global recession was the order of the day. Not helped by comments by Alan Greenspan that the current crisis was "a once-in-a-century credit tsunami,"[7] stock markets got smashed again.

INTEREST RATE CUTS IN OCTOBER

The week of October 27 saw some relief for the markets as hope for aggressive central bank rate cuts brought some calm. While the follow-through from October 24 hit Hong Kong and Japanese stocks on the 27th, the Dow was relatively stable. On the 28th, it rallied nearly 11 percent. On October 29, the Fed duly delivered an interest rate cut of 0.5 percent, its second half-point cut of the month, the first being on October 8. The Fed funds rate now stood at 1 percent in the United States, having been at 4.5 percent just one year earlier.

If on a macro-scale, the world had seen the devastating effects of excessive leverage, then so too on a micro-scale, many retail investors got toasted. The long CFD trade turned into a disaster as stock losses compounded by leverage obliterated portfolios. For the thousands of yen carry traders in Japan, the pain of failure was also felt. As worldwide interest rates came down, the yen strengthened aggressively against many currencies. Many clients were stopped out of their long positions.

LEVERAGE AND RISK MANAGEMENT

Brokers fared differently. Those who had genuine B Books in currencies cleaned up as the yen strengthened and clients were stopped out. When clients had initiated long trades, brokers who had taken the opposite side were short. As clients stopped themselves out, selling their long positions, brokers bought them, offsetting their own existing short positions and thus making fortunes.

Some brokers who operated guaranteed stops using an "agency model" were somewhat less fortunate. If the market gapped through their clients' stop level, the clients would be guaranteed the price of their stop, and the brokers would assume the loss between where they bought currency off a client and where they sold to the market. Other brokers who guaranteed that clients could not go into negative equity also ran the risk, by using an agency model, that they could not cover their clients' positions fast enough. Although this happened in one or two rare instances, most brokers' risk management systems held up robustly. This certainly would not be the case in 2015 when the Swiss National Bank removed its currency peg of supporting the euro against the Swiss franc. By then, the markets had moved on with many new players and high-frequency traders added to the mix.

All in all, 2008 was good and bad for retail brokerages. With the spotlight on leverage, many regulators looked to act to reduce the risk of clients blowing up. Other regulators looked to squeeze out poorly capitalized boutique brokerages. In Japan new measures were introduced to curb excessive risk taking in foreign exchange with progressive increases in margin requirements to be incrementally put in place, cutting leverage to 25 times by mid-2011. In the United States, on October 22, 2008, the Commodity Futures Trading Commission (CFTC) approved increases to the capital requirements of the National Futures Association (NFA) for Forex Dealer Members (FDMs) to $10 million as of October 31, 2008, $15 million as of January 17, 2009, and $20 million as of May 16, 2009.

QUANTITATIVE EASING

After a rout, it takes time to recover. The fallout from the global financial crisis had been harsh, and worldwide interest rates collapsed. Governments and central banks from all over the globe engaged in "quantitative easing" and pumped money into the system in order to encourage companies to borrow cheap funds and use it to grow their businesses.

Many banks and brokers that dealt in shares proposed strategies of buying single stocks or indexes in monthly increments. "Doubling down" for an inevitable recovery was a viable strategy. Stock markets started to recover in leaps and bounds. Consumers gained confidence.

NEW FX TRADERS: EXPERT ADVISORS AND HFT ALGORITHMS

Two new breeds of traders joined the FX market. The first were *Expert Advisors*—that is, robots that could trade on behalf of clients or provide chart buying and selling points. Momentum for the use of Expert Advisors had been growing in tandem with the improvement of functionality for the Metaquotes MT4 platform. The second were *high-frequency trading algorithms*—that is, predatory computer programs trained to buy and sell currencies in fractions of a second.

A simple HFT algorithm might be a latency arbitrage scalping model. It could be programmed to sell and buy bids and offers from two different providers in a split second based on the times it took for the price data to reach the algo (and go back to the providers) to take advantage of any favorable price discrepancies caused by the time latency. HFTs will be explained in more detail in the next chapter.

ONLINE PLATFORMS AND TRADING VOLUME INCREASES

Trading volumes in equities and FX exploded. The ease of programing in MetaQuotes MQL4 and MQL5 gave many programmers the capacity to create chart signals and trading robots. MetaTrader MT4 for retail traders and Currenex, which catered to larger traders, were two of the de facto platforms that brokers without their own proprietary platforms really needed to offer in order to be competitive and to on-board clients. Fairly soon there were multiple brokers to choose from with whole arrays of platforms. Some brokers could offer a complete suite of platforms, including Currenex, MT4, Integral, Hotspot, and FXall. CMC Markets and Saxo Bank continued to focus on upgrading their own platforms. FXCM added Currenex and MT4. GAIN Capital added MT4.

A rising equity market means good profits for all involved in CFD trading. In general, leverage works for clients, and brokerages benefit from agency commissions and from charging overnight interest on CFD positions. In the United States, FXCM bought some smaller FX brokerages squeezed out by the NFA's new capital requirements. In May 2010, it also acquired ODL Securities, a London-based FX, equities, derivatives, and commodities brokerage. Saxo Bank launched a new equity platform that had the functionality to offer 11,000 equities on 23 exchanges worldwide. It also white-labeled its platform to Barclay Stockbrokers Ltd. and Microsoft. FXCM and GAIN Capital were working hard in preparation to list on the New York Stock Exchange. They both reached their goal in December 2010. On December 1, FXCM raised $211 million from its initial public offering, valuing the company at just over $1 billion. Two weeks later, on December 15, GAIN Capital raised $81 million, giving the company a market capitalization of just under $280 million.

Shortly afterward, a new entrant appeared in the market: ADS Securities, a well-capitalized Middle Eastern brokerage that opened for business in Abu Dhabi in March 2011. In May, Saxo Bank revealed it had white-labeled its platform to TD Waterhouse in the United Kingdom.

The emergence of high-frequency traders and trading robots has significantly changed the dynamics of FX trading. In its 2013 triennial survey, the Bank of International Settlements (BIS) revealed that overall daily FX volumes had increased by 30 percent since 2010, from $3.971 trillion to $5.345 trillion. Of this volume, spot FX had increased by over $500 billion, or 37.5 percent, from $1.488 trillion to $2.046 trillion. Nonfinancial institutions such as governments, corporations, high-net-worth individuals, and retail traders accounted for 9 percent of total volume, with hedge funds and proprietary trading firms claiming 11 percent. In the 15 years since retail online platforms have really been in existence, the spot market has seen its volumes grow 260 percent from an average daily volume of $568 billion in 1998.

MERGERS AND ACQUISITIONS

After its initial public offering, FXCM used some of its proceeds to expand into the HFT and algorithmic trading space. In June 2012, FXCM announced it was purchasing 50 percent of little-known Lucid Markets for $176 million, net of Lucid cash. Lucid at that stage was trading $35 billion per day in its capacity as a non-bank market maker. In the 12 months ending December 31, 2011, under U.K. generally accepted accounting principles (GAAP), Lucid had revenues of $148.9 million and earnings before interest, taxes, depreciation, and amortization (EBITDA) of $113.4 million. The CEO of FXCM, Drew Niv, commented, "The acquisition of Lucid—a leader in market making and trading in the institutional FX market—is a natural extension of the evolution of our institutional business."[8] FXCM had also been developing its in-house trading platform. The combination of Lucid's market making abilities, its own proprietary software, and cash from the IPO positioned FXCM strongly as it diversified its business from a mainly retail client base to strengthen its institutional offerings and grab market share. One month later, in July, Reuters announced it would absorb FXall; this time the price was $625 million.

Consolidation and acquisitions continued into 2013. In April, FXCM audaciously offered to buy GAIN Capital for $210 million in an all share offer. GAIN Capital spurned the offer and simultaneously announced it would acquire Global Futures and Forex Ltd. (GFT) for $107.8 million, having already taken GFT's U.S. client base in December 2012 as well as the U.S. client base of City Index in February 2013 for a "small fee." In October 2014, in one of the last deals to be announced before the Swiss National Bank disaster of January 2015, GAIN Capital announced that it had entered into a definitive agreement to buy City Index (Holdings) Limited for $118 million.

In the race for online FX dominance, CMC Markets, Saxo Bank, FXCM, GAIN Capital, and the fledgling ADS Securities were all well capitalized, with decent global reach, solid platforms, and product suites. They all had strengths and weaknesses and their fair share of good and bad publicity. There were subtle differences in their modi operandi, but profits for all of them revolved around client volumes, commissions, spreads, and financing charges. In some cases, additional profits were made by running certain trading books. FXCM and GAIN also had the additional scrutiny of being companies listed with all the differing reporting requirements that are attached to being in the public eye. The beginning of 2015 would radically change the pecking order of these top five companies in an astonishing few minutes that brought many clients and companies to their knees.

SWISS NATIONAL BANK 2015

In September 2011, the Swiss National Bank (SNB) pledged to peg the Swiss franc to the euro at a rate of EUR/CHF 1.20 and to buy unlimited quantities of foreign currencies to maintain the "floor" on EUR/CHF—something they would do with "utmost determination." As late as December 2014, the phrase "utmost determination" was reiterated with reference to maintaining the currency floor as the SNB introduced negative interest rates on short-term deposits in an effort to stem the pressure on Swiss francs from safe haven buyers. In January 2015, the SNB abruptly changed its policy.

The only words that can adequately describe the aftermath of the Swiss National Bank's decision to abandon the floor of 1.20 that it had been holding on EUR/CHF would be "flash crash"! The announcement came at 4.30 a.m. Eastern Standard Time (9.30 a.m. London, 10.30 a.m. Switzerland). According to data released by FXCM, just one minute and eight seconds later, they had only one bid to hit at 1.1094. Just two and half minutes later at 4.33 a.m., one bank was quoting 0.6374. At 4.42 a.m., the price was somewhere around 0.9600, and not until 5.10 a.m. did the market stabilize around 1.0400. Where brokers got filled by banks was something of a lottery. The price had dipped as low as 0.8517. The lottery was passed on to clients.

Irrespective of where clients got filled by their brokers, whether it be 0.85, 0.9235, 0.9625, 1.00684, 1.02, 1.04, or anywhere inside or outside of that range, the fact is that the consequences of a freak action on the part of the SNB, a freak reaction on the part of liquidity providers, and millions of algorithmic programmed computer-generated orders in between literally short fused the market. There are no stories of FX salespeople clambering over each other to pick up phones and bellow panicked instructions to brave traders to get a price. The market was zapped.

And dealers had no part to play. The market dumped 20 percent and more in three and a bit minutes and went much lower before it stabilized. As one dealer said, "We just looked at each other and asked what the heck happened to EUR/CHF? Then it was a question of finding out how badly our stops had been filled."

It was a very dire situation. As rumors made their way around the markets, it was becoming clear that some brokers who offered high rates of leverage and that ran "agency straight-through process models" had fared very badly indeed. The very customers who were supposed to blow themselves up had done that in style and at the same time blown up the brokers. Alpari, a U.K. broker, offered some of its clients 400-to-1 leverage. Imagine a EUR 20,000 account leveraged 400 times. That EUR 20,000 could theoretically maintain a position of EUR 8 million and earn a very small carry against Swiss francs. If an 8 million EUR/CHF position falls 20 percent in three minutes, then it loses 1.6 million Swiss francs. Marked-to-market at EUR/CHF 0.96, and the loss is EUR 1.667 million.

Alpari had many clients employing ridiculous amounts of leverage who in an instant went massively into negative equity. Unsurprisingly, the bulk of them would not be able to pay their margin calls. If clients can't pay, then it falls upon the broker to cough up. Alpari applied for insolvency on Monday, January 19. FXCM and Saxo Bank also prepared for huge losses, with FXCM's clients dropping in the region of $225 million and Saxo Bank's clients losing about $107 million. FXCM hastily arranged a rescue loan of $300 million from Leucadia National Corporation in order to stay in business. CMC Markets said some clients lost but it was "business as usual." GAIN Capital "made a gain," and ADS Securities posted "a record trading day."

It is worth bearing in mind the folly of the situation, not just from a client perspective and a brokering perspective but also from the point of view of a prime broker:

1. *Client:* Unless you are just gambling, it is totally reckless to trade with such high degrees of leverage!

2. *Broker:* However morally reprehensible it is for so-called brokers to run B Books on client trades, it clearly makes no sense to pass 400-to-1 leveraged clients through to prime brokers in an agency model.

3. *Prime broker:* Risk and credit managers are paid to look at concentration risk for currencies and at balance sheets of counterparties. Could they have done better?

It may be wrong, in hindsight, to point the finger at prime brokers here because concentration risk in Swiss francs may not have been that high. Nobody expected a crash of such speed and magnitude. But there must have been warning signs. The world had recovered somewhat from a situation in which Greek, Spanish, Portuguese, and Irish sovereign debt was under pressure. True, Russia's currency was suffering, but risk managers and currency traders in Swiss francs must have been aware of the huge cost of maintaining the floor for the euro against the Swiss franc that the SNB was facing, especially because the EUR/USD had depreciated from nearly 1.4000 to 1.2000 in the year preceding the announcement.

Where prime brokers can be called into question is where they supported brokers with flaky balance sheets offering excessive leverage to a largely retail clientele. Fundamentally, the fault lies with brokers, though, in assessing the suitability of their clients to trade foreign exchange and in containing their own risk. To be fair to GAIN Capital and Saxo Bank, they had raised their margin levels to 5 and 8 percent, respectively. Saxo Bank therefore potentially mitigated some of its client losses. FXCM had been going to great lengths to diversify its business, but no doubt there were some institutional casualties too.

While Alpari, FXCM, and Saxo Bank made the headlines, there were many smaller brokers that disappeared in a puff of smoke. Prime brokers and their trading desks also fared quite badly, with both Deutsche Bank and Citi rumored each to have lost $150 million. Barclays too was hit for losses in the region of $100 million. All in all, "long EUR/CHF" was a massively risky trade at elevated levels of leverage for negligible returns.

As much as the SNB episode was a disaster for retail clients, some hedge funds, brokers, market makers, and banks, there is always some good that comes out of such events. Regulators will no doubt scrutinize retail brokers more thoroughly, and so too will banks offering prime brokerage services. One can reasonably expect capital requirements for brokers to be raised, and so too margin levels. Clients who are more of the gambling mindset may migrate to less safe regulatory jurisdictions, where their cash is not as well protected. In essence, it is totally the customer's right to trade where she pleases, and so it is also her risk.

The Australian Securities & Investment Commission (ASIC) on its *MoneySmart* financial guidance website has added its views on CFD trading, saying, "Contracts for difference (CFDs) are a way of betting on the change in value of a share, foreign exchange rate, or a market index." The ASIC adds, "You are not buying the underlying asset, just betting on the price movement." It even goes as far as to say, "You're effectively gambling a much larger amount of money than if you went to the casino or racetrack. You face potentially unlimited losses so think carefully before investing in CFDs."

But somewhat paradoxically, while alerting clients to the dangers of excessive risk taking and gambling, the Australian regulator ASIC only requires FX and CFD brokers to pay up capital of AUD$1 million. Barriers to entry to operate as FX and CFD brokers therefore remain low compared to the United States, and unlike Japan and Hong Kong, leverage of 400 to 1, or in some cases more, can still be obtained!

GROWING PAINS FOR
FX AND CFD TRADERS

The rise of retail FX and CFD trading has been incredible. And it is fascinating how some of the "headline brokerages" have evolved. The flamboyant Peter Cruddas finally took CMC Markets to IPO in February 2016, achieving a market value of GBP 691 million. He has an excellent platform and great charting facilities. Saxo Bank too and its founders Kim Fournais and Lars Christensen have shown incredible awareness and vision in developing their platform and product suite and in extending their global reach by entering into some significant white label agreements. GAIN Capital and Glenn Stevens have subtly been growing their business by entering into strategic partnerships and acquiring competitors.

The well-capitalized ADS Securities continues to expand. FXCM, until January 2015, had shown an instinctive ability to expand and diversify and try to "stay ahead of the curve." These are some of the well-known brand names in online trading.

But do they have a competitive advantage? Niv unfortunately has been quoted as saying "If 15 percent of day traders are profitable, I'd be surprised!"[9] with all the aplomb of Gerald Ratner saying his jewelry was "crap." If 15 percent of day traders are profitable, then, by definition, 85 percent are not. That is good news for companies that run a B Book, but it is not so profitable for companies that run an agency straight-through process. With such a high attrition rate for customers, only excellent marketing or client on-boarding networks can fill the "leaking bucket." But marketing is expensive, and the market is finite, and so it is questionable if this strategy is sustainable in the long term. Events such as "SNB 2015" do nothing to instill confidence in retail brokerages or FX as a product.

High-frequency trading scalping algorithms and arbitrage models, while profitable in the short term, eventually make the market efficient and returns diminish. As brokers fight for clients in the CFD market, exorbitant overnight interest charges, spreads and commissions, and the like will all erode as in other markets. MT4 is a fabulous product, and social trading is an innovative concept, but once again, even in a fair market with zero spreads and commissions, only 50 percent of clients will make money. Expert Advisors get paid out of spread from the people who follow their trades. If you combine spread and leverage and excessive trading, profitable traders may well diminish to 15 percent, as Niv opines.

Is the market scalable? The answer is still yes, but the message to customers needs to be refined, and regulators must work with providers to really train or educate clients to approach FX and CFD trading as they would any other investment. It is essential that clients understand the notion of churning—an unethical and in some cases illegal practice of excessive buying and selling of a product in a client's account in order to create commissions. If clients subscribe to trading algorithms that trade on short-term price signals and there is a commission (or spread rebate) going to the manager, clients need to know that.

The risk of how leverage can lead to losses needs to be communicated more effectively, as does the attritional effect of financing charges. Of course, the positives of leverage should be explained, but somehow, clients should be made aware that trading FX and CFDs is a high-risk strategy. No one in his right mind would invest in equities if he believed he had only a 15 percent chance of winning. And yet people leverage up in CFDS. Clients need to have confidence in what they are trading; otherwise, ASIC is right: "You're effectively gambling a much larger amount of money than if you went to the casino or racetrack."

If brokers are running large amounts of risk, they need to have the capital to support their operations. SNB 2015 tested the value-at-risk models of some banks and brokerages well beyond normal parameters. It is testament to many that the models held up. It is difficult to proffer an adequate solution aside from taking excessive leverage out of the system because in this example, as in other flash crash scenarios, the likelihood of the event was rare and the move was so extreme.

FX has had a good shake-up, and a few stronger brokerages will evolve in strongly regulated centers. They will always be flanked by poorly capitalized brokers, based out of less recognized regulatory jurisdictions. Clients will migrate to where they feel most comfortable. In terms of the evolution of retail FX and CFD trading, a small number of brokerage names have evolved from the outset. To the owners of these brokerages and in particular Peter Cruddas, Kim Fournais, Lars Christensen, and Glenn Stevens, who are consistently at the forefront of the industry, whether they are worth millions or billions, they all rank as Currency Kings!

Jim Simons:
Quant King

6

When the Renaissance men stepped into the MF Global office in Hong Kong, it was a somewhat surreal moment. To say they stepped in could better be described as wafted or floated in, such was their calm demeanor. I couldn't help noticing how relaxed they were and how super cool and confident. I don't remember if it was Mark Rhoades-Brown or Gudjon Hermannsson or one of the others who wasn't wearing socks, but it triggered a memory of the successful Goldman trader who used to sit on the end of a desk in London and who had dispensed with suit, tie, and shoes in preference for jeans and a T-shirt and grew his hair that little bit longer in a nonchalant, nonmaterial display of wealth and power—someone who was so self-assured and perhaps too successful to conform to normal dress habits and maybe also too important profitwise for management to question his comfortable attire. The Renaissance men had this aura. Why wouldn't they?

We'd all heard of Renaissance Technologies of course—that hedge fund from East Setauket, New York, staffed with the smartest quants on Wall Street; the fund with one of the best winning runs in the markets that consistently delivered high double-digit, if not triple-digit, returns; the fund founded by a mercurial math professor and Cold War code breaker, Jim Simons. Our visitors had confidence in spades, the same assuredness in their abilities and system that you would attribute to John Henry. They were also backed up by a huge amount of capital. Now they were in our office and possibly about to give us a small piece of their secret. We were all ears!

Over dinner at the restaurant of the New York chef and Hong Kong gastro celebrity Harlan Goldstein in the International Finance Centre, the Renaissance men told us what they wanted: colocation of servers (in other words, proximity to the exchange) and also feeble commission charges for trade execution. Two essential elements to secure their trading edge. They were going to trade huge volumes! Speed was an essential element to complement their competitive advantage. How they would use that speed was open to debate and conjecture. They didn't let on. After all, Renaissance was secretive in its affairs. Today you would guess it was a high-frequency trading strategy. Back in 2008, high-frequency trading was not nearly as prevalent. They wanted to eliminate erosion of profits due to excessive commissions. Their margins of profitability were obviously small. The quid pro quo would be high volumes. Our commission earnings would grow very quickly even though the cost per trade was tiny. Their profits would increase with the volume they could trade. If we could meet their demands, we might get a sniff of the action in executing their business.

ARBITRAGE

Speed is an essential element of most financial markets arbitrage: "The early bird catches the worm." And arbitrage in the financial markets has been going on for years. Arbitrage in its basic form is the simultaneous buying and selling of the same product in two different venues to capture favorable price discrepancies. "Arbing" has become less crude and more refined nowadays as computers have displaced traders, but despite this, it still happens, and it is traded by many participants, in large amounts on a daily basis on the world's markets and exchanges. Foreign exchange is one such market, and the volumes traded are colossal.

Arbitrage and trade have gone hand-in-hand for many centuries. Nowadays we choose to describe arbitrage as a simultaneous purchase and sale, but in many physical trading activities—that is, delivery of a physical good against payment—arbitrage historically involved a time lag between a purchase and sale. *Arbitrage* and *trade* were effectively interchangeable. Buying goods in one country, transporting them to another, and selling them for a profit would be considered trade hundreds of years ago; buying and selling that same good by telephone in the two different centers, having taken into account the transport costs, might well be classed as an arbitrage in modern times. Buying and selling an essentially similar good for a profit on two different exchanges by clicking on a computer mouse would be considered an arbitrage today.

The words "Silk Road" can evoke romantic visions of traders and merchants in times past, traversing vast wildernesses transporting goods from east to west, whether they be textiles, metals, or spices, and exchanging them for gold, silver, or other goods. Gold and silver were considered currency—a benchmark or measure of value. The price achieved for gold and silver could vary from country to country, and savvy merchants knew where to "arb" the precious metals—not without risks to their lives as there was often a high chance of ambush by bandits because not all routes were protected, and those that were required that a tax be paid for safe passage. Similarly, as *bills of exchange* (BOEs) evolved in Europe from the seventeenth century onward, an arbitrage evolved between the stated currency value on the bills of exchange and the price of its convertibility into physical gold and silver in two different geographical locations.

Arbitrage is present in all our lives. Banks wouldn't exist without arbitrage. What banks pay out on savings and what they charge on loans is an arbitrage. If a mortgage lender engages in selling a fixed mortgage at the LIBOR, Euribor, SIBOR, or any other benchmark interest rate and the lender adds 0.5 or 1.0 percent or whatever else it can get away with, then consider yourself arbed by the mortgage lender. The spread over the benchmark is the lender's arbitrage—that is, the lender's profit. The lender can cover the trade far less expensively than the price you pay.

Arbitrage has many forms and guises. Some multinational companies go to great lengths to avoid paying taxes by booking profits in one location (where they pay less tax) and booking losses or booking smaller profits in another location (where they pay more tax). To elaborate on an example of a hypothetical tax arbitrage, let's consider a company that has business interests in both Australia and Hong Kong. Let us assume a corporate tax rate in Australia of 28.5 percent and in Hong Kong of 16.5 percent, a difference of 12 percent, and for the sake of the example, a notional taxable profit of AUD$1 million is made in both centers after any taxable relief.

It could be argued that the company might pay AUD$120,000 less in taxes if its profits were booked in Hong Kong. A potential way to get around this tax burden might be to buy out-of-the-money FX option strangles in Australia and sell out-of-the-money FX option strangles in Hong Kong. In Australia, you would pay a premium to put this trade on and hope the trade expired worthless. In Hong Kong, the same option would expire worthless too, and you would collect the premium. This example is of course hypothetical, but it could happen in any two financial centers around the world. It would make even more sense if somehow the sold strangles made more premium than the bought strangles. This trade could be put on monthly to allow "time" to quickly work its decay on the option value. There may be subtle discrepancies in option prices on the exchange versus the OTC market. If the trades are booked as legitimate hedges in both centers, then the transfer of wealth is effectively made.

In the financial markets, some companies may headquarter or house subsidiaries of their businesses in locations where there is a less severe regulatory burden. Some might consider this regulatory arbitrage. It happens a lot in the foreign exchange markets. Generally these locations may require companies to pay up less capital and may well allow companies to offer excessive leverage to retail investors. Customers of course may choose where they trade, and it may well suit some customers to trade where they can obtain higher degrees of leverage. Less recognized regulatory centers are less likely to provide protective measures when it comes to the safety of client funds. That is the customers' risk of course. In general, wherever there is a discrepancy, whether it be price, tax, or regulation, arbitrageurs will try to maximize their gain from the situation.

Modern-day arbitrage opportunities are traditionally found on futures exchanges where the same or very similar products are traded. A gold contract, for example, might be traded in ounces or in grams. There might be subtle differences in the quality of the gold—99.5 percent purity versus 99.99 percent. The contract might be traded in different currencies and countries. Each variable adds an opportunity for arbitrage—especially latency arbitrage! Trading on exchange versus over the counter also adds another variable. In commodities prices, there may be opportunities due to a market in contango or in backwardation. *Contango* is a situation in which the spot or cash price of a commodity is lower than the forward price. *Backwardation* is the opposite. It is a situation in which the spot or cash price of a commodity is higher than the forward price. The development of a backwardation is associated with supply shortage.

One other aspect of trading on exchange is that while there are a great many speculators, trend followers, and high-frequency traders now trading the markets, there are also bona fide hedgers.

In perishable commodities, or in commodities that can be affected by the weather such as coffee, there will naturally be fluctuations in price that can lead to normal backwardation or contango markets. There is also the aspect of physical delivery. Add to the mix storage costs, transport costs, and interest rates, and soon the complexities exist to create enough potential distortions in pricing for sophisticated computer programs to juggle the numbers and arb the exchanges.

Exchanges thrive on volume, commissions, and clearing fees, and many new exchanges have popped up across the globe, more so since the explosion in high-frequency trading. If there is a genuinely liquid market for a product, an exchange (and an HFT) can quickly prosper. Not all contract specifications suit exchange participants, and some exchanges and their products have failed. Others have had teething problems when dealing with physical delivery.

In Oxfordshire, England, home of one of the oldest and greatest universities in the world, a farmer brought a nascent exchange to a standstill in an example of physical delivery arbitrage in which you have to admire him for his audacity and derring-do. His name was Clive Hawes, a giant of a man with an iron will to match. Hawes's particular skill was that he was a livestock farmer and trader par excellence on the sheep and cattle markets. He had grown up as a boy learning from and watching his father, and he had taken over his father's sheep flock, cattle herd, and other farming interests after his father's untimely death.

At this stage as a 21-year-old, he was already importing and exporting cattle with his longtime school friend Ben Sparrow. While their career paths diverged soon afterward, Hawes and Sparrow would remain great friends until Hawes's own untimely death at the age of 61. Hawes was never a man who did things in half measures, regularly buying vast amounts of livestock at Banbury Stockyard—reputedly Europe's largest livestock market. In some years it would be sheep, but in 1990, his attention was drawn to an arbitrage on the recently created beef futures market. Hawes spotted that he could buy steers in the physical cattle market far cheaper than the price at which he could sell them on the futures exchange. And so he did. He bought pen after pen of steers, brought them home to correctly specified pens at his farm, and fed them appropriately to ensure that they reached the stipulated weight. A week before the contract was due to roll over, he instructed the exchange that he would deliver!

On a frosty winter morning, an impressive convoy of articulated lorries arrived at his farm, and several hundred cattle were loaded and sent to the abattoir. All was going to plan! But then of course a hitch arrived. The trader who had been buying the futures was none other than the owner of the abattoir—a burly man of rubicund complexion whose demeanor was changing by the second as lorry after lorry of braying steers arrived at his doorstep. As he fidgeted in his boots, his brow became increasingly furrowed, his fists clenched, and he reddened to the point of apoplexy.

The abattoir owner resorted to rejecting pens of cattle for the most obscure and tenuous reasons. He also refused to pay for the hides (or skins) of the slaughtered beasts, which would normally be the case. Tension mounted on both sides. While an abattoir in the middle of nowhere might have made an excellent location for a bare-knuckle fistfight, the two men were normally friends and well respected in the industry. The supervisors of the futures exchange were called in, and a gentlemen's settlement was negotiated. The two men would laugh over it for many years. More important, they both learned lessons about risk!

Currency arbitrage generally happens between currencies traded on futures markets versus the OTC market. However, in the OTC market, subtle price discrepancies due to different quotes provided by genuine market makers can create moments when bid prices exceed offer prices, and in this area there is a phenomenal amount of what is called *latency arbitrage*. It must be said that brokers and platforms have mechanisms to avoid quoting inverse pricing, but trading companies that have multiple price feeds via an application programming interface can combine them into an aggregated price and then create a trading algorithm to capture any inverse prices and therefore capture free profits. (An *application programming interface*, or API, is defined as a set of functions and procedures that allow the creation of applications that access the features or data of an operating system, application, or other service.)

To illustrate a simple arbitrage in the spot market in euros versus U.S. dollars:

Provider 1 quote: EUR/USD 1.10101/1.10104

Provider 2 quote: EUR/USD 1.10105/1.10108

Provider 3 quote: EUR/USD 1.10107/1.10110

The best offer is 1.10104, and the best bid is 1.10107. The algorithm would sell the bid at 1.10107 and pay the offer at 1.10104. In this example, if the notional amount was EUR 1 million, the profit would be $30—(1 million × 0.00003). Prime brokerage and platform or API charges might add up to US$8 per million, or 2 million × 1.10, or roughly $17.6 for the trade. Profit works out at $12.4—not much, but if executed 1,000 times per day, it adds up to $12,400!

On January 4, 1999, the euro started trading on the over-the-counter market as the common currency of 11 countries. It wasn't long before arbitrageurs noticed significant profitable opportunities in what became known as a triangular arbitrage between EUR/USD, USD/CHF, and EUR/CHF. The arbitrages were much larger than the fifth decimal arbs we see today. In early 2000, prices were quoted only to the fourth decimal. Societe Generale, a French bank, set up teams of arbitrageurs in London and New York to take advantage of the arbitrage. The requirements for inclusion in the teams were nimble fingers and the ability to handle quick mental arithmetic. For a period of time, especially the years from 2001 to 2005, Societe Generales's profits were in the multimillions from this activity.

The arbitrage is slightly more complicated than the EUR/USD example, but it is easily explainable.

EUR/CHF is known as a *cross-currency*. It is quoted as EUR/CHF, or it can be created synthetically by combining EUR/USD and USD/CHF. For this example, I use fourth decimal quotes, typical of the early 2000s.

Say EUR/USD trades at 1.1010/1.1013 and USD/CHF trades at 1.0200/1.0205.

To buy EUR against Swiss francs, synthetically, one would first have to buy euros versus dollars (Buy EUR, Sell USD) and then buy U.S. dollars versus Swiss francs (Buy USD, Sell CHF).

So, to buy 1 million EUR/CHF, the following trades would need to be executed:

Buy 1 million EUR/USD at 1.1013 (it costs US$1.1013 million).

Buy 1 million, one hundred and one thousand, three hundred dollars against Swiss francs at 1.0205.

The cross-price is therefore 1.1013 × 1.0205, or 1.12387665 rounded up to 1.1239 to buy 1 million EUR/CHF. Similarly the bid price can be calculated as 1.1010 × 1.0200, or 1.12302 rounded down to 1.1230. Traders would most likely quote this pair at 1.1230/1.1240.

In the first instance, it seems highly unlikely that anybody could arbitrage a price as wide as 1.1230/1.1240, but as will become evident, a vast opportunity existed for this arbitrage, and the market lasted for several years. Societe Generale was not the only bank to profit from the arbitrage. Other traders at Bank of America and Fuji Bank were also most proficient at trading this particular triangular cross-trade. The trick was simple and something that Renaissance and others would copy and apply electronically to many other triangular cross-trades in the future. In the early 2000s it was sharp human minds, aided by real rather than artificial intelligence and by Microsoft Excel spreadsheets and two or three trading platforms, who executed the EUR/CHF arb in enormous quantities.

In reality, spot EUR/CHF did not trade at a 10 point spread. On the EBS platform, it might trade at 5 pips or even 3 pips, so the price seen by the traders might be 1.1235/1.1238. There were other factors in the market that helped give confidence in the trade, even if momentarily, one of the trading legs—there are three in a triangulation trade—was losing money relative to the spot price.

As an ex-Societe Generale trader explained, "Quite often you would have banks doing lots of Fix types of trades where they would come in and bid through the offer on the amount that was available on EBS. So, for example, on New York open a bank might receive an at-best order to buy 50 million EUR/CHF at market. The bank trader would basically bid through the offer. So say the market was 1.1210/13 in 3 million by 5 million. The bank might go 1.1214 bid for EUR $30 million. And he might execute the rest at the 1.1215 offer.

"On our side we had traders who could sense the weak side and so therefore might have offers in EBS for 5 million at 14 and 5 million at 15. Our trader would therefore be short 10 million EUR/CHF at the offer price. Eventually the market goes back into line, and during those times [the early 2000s], EUR/CHF would be in, say, a 30 pip trading range, so even if you were short at 17 in a 19 to 21 market, you knew you would have a chance to leg out at some point or the cross would come back lower." He went on to say, "The bank trader would just jam the market because he had the at-best order. Regardless of how well he filled that order, he would just add a pip or two for himself and fill the client accordingly! So arbitrage was literally profiting from inefficiencies in the market."[1]

"Arbing through the legs"—that is, creating a synthetic EUR/CHF buy trade to cover the short trade—was made easier by connecting price feeds in EUR/CHF, USD/CHF, and EUR/USD into an Excel spreadsheet. If the trader was indeed short at 17, he might be able to buy EUR/USD and buy USD/CHF and perhaps pay 15. Therefore making 2 pips. The traders would use a combination of EBS and Reuters platforms. In addition, they could call out to other counterparties to get quotes. Trading electronically was much faster, of course, and time was of the essence. So was saving commissions. On EBS, aggressors—or clients who "paid" offers or gave "bids"—would pay a commission, usually in the region of $20 per million U.S. dollars traded. Those who left resting orders would not pay the commission.

Traders typically had profit objectives of $2 million to $3 million annually with incremental bonus potential above those numbers. Some traders were not salaried and were just paid a percentage of performance. Interestingly, a lot of the traders were older, more experienced people. They were FX professionals who had been dealers for years and who had watched the ebb and flow and interaction of EUR/USD and USD/CHF through countless economic announcements over the years. They knew where the support and resistance were, had their ears to the ground for information, and were quick witted enough to instinctively feel when they were in profit or in loss. There was one trader who was so good he made in the region of $65,000 to $70,000 every day with just one or two trading losses per year. As his ex-colleague revealed, "Only when EBS allowed API trading did the machines take over. I never saw them perform like my friend. He was unbelievable. He saw moves before they happened. He smelled out the market."

SIMONS THE MATHEMATICIAN

There are few in the market who have extrasensory perception—perhaps George Soros is one of them. And perhaps, in his capacity as an EUR/CHF arbitrage trader, the Societe Generale trader was another. Jim Simons, the founder of Renaissance Technologies, is most definitely in that league, and his credentials for sniffing out opportunities in the market, developing algorithms to do his sniffing for him, and capturing unbelievable profits are second to none.

Simons was not always a financial wizard. His background is in mathematics and academia. Born into a Jewish family in Brookline, Massachusetts, Simons excelled in mathematics and logic, often spending his nights thinking or "pondering" about solutions to problems, solving them, and then promptly forgetting them. He studied mathematics at the Massachusetts Institute of Technology and also at the University of California, Berkeley, where he gained a PhD at age 23. His pet subject was geometry, and along with Shiing-Shen Chern, he developed the Chern-Simons theory in secondary characteristic classes of 3-manifolds, a close relation of string theory. This concept is best described as the way in which point-like particles of particle physics are replaced by one-dimensional objects called *strings* and how these strings propagate through space and interact with each other.

After teaching at both Harvard and MIT, Simons moved to Princeton, where his love of geometry and skill at pattern recognition led him to work as a code breaker for the Institute of Defense Analyses albeit under the auspices of the National Security Agency (NSA). When he publicly contradicted his boss, retired four-star Army General Maxwell D. Taylor, in the *New York Times Magazine* over the merits of the Vietnam War, he soon found himself looking for alternative employment. And he found it at Stony Brook University on Long Island, where he took over as chairman of the math department in 1968.

Simons spent the next 10 or so years aggressively building up the department into a first-class operation. Along the way he would inspire and nurture a new generation of mathematicians, some of whom would eventually join him at Renaissance. He was recognized for his contribution to geometry in 1976, when he won the Veblen Prize of the American Mathematics Society for his work in this area.

One year later, in 1977, he set up Monemetrics, the precursor to Renaissance Technologies. His business partner was Lenny Baum, with whom he'd worked at the Institute of Defense Analyses. Baum was a cryptanalyst. An expert at code breaking, he could solve riddles of infinitesimal tininess in mammoth data streams, and, in theory, he and Simons would apply Baum's algorithms to huge amounts of financial markets data in order to find hidden patterns and calculate the probability of their recurring. A small probabilistic edge would give them a statistical chance of beating the market! Two outstanding mathematicians—a geometer and a cryptanalyst—looking to crack the financial "Enigma code."

THE MEDALLION FUND

In practice, Baum turned out to be a master fundamental trader and had little incentive to apply the algorithms he'd created. Enter James Ax, a probability theory expert who had worked for Simons at Stony Brook. Ax determined that Baum's algorithms could be applied to securities, commodities, and currency markets, and so between Ax and Simons, they set up Axcom Ltd., an offshoot of Monemetrics that in due course would be renamed the Medallion Fund, at first a subscription fund but later the coveted employee-owned moneymaking machine that Renaissance Technologies is now so famous for.

Axcom's double-digit profit making years abruptly stalled almost immediately after it was renamed Medallion. A nausea-inducing drawdown of 30 percent occurred from late 1988 until April 1989, testing the nerves and resolve of the two partners. Ax's and Simons's opinions diverged on how to deal with the problem, straining their working relationship to breaking point. Ax considered the drawdown acceptable within the model's trading parameters and wanted to continue to trade. Simons wanted to stop, analyze, cogitate, and get to the bottom of the problems facing the fund. Both men remained resolute in defending their opinions, and so a standoff ensued. Elwyn Berlekamp, a fellow PhD and game theory expert at Berkeley who acted as advisor to Axcom, intervened and offered to buy out James Ax's stake. The three men agreed. Ax left the fund, and Simons and Berlekamp worked out a way to get things back to profitability. It involved shortening the holding period of their trades—something that as the years passed developed into a much higher frequency trading strategy.

What was so powerful and different about Simons's recruiting and trading approach compared to other funds was that he set about incrementally building up his business and its intellectual firepower by plucking the best brains he could find from the different fields of mathematics, physics, engineering, and computer science—himself, a geometer; Baum, a cryptanalyst; Ax, a probability expert; and Berlekamp, a game theorist. It was as if Simons was a modern-day John Galt. PhDs would be enticed to a utopian moneymaking phenomenon, each adding his or her particular skill and all working harmoniously under an avuncular visionary. Applying science to beat the markets was the name of the game. The people at Renaissance all added something to the mix, and just as he had done at Stony Brook with his math faculty, Simons kept building and adding different skill sets to keep his fund at the top of its game.

Aside from Ax, few Renaissance employees have voluntarily left the fund. There has been no seemingly sound reason to do so. Berlekamp is an exception; having brought the fund back to profitability and returning 55.9 percent (net of fees) in 1990, he also left. His desire was academia, and his passion was game theory, and he returned to UC Berkeley to teach math, where he remains today as professor emeritus. Money and the financial markets were seemingly less relevant to him. He found financial types "dull" compared to academics. It is a shame for Ax that he left under acrimonious circumstances and that he would not figure in the firm's unparalleled successes over the next three decades.

THE RENAISSANCE TECHNOLOGIES PHILOSOPHY

Ax certainly had ideas, and for a while he made money using a relative value strategy. In the commodities markets, he would sell futures that had opened sharply higher and buy futures that had opened sharply lower from their previous day's close, hoping to benefit from retracements to more normal levels. Simons alluded to employing the same tactics in stock picking when testifying to Congress after the global financial crisis in 2008. "Our trading models tend to be contrarian, buying stocks recently out of favor and selling those recently in favor," he said. In a rare interview with *Institutional Investor* printed in November 2000, he explained his trading philosophy in a little more detail: "We look at anomalies that may be small in size and brief in time. We make our forecast. Then, shortly thereafter, we reevaluate the situation and revise our forecast and our portfolio. We do this all day long. We're always in and out and out and in. So we're dependent on activity to make money."

The Renaissance philosophy is one of treating the financial markets as one giant experiment. The markets are in dynamic evolution. Simons's quants or code breakers analyze any hypothesis and apply it to multiple markets. If technical analysts like Edwards and Magee look for patterns, then Simons and his analysts look for patterns within patterns. He has said, "We search through historical data looking for anomalous patterns that we would not expect to occur at random. Once we find one, we test it for statistical significance and consistency over time. After we determine its validity, we ask, 'Does this correspond to some aspect of behavior that seems reasonable?'

"Many of the anomalies we initially exploited are intact, though they have weakened some. What you need to do is pile them up. You need to build a system that is layered and layered. And with each new idea, you have to determine, is this really new, or is this somehow embedded in what we've done already? So you use statistical tests to determine that, yes, a new discovery is really a new discovery. OK, now how does it fit in? What's the right weighting to put in? And finally you make an improvement. Then you layer in another one. And another one."[2]

The quest is to beat the markets because in the view of Simons and his analysts, the markets are still inefficient, although Simons contends that the markets are "considerably more efficient" and that "efficient market theory is correct in that there are no gross inefficiencies."[3] About a third of Renaissance's 275 staff members hold PhDs in all manner of disciplines. Bob Mercer and Peter Brown, who both joined Renaissance in 1993, are the founders of a speech recognition group for IBM. Gudjon Hermannsson has a PhD in computer science from Stony Brook. Mark Rhoades-Brown, himself a nuclear theorist by training, pointed out at the University of Tennessee, Knoxville, Graduate Awards Ceremony in 2002 that the biggest chunk of Renaissance's scientists are physicists. He also said that the value of critical thinking is as an asset that many scientists possess and one "that has value in the outside world beyond physics." In quantum physics, small causes can have large effects. It is known as the *butterfly effect*, and it forms part of chaos theory. If any hedge fund can make sense out of chaos, it is Renaissance. In the quant world, everything is relevant!

Such is the culture at Renaissance that freedom of expression is paramount on the totem pole of values; critical thinking and problem solving are passions, and moneymaking is an inevitable side reward. The people at Renaissance are living the American dream in real time and using their brainpower and brilliance to continuously beat the market. Their results of the last 28 years are testament to the fact the markets can be beaten and also that one must evolve with the market to keep winning. One can expect that with the caliber of personnel that they employ and the techniques that they utilize, Renaissance will stay at the top of the pile for many years to come.

THE MEDALLION FUND UNDER MERCER AND BROWN

Simons stepped aside from leading Renaissance Technologies at the end of 2009, handing the reins to Bob Mercer and Peter Brown, who were by then 16-year veterans of the company. Their privilege was to take over the Medallion Fund with average annual returns above 40 percent with only one losing year in 1989. Simons, who had set up Math for America in 2004, whose mission is to improve mathematics education in the U.S. public schools, would concentrate more on his philanthropic activities. By 2009, Renaissance was managing other funds, including the Renaissance Institutional Equities Fund and two "diversified alpha" funds. Its assets under management were north of $20 billion.

The question that would be asked was whether Brown and Mercer could continue making stellar returns. The answer was a resounding yes, certainly for their in-house fund, as Medallion posted a 33.9 percent return in 2010 (Table 6.1).

In the 27-year period from 1990 to 2016, Renaissance had turned $1,000 in its Medallion Fund into over $13.2 million.

TABLE 6.1

Renaissance Medallion Fund Returns for 1990 Through 2016

Year	Percent Returns
1990	56.0
1991	39.4
1992	34.0
1993	39.1
1994	70.1
1995	38.3
1996	31.5
1997	21.2
1998	41.5
1999	24.5
2000	98.5
2001	33.0
2002	32.7
2003	27.3
2004	28.7
2005	32.7
2006	51.3
2007	85.9
2008	98.2
2009	47.0
2010	33.9
2011	36.6
2012	28.8
2013	46.9
2014	39.2
2015	35.6
2016	21.0*

Source: Bloomberg.   *Through June 2016.

And this was after fees, which ramped up over the years to a 5 percent management fee and a 44 percent performance fee. It is quite the most remarkable performance record of any fund, and it also shows how compound interest works in the most extraordinary way.

Mercer and Brown would increasingly focus on high-frequency trading, and along with other hedge fund giants such as Ken Griffin's Citadel, they would extract profits not just by sniffing out patterns but by employing powerful computers to provide split-second liquidity to any manner of markets and then just as rapidly off-loading any positions that might be accumulated straight back to the market. Their split-second intervention, often using large amounts of leverage, would collect small favorable price discrepancies in what amounted to a large-scale arbitrage operation.

HIGH-FREQUENCY TRADERS

In the currency markets, other HFTs have become very well known, certainly among brokers and electronic communication networks. Names that keep cropping up are Lucid Markets, GSA Capital, and Virtu Financial. All have pretty much the same modus operandi and similarly describe their "liquidity provision" in glowing, nonpredatory terms.

Virtu, a company listed on Nasdaq, in its company overview says, "Virtu's liquidity provision plays a vital role in the overall health and efficiency of the global financial markets, especially in times of market turbulence." And it also says, "As market makers, we lower costs for both retail and institutional investors by supplying competitive bids and offers, without seeking to take on risky directional positions."

Lucid Markets, owned by FXCM and founded by ex-Goldman Sachs alumni Mat Wilhelm and Dierk Reuter, is "focused on delivering a compelling liquidity offering for FX markets accessible via API." Reuter, incidentally, is a former global head of algorithmic trading at Deutsche Bank, and he holds a PhD in aerospace engineering from the Georgia Institute of Technology.

Founded in 2005 by Oxford University math graduate Jonathan Hiscock, who is a former managing director of statistical arbitrage at Deutsche Bank, GSA Capital is somewhat more transparent, if only insofar as the company admits to being a prop shop. "We run a number of absolute return, alternative strategies focused on systematic trading across liquid equities, futures, and foreign exchange markets globally." They do this on a "world-class" proprietary platform and trade on "multiple time frames."[4]

SPINNING THE STACK

Collectively, these non-bank market makers have challenged the more traditional liquidity sources provided by giants in the FX market such as UBS and Deutsche Bank, but at the same time they have incurred the wrath of some less adept providers by continually picking them off in a game of cat-and-mouse arbitrage. Some banks have complained that HFTs have been "spinning the stack" in aggregated liquidity pools. The concept is not too dissimilar to "whale order hunting" in equity markets.

An example of a *liquidity stack* is shown in Figure 6.1. This is an aggregated stack of liquidity in USD/JPY. Anybody wishing to buy $40 million would be able to do so theoretically at no worse than 118.03. The *volume-weighted average price* (VWAP) is actually 118.0238. (To get this, you multiply volume by price for all the amounts offered to achieve an average price, which in this case was $40 million.)

HFTs scrabble to be *top of book*—that is, to be the best bid and offer, or 118.01/118.012. And they will trade against small orders (and each other) to maintain the top-of-book position. If

Currency Pair: USD/JPY			
Millions	**Bid**	**Offer**	**Millions**
2	118.01	118.012	2
3	118.009	118.014	3
5	118.007	118.017	5
10	118	118.02	10
20	117.98	118.03	20

Figure 6.1 Liquidity stack, USD/JPY.

the 118.012 offer is taken out by a large order, the HFT is quick enough to buy at 118.014 in front of the big order and resell at a higher price. Say the order is for $40 million. The price might get distorted as shown in Figure 6.2. An HFT "spins the stack" to its advantage.

Currency Pair: USD/JPY			
Offer	**Millions**	**HFT Buy**	**HFT Sell**
118.012	2	118.012	118.012
118.014	3	118.014	118.016
118.017	5	118.017	118.019
118.02	10	118.02	118.029
118.03	20	118.03	118.04

Figure 6.2 Liquidity stack with HFT intervention.

The new VWAP for $40 million is 118.0314 compared to 118.0238. A profit of 0.0076 pip in $40 million. This amounts to 304,000 yen, or $2,575.4 (marked-to-market at 118.04). Far from delivering a compelling alternative liquidity source, the HFTs have just imposed a rather noxious trading tax.

THE PROFITABILITY OF HFTs

In the year ended December 2011, Lucid, whose focus was entirely on FX, made operational profits of $113.4 million on $13.4 trillion of volume using its market maker/taker model. GSA Capital split profits from its multiple asset strategies of GBP 71.4 million among its partners for the period up to March 2013. Virtu reported that 20 percent of its $414.5 adjusted net profits for the year ending December 31, 2013, or about $82.9 million, came from FX. It was a maker/taker on the following platforms: CME, ICE, Currenex, EBS, Hotspot, Reuters, FXall, and LMAX. Virtu listed on Nasdaq on April 15, 2015, raising $314 million from its IPO and valuing the company at over $2.5 billion.

In the high-frequency game, Renaissance's Medallion kept returning profits of 20 percent plus, but some of its other funds were posting distinctly mediocre returns. In 2012 Renaissance Institutional Equities Fund posted profits of 8.43 percent, and Renaissance Institutional Futures Fund (RIFF) actually lost 3.17 percent. In October 2015, Renaissance announced it would close RIFF, citing a lack of investor interest. The reality was that the fund was a relative underperformer, posting average annualized returns of 2.86 percent (after fees) since its inception in September 2007. A fund holding about $1.46 billion in 2013, it posted profits of just 2.15 percent, or about $31 million. Compare this to Virtu's roughly $95 million from Global Commodities in 2013 (Global Commodities' trading accounted for 23 percent of Virtu's adjusted net earnings of $414.5 million), and it would seem that Renaissance had either at least partly lost the battle in latency arbitrage or had an issue with its algos. Other viable explanations are that the market had reached saturation levels with many HFTs employing the same strategies or that markets had indeed become efficient and arbitrageurs had served their purpose.

It's interesting to read Virtu's stated "competitive strengths" in its prospectus summary:

1. Critical component of an efficient market ecosystem

2. Cutting-edge, proprietary technology

3. Consistent, diversified, and growing revenue base

4. Low costs and large economies of scale

5. Real-time risk management

6. Proven and talented management team[5]

It would seem that points 2 and 4 are definitely competitive advantages. Scale and low costs are highly beneficial to making outsize profits. Virtu has had only one losing day in over 1,200 trading days. Their proprietary software is working for now. Point 3 is debatable: other companies such as Renaissance prefer to concentrate on stocks, bonds, commodities, and currencies that are publicly traded, liquid, and amenable to modeling. So diversification into non-liquid investments has plenty of associated risks.

Thankfully, Virtu has "real-time risk management"—a must have for the frequency of the company's trading. There will be plenty of discussion about point 1. In some respects, HFTs make for an efficient market ecosystem, but only in very small trading amounts. Pension funds might well grumble that order execution is far more difficult and less efficient due to the many thousands of orders that flurry through the system the instant they try to execute a large trade. One would hope that Virtu's management team is proven and talented. It certainly seems to be: $414.5 million of net adjusted profits in 2013 is an enormous amount of money.

But what of the weaknesses that could hinder profitability? These would apply to Renaissance, Citadel, GSA, Lucid, or any other HFT:

1. Because our revenues and profitability depend on trading volume and volatility in the markets in which we operate,

they are subject to factors beyond our control, are prone to significant fluctuations, and are difficult to predict.

2. We are dependent upon our trading counterparties and clearing houses to perform their obligations to us.

3. We may incur losses in our market making activities in the event of failures of our customized trading platform.

4. We may incur material trading losses from our market making activities.

5. We are exposed to losses due to lack of perfect information.

6. We face competition in our market making activities.

7. We are subject to liquidity risk in our operations.

8. Rules governing designated market makers may require us to make unprofitable trades or prevent us from making profitable trades from time to time.

9. Regulatory and legal uncertainties could harm our business.[6]

There's plenty to sift through here, but most glaring are volume, volatility, liquidity, competition, and regulators. Much to the chagrin of many HFTs and some exchanges, there have been several recent books that expose some of the moneymaking methods of HFTs. In addition, a new phenomenon in the markets known as "flash crashes" seems to be a constant risk to stability and order in the markets—the blame for which some have placed squarely at the door of HFTs. The begging questions are whether HFTs actually add value in the sense of "liquidity provision" and whether their outsize profits are genuinely sustainable. In the long run, markets become efficient because arbitrageurs iron out inefficiencies. A hotter topic, and one that will undoubtedly cause debate and perhaps uproar, is the extent to which retirees suffer in their pension schemes due to market slippage.

SMALL AND MEDIUM-SIZED
ARBITRAGE TRADING FIRMS

It would seem pretty daunting for anyone, especially a layman foreign exchange trader, to even contemplate arbitrage trading, and yet it is possible—no PhD required! To trade in anywhere near the scale of a Virtu or a Renaissance firm would require a huge capital outlay, investment in infrastructure, technology, and key personnel. But even faced with such daunting competition, smaller traders with normal accounts can make money using an arbitrage strategy without eating into their life savings. How is this possible? A small capital investment will not lead to billions in profits, but it can produce positive, relatively risk-free returns—something that no other single FX strategy can match.

The key is to trade products that are less liquid and are found in more remote parts of the world. Somewhere outside the reach of algorithmic HFT behemoths. Trading new products on fledgling exchanges against established OTC products can lead to potential arbitrage opportunities. Triangular trades in different centers add complexity, as does trading longer time frames. Increased leverage magnifies small gains into acceptable returns. In using arbitrage strategies, it is essential to keep trading and borrowing costs to a minimum. It is also a prerequisite to use a broker or bank that is well capitalized and has a stable balance sheet.

In recent years Dubai and Abu Dhabi have emerged as alternative trading centers that span the crossover between Asian markets and London. ADS Securities in Abu Dhabi is the region's largest regulated retail FX broker. Dubai, originally known for oil production and as a center for international trade, has emerged as an incredible twenty-first-century city, with excellent infrastructure, a superlative airline, outstanding architecture, and unbeatable facilities. During this time, it has welcomed many new inhabitants from many cultures while maintaining its own heritage, dignity, and traditions.

Dubai is a city that has embraced change, encouraged technology, and promoted entrepreneurialism, new business enterprises, and commerce. In the financial services sector it now ranks as a respected alternative for the establishment of hedge funds or indeed foreign exchange brokerages, under the auspices of the Dubai International Finance Authority. Its futures exchange, the aptly named Dubai Gold and Commodities Exchange (DGCX), has seen 10 years of impressive growth as the premier futures exchange (outside of India) for trading Indian rupees and now other less readily traded currencies such as the Russian ruble, Chinese renminbi (yuan), and South African rand.

NON-DELIVERABLE FORWARDS (NDFs)

The DGCX commenced trading in November 2005, and it launched the world's first Indian rupee (INR) futures contract in 2007. Beginning in 2010, the DGCX started to see unprecedented levels of volume as arbitrage opportunities arose on contracts traded on DGCX INR futures versus non-deliverable forwards (NDFs) offered by banks and accessed through FX brokers. In Dubai there was a natural requirement for trade in Indian rupees because a large proportion of Dubai's 2.5 million inhabitants hail from India. There are many merchants and business owners who are non-resident Indians. The DGCX formed a natural exchange for the many businesses located in Dubai that wanted to transact "on exchange" in Indian rupees.

As the market developed, slight disparities appeared between locally traded Indian rupees on the DGCX and the more globally traded non-deliverable forwards offered by many banks with a presence both in India and outside of India. Banks such as Deutsche Bank, Standard Chartered Bank, HSBC, and many others have a presence in India. They are also providers of an NDF outside of India. Non-deliverable forwards allow for trading in currencies such as the Indian rupee, Chinese renminbi (yuan) (CNY), Brazilian real (BRL), and South Korean won (KRW), among others, outside of these countries. Settled in dollars, the local currencies are never delivered. The conversion rate—known as "the Fix"—for both onshore and offshore markets in the Indian rupee is set daily by the Reserve Bank of India (RBI).

Globally, NDF volumes remain surprisingly small, with estimates ranging for daily turnover of $17 billion in INR and $19 billion in KRW, with $16 billion in BRL and CNY trading up to $17 billion per day. The Bank of International Settlements Triennial Survey of 2013 estimated that the total daily turnover for the whole NDF market came in at a mere $125 billion. The populations of these countries—as well as Russia, Malaysia, Indonesia, Colombia, Taiwan, and the Philippines—whose currencies can be traded offshore as NDFs, far exceed those of the G10 countries, yet offshore turnover in their currencies accounts for only 2 percent of the whole. The non-deliverable option (NDO) market is even less sophisticated and represents a huge potential market. NDF trading is largely unchartered territory with massive potential both for growth and for arbitrage trading. The fact that the DGCX now offers contracts in Russian rubles and Chinese renminbi (yuan) presents undoubted opportunities.

The Indian rupee arbitrage really gathered momentum from the years 2011 to 2014. In Dubai, the exchange-traded U.S. dollar price would tend to open up bid versus the rupee and relative to the NDF price, especially in the early part of the month. The price on the DGCX more or less mirrored the onshore price on the Indian MCX exchange, reflecting demand for U.S. dollars to buy, among other things, oil. The NDF price in USD/INR was affected by a whole basket of different currency interactions and often lagged the pure onshore price. Indian rupee forwards were calculated to mirror the impressive interest rate "carry" in India, which represented attractive yields for those offshore willing to accept exchange risk.

In many instances the dollar was sold offshore as speculators accumulated rupees. The arbitrage, therefore, was to buy U.S. dollars in the NDF and sell U.S. dollars on the futures exchange. In periods of rupee strength, as investment in India and demand for rupees accelerated, carry trading became doubly attractive as traders were paid interest to hold on to rupees and also benefited from an appreciating currency. Almost in tandem, arbitrage opportunities came around much more frequently. And virtually on a daily basis the arbitrage would fluctuate between 2 and 5 pips and sometimes reach 7 pips. On rare occasions it could reach 15 or more pips.

To work out the profit on a USD$1 million position capturing 5 pips, an example calculation is as follows:

Buy $1 million USD/INR one month forward at 65.00.

Sell $1 million USD/INR one month forward at 65.05.

Profit = 0.05 × 1 million, or 50,000 rupees. Marked-to-market at 65.00 = 50,000/65, or $769.23.

Brokers typically offered 3 percent margin or 33.33 times leverage. So in order to put on a $1 million position, it would take just $30,000 in capital. Multiply this by 2 because two positions (a buy and a sell) were involved to lock in the profit one month forward, and the monthly return on $60,000 was an impressive 1.282 percent, or over 15 percent per year. In reality traders made much more as the arbitrage would tend to from 5 pips to zero as the month end approached and might even reverse. Positions could thus be unwound and put on in the next calendar contract. The opportunities were vast, and the trades could be done with the click of a mouse. And what's more, the trade was open to anybody who could access the DGCX and offshore NDF pricing. And it still is.

LIMITATIONS ON TRADING NDFs

There were some limitations to the trade, scale being one of them. Many brokers had concentration risk limits set by their prime brokers. These tended to be in the area of a $300 million to $500 million net open position. There were only seven or eight brokers offering the NDF, and these tended to use the same prime brokers. As the arbitrage generally favored being long U.S. dollars in the NDF, and since brokers passed the positions via a straight-through process to prime brokers, brokers were left holding large quantities of short U.S. dollar positions at prime brokers such as UBS, Deutsche, and Citibank.

Other limitations to the trade were the brokers themselves. In 2011, MF Global collapsed, and many of its clients trading NDFs had difficulty retrieving their funds during the bankruptcy proceedings. In September 2014, Marex Spectron confirmed that it was to close its FX business, and in May 2015, Fixi Plc ceased to offer NDF trading. One client of Refco and then MF Global has warned investors that it is imperative that they find a stable broker. The ability to withdraw funds in a timely manner is essential if you are trading with high degrees of leverage and at several brokers. Profits from one broker have often been withdrawn and used to meet margin calls at another broker. Any disruption to the flow of funds can mean trades getting closed out—a risk in itself because the other side of the trade remains open and to close that out too means paying away the spread. But finding funds to trade when your own legitimate funds are tied up elsewhere through no fault of your own is extremely galling. Brokers going bankrupt only ramps up the stress.

There is in an old saying in the financial markets: "Nothing kills success like success." It is true that its success in Dubai led other exchanges to try to offer an Indian rupee contract. In December 2012, the CME launched an Indian rupee futures contract, followed in November 2013 by Singapore's SGX. Some CME salespeople made a habit of touting the arbitrage opportunities as a fait accompli and reason to trade Indian rupee futures, and sure enough, new participants including high-frequency trader Indian rupee market maker/takers joined the party. The arbitrage subsequently virtually disappeared. A new saying that might be coined is "Nothing kills a successful arbitrage like an HFT," and yet from time to time, certainly in Dubai, where there is a natural flow of Indian rupees and genuine market hedgers on exchange, there still exist opportunities to arbitrage. And in the cyclical ebb and flow of the markets, that arbitrage may come back in reasonable proportions when the dollar weakens!

One hardened and successful arbitrage trader has reiterated that the stability of counterparties is a prerequisite in trading arbitrage, especially if you are to put down significant amounts of capital. Safety of client funds is paramount! A recent arbitrage in Australian dollars on exchange versus OTC illustrates this point.

In the burgeoning market of retail foreign exchange, many incentives are offered to entice new traders to start trading, one of which may be on rollover costs. If a client holds a currency that pays interest, he should receive interest on his position. The counter is true also. If he is short that currency, he should pay interest. Retail brokers who expect their clients to "blow up" sometimes offer a loss leader and might not charge interest on short positions. The Australian dollar is a good illustration of this. The Reserve Bank of Australia (RBA) may, for example, hold interest rates at 2 percent. One would reasonably expect to earn 2 percent annually for holding Aussie dollars and pay 2 percent annually for borrowing them. Naturally if a counterparty doesn't charge interest on short positions, if you can find one that does pay interest on long positions, you have an arbitrage. Thus 2 percent multiplied by leverage of, say, 50 times makes for a 50 percent annual return (100 percent/2 as there are two trades: one at the broker and one at the futures exchange). One such arbitrage arose between a broker in a less recognized jurisdiction and the CME.

Here's the trade:

Sell AUD spot at the offshore broker. Let's say 0.7268.

Buy three-month future, say, 0.7238.

Arbitrage is 30 pips, or US$3,000 per AUD million.

The profit is locked in.

There are a couple of issues for the retail broker here. First, he is expecting his clients to overtrade, or he is expecting trades on the long side to cover the client short positions. If he is running a B Book, his profits magnify as trades net off. What the B Book doesn't want is to be on the other side of a large short AUD trade in a market where the AUD is weakening. Unfortunately for the broker, this is precisely what happened. If a short 100 million AUD/USD position moves 100 pips lower, then the B Book will lose $1 million. If the broker is capitalized at less than $1 million, then all things being equal, he is insolvent.

In the period from October 2014 to October 2015, the AUD dropped from 0.89 to 0.69. The arbitrage worked for sure. The broker was not as successful.

The advice from the arbitrager, who luckily got his capital back but whose broker reneged on the free rollover, causing him to lose money, is as follows: "There will always be arbitrages, but make sure they are genuine and accessible to everyone. Your returns might not be so large, but you won't lose your capital." He goes on to say, "A lot of products seem genuine, but they are not. Avoid lucrative no-brainer trades, and ask yourself the questions

'How come?' and 'Why?' You will save yourself a lot of pain later. Above all, you must protect your capital. And that can only happen if you select your counterparties who are appropriately regulated and have correct protection of client funds."[7]

THE MONEYMAKING POTENTIAL IN ARBITRAGE

Making money can be a tremendously exciting business. And making tons of money for free is every arbitrageur's dream. There are plenty of success stories of smaller-scale arbitrageurs who have made many thousands if not millions of dollars. What unites all of them is that they tend not to shout about their moneymaking edge. Arbitrage is the business of making money from inefficiencies in the market. It makes no sense whatsoever to share that competitive advantage because doing so limits the life span of the trade. There will always be arbitrages across markets and exchanges, and savvy investors can profit from being alert and prepared.

On a grander scale, the progress in computer technology and wizardry has meant that a few cutting-edge super quants with powerful computers, excellent communication networks, and proximity to pricing servers have evolved as giant moneymaking machines.

With respect to Renaissance, while secrecy is paramount, it also has super brain power in the sciences as one of its competitive advantages. Under its roof, it accommodates PhD scientists in math, physics, aeronautical engineering, and computer science, among others. Brilliant people who can spot patterns in charts before they become patterns, who study speech, and who model behavior. Sure, they have gone down the HFT route, but they had the scale to invest in infrastructure and the ability to apply their models over ever diminishing time frames.

AN INSPIRING LEGACY

Jim Simons is surely one of the smartest people ever to have traded the markets. Over a 20-year period, his returns were astronomical, and he built a phenomenal legacy to hand off. His Renaissance fund is among the most successful funds ever launched, and it is the beacon for professionalism and performance. His staff members have been rewarded for being critical and creative and for challenging the norms. They have mostly made a fortune from trading stocks, bonds, currencies, and commodities that are "liquid, publicly traded, and amenable to modeling." If there are indeed patterns in the market, Renaissance has discovered them, which can give hope to any budding trend follower, although Simons has observed that "efficient market theory is correct in that there are no gross inefficiencies."[8]

You cannot help but like and admire Jim Simons. He's done his bit for his country as a Cold War code breaker. He created an outstanding mathematics faculty at Stony Brook University. He has shown the world of finance that you can beat the markets, and he now acts in a philanthropic capacity promoting and sponsoring Math for America. Among the quants, he is the best of the best, and he has created the same in Renaissance Technologies. He is a financial markets genius and stands without equal as the ultimate Quant King.

Renat Fatkhullin: Social Trading and MT4

f Mark Zuckerberg and Renat Fatkhullin were standing side by side in a taxi stand, a few heads might turn. Most people would instantly recognize Zuckerberg. "He's that guy from Facebook!" or "It's that social media guy," some might say. "Why's he waiting for a taxi? He's worth billions. Who's that person he's standing next to?" It would be hardly surprising that anybody outside of the computer programming world or very few inside or outside of FX would not recognize Fatkhullin.

A man more secretive than option trading Swiss billionaire Urs Schwarzenbach, Fatkhullin is to social trading as Zuckerberg is to social media. His products are so sought after that they are a must have for almost every currently operating retail FX and CFD brokerage. Several companies have tried to issue an IPO on the back of "their" client bases using "his" software. The scale and reach of his platform and associated products is unsurpassed by any of his FX market making contemporaries. He does not have many serious competitors, such is the demand of brokers in the retail space to license his software. He remains humble, down to earth, and reachable by like-minded technology and computer individuals. He doesn't boast of his wealth and remains selfless. No "rich lists" for him, although if he were in them, he would surely be near the top.

His company is MetaQuotes; his trading platform is Meta-Trader. It is the single most popular and successful trading platform ever to reach the market. If there were one person who symbolized everything to do with the success of retail FX and CFD trading, it would be Renat Fatkhullin, and yet he is neither a trader nor a market maker. He is, rather, an enabler. He has enabled brokerages to offer a low-cost scalable platform to their client bases. He has adapted his platform for ease of use on mobile and Android devices. He has created a programming language that allows for Expert Advisors and robots to provide either trading signals or algorithmic trading. His platform has charts, allows for up-to-date news, and is user-friendly. He fills the need for clients new to trading to trade in very small sizes or utilize many of the "expert" tools provided side by side on iterations of his platform. His software allows brokers to manage the risk that they take on by being counterparty to trades or pass it on to their banks. In short, he offers many things to many people. In the process, he has become a billionaire. He has achieved this in a little under 16 years.

Fatkhullin's success story initially ran in tandem with that of Alpari, the now defunct London-based FX and CFD broker. While Alpari was formed on Christmas Eve 1998, it wasn't until November 2000 that MetaQuotes Software Corp. was established. In what the Alpari founder and chair, Andrey Dashin, has described as a "historic" meeting with Renat Fatkhullin, in that same month, Alpari would take its trading online using the newly developed MetaQuotes platform. Retail FX trading was in its nascence with as yet no broker or platform dominating the market. Alpari would join the likes of CMC Markets, FXCM, CMS, Saxo Bank, and GAIN Capital and would initially offer online trading in 11 currency pairs.

Apart from envisioning the most outstanding opportunities of scale and profits, many of these companies had other common similarities, not the least of which was a connection with Russian computer programming engineers. There are many schools in Russia that offer computer science and information technology degrees, and for some reason, there seem to be a great many Russian computer engineers and programmers working in the field of FX—and nowadays, more and more in the fields of algorithmic and high-frequency trading. Perhaps a few were inspired by George Soros, who donated many tens of millions to projects in Russia as part of his efforts as a philanthropist and whose George Soros Foundation constructed 32 computer centers at universities in Russia's major cities.

In an interview with *FX-MM* magazine, Denis Sukhotin, Russian founder of FxPro, says of his desire to succeed that his motivation, in part, came from *not* wanting to be part of the previous Soviet system. He said, "I think this is why many who came of age after the collapse of the Soviet Union are so driven."[1] It is true that Sukhotin and other like-minded Russian entrepreneurs have raised the bar in terms of product offerings in the foreign exchange market. And many FX brokerages have used Russian-inspired technology. Saxo Bank outsourced work to St. Petersburg-based Reksoft from 2003 to 2006. MF Global used Russian developers from Rostov to work on its retail platform—a hybrid of VT Trader, also used by CMS. Before moving its headquarters to Limassol in Cyprus, MetaQuotes found its origins in Kazan, Russia. Then of course there are the Russians who either founded brokerages or hold high-ranking positions in them. Alpari's founders, Andrey Dashin, Andrey Vedhikin, and Gleb Petrov, all hail from Russia. As does FxPro's Denis Sukhotin. Eduard Yusupov has been the global head of dealing for FXCM since 1999. With very few exceptions, almost all retail FX brokers offer MetaQuotes products and therefore have an association with Russian-built software.

But how was it that MetaQuotes extended its reach when on a relative basis, brokers using their own software simply stood still? The answer for the most part is found in the question! In the late 1990s several brokers launched retail FX using their own software. The intellectual property rights belonged to them, and they were constrained by the capital they invested. At the same time, profits from retail trading were enormous given the spreads involved, the frequent use of B Booking clients, and the propensity of novice retail traders to blow up. Brokers were motivated by greed and dollar signs, and far from developing white label solutions to quickly accumulate worldwide client bases as part of a parallel business strategy, many were content to gather quick and easy profits in their own backyards. Retail brokers were relatively small and comparatively understaffed.

Some early versions of platforms were clunky and not so user-friendly. White label solutions did evolve, but generally they involved a not insignificant profit share between the enabling party for all the associated add-on services necessary in providing the white label. The B Book also remained and belonged fairly and squarely to the broker offering the white label solution! The demand for retail FX far outweighed the supply of platforms scalable enough to handle the business. Trust was also an issue. Smaller brokers in less heavily regulated jurisdictions and with smaller capital bases wanted to offer FX and profit from it without the punitive tie-ups and risks to partnering with marginally better known FX start-ups.

Fatkhullin spotted an opportunity, and he had several competitive advantages that quickly led to him and MetaQuotes gaining a global footprint. First, he had a highly intellectual and like-minded workforce on his doorstep. Second, his cost of labor was not high. If he could develop a scalable, inexpensive, user-friendly platform, then he could issue multiple instances of it for a one-off license fee and a monthly recurring commitment fee. His staff members were galvanized by his vision. It provided a quick, relatively cheap, and viable alternative to brokers wishing to benefit from their client bases and also wishing to manage their own risk. Crucially, it also allowed clients to sign up with brokers they might be more comfortable with rather than sending their money offshore. Fatkhullin and his team had created a company with a product that generated an excellent positive monthly cash flow and that would grow incrementally with the number of licenses they sold. He absolved himself of any risk taking and from paying for expensive marketing and simply focused on something that he did best: computer software development. At the same time he delivered to brokers and clients an outstanding FX platform.

The entwined stories of MetaQuotes and Alpari took a leap forward in 2005. MetaQuotes had progressively been improving its software and applications for the previous four years, upgrading its MetaTrader platform, and it launched a trading platform for use on Palm devices. Alpari celebrated attracting its 10,000th customer in March 2005. By then, MetaQuotes had reached out to many hundreds of thousands of clients worldwide through its network of subscribing brokers. July 1, 2005, marked the official release of MetaTrader MT4, by far MetaQuotes' most advanced platform to date. For one thing, it could offer FX, CFDs, and futures on the same platform. In addition, the platform was much more reliable and secure and able to efficiently resist "net attacks." The client graphical user interface was more functional, and on the back-office side, additional tools were provided to brokers to process trades. In short, it was a vast improvement on the previous version of MetaTrader. What's more, and momentous to the chronology of social trading, is that the platform also featured MQL4-IDE—a development environment for creating trading strategies. This was a tool that would help transition automated trading strategies and ultimately social trading from an inchoate idea to something of enormous magnitude.

SOCIAL TRADING

The adjective "social" has been popularized in this millennium, especially since the advent of companies such as Facebook, Twitter, and LinkedIn. Facebook has more followers than many religions, and it has added WhatsApp and Instagram to its suite of offerings. For its owners, it has become a cash cow with earnings before interest, taxes, depreciation, and amortization (EBITDA) at well over $6 billion at the time of this writing. The company joined the Fortune 500 list of companies by revenues earned in May 2013, and its founder Mark Zuckerberg is worth many billions of dollars.

Zuckerberg's rise to stardom was swift, as was his company's. Facebook was launched in February 2004 as an Ivy League networking website. By 2006, it opened up to anyone over 13 years old with a valid e-mail address. By 2007 it had attained a theoretical paper value of $15 billion when Microsoft acquired 1.6 percent of the company for $240 million, and by 2010 it had half a billion users. In April 2012, Facebook bought Instagram for $1 billion, and in February 2014, it bought WhatsApp for $19 billion. By August 2015, it had eclipsed 1 billion users, and its market capitalization topped $300 billion by November 2015.

While the concept of social media equates to massive marketing opportunities and Internet boom types of valuations for Facebook and others, the application of shared networks has not been lost on the online trading fraternity. It is perhaps due to social media that the term *social trading* came about. The benefits to marketing are relatively straightforward and clear vis-à-vis social media networks. Sample populations with similar characteristics can be segregated and targeted with any number of promotions. The advantages of social trading are less clear. But first we need a better understanding of what social trading is and how it came about.

In all walks of life, there are leaders and followers. In the financial markets, people's spirits and wealth are generally buoyed by advancing equity markets. Positive equity markets tend to mean that companies are doing well, and so job security (or the chance of finding a job) is that much better. People can borrow more and spend more. People are more content and sanguine and feel far more reassured about their investments and also when they listen to and watch bull market experts opine effusively about the favorable aspects of holding stocks and the potential upward trajectory of the various stock indexes. It beats listening to bear market naysayers who predict imminent doom and catastrophe!

This cognitive human fallacy is known as the *optimism bias* or *positivity illusion*. The optimism bias holds true in declining markets as people tend to hold on to losing positions far longer than they should by somehow thinking that (a) they know better than the market or (b) they know better than their peers. Amos Tversky and Daniel Kahneman have put forward a theory in behavioral economics known as the "prospect theory." They contend that the pain of loss in terms of utility far exceeds the equivalent pleasure of winning a similar amount. Humans will go to great lengths to avoid feeling pain. The theory explains, in part, why humans cut winnings quickly and run losses—something not lost on the many retail FX brokerages that run B Books.

The optimism bias is the reason that many people follow financial market gurus. There is a high chance that those gurus became gurus due to "survivorship bias." (They outlived other gurus who got something wrong just that little bit earlier.) Think of a roulette table and watching somebody who correctly predicts either black or red successfully several times over. He might put all his chips in for the next spin of the wheel. The optimism bias might mean that you back him and you put your own money on "the survivor" to win. As is true of a lot of financial market gurus, he's only as good as his luck. He is just as likely to get it right as he is to get it wrong. You either double your money in this example or your chips disappear with his.

Financial gurus tend to crop up in rising or bull markets. In Hong Kong, there was one revered guru who had such a following that crowds of people would pay significant entrance fees to attend his seminars. They would listen most attentively and hang on to his every word; they would applaud him rapturously; and some might even ask for his autograph at the end of his sessions. He was an older, bespectacled, not unintelligent man who said the right things at the right time, and he appealed to a great many people. He was a great one-man marketing machine, and no doubt he did very well from his local infamy. His candle fizzled out in the year 2008 as the global financial crisis hit worldwide equity markets.

The point here is not to deny this man his luck but to point out how many small lucky gurus could and still can monetize their luck without going to the great expense of setting up hedge funds. The answer comes in two forms: (1) trading for another person or persons with a *limited power of attorney* (LPOA) and (2) using either a *percentage allocation module management* (PAMM) *structure* or a *multi-account manager* (MAM) *structure* to allocate trades. Trading with an LPOA and either a PAMM or a MAM structure is where social trading traces its origins.

TRADING WITH A LIMITED POWER OF ATTORNEY

Allowing somebody to trade with a *limited power of attorney* (LPOA) on your account essentially means that you delegate trading authority to somebody else. The "limited power" part of the agreement generally stipulates that your trading agent cannot withdraw your money, but in most other respects, he has complete control over your account and certainly with respect to trading decisions. Before entering into an LPOA agreement with anybody, it would pay to be totally sure that the individual to whom you entrust your money is of the highest caliber and integrity. It would probably pay to have references from other people who have utilized his services.

You might also wish to check out which broker the trader uses. The temptation of some traders who trade with LPOAs is to "overtrade." You may well have agreed on some performance incentive with the trader to pay her when you make money. The chances are, she gets a kickback from the broker from trades she executes on your behalf, and if she trades frequently, these hidden rebates can quickly add up. Performance can soon become secondary to the spread kickbacks she receives.

PAMM AND MAM ACCOUNTS

A progression of limited power of attorney comes with percentage allocation module management (PAMM) or multi-account manager (MAM) accounts. If two or more people give limited power of attorney to a money manager, he might use either a PAMM or a MAM structure to trade the accounts. PAMM is quite straightforward. Say the manager has a pool of funds from four different investors. When the manager executes a trade, then the trade is automatically split in the proportion that each investor holds in the pool.

For example, a pool of funds comprises $100,000:

Investor 1: $25,000 (25 percent)

Investor 2: $10,000 (10 percent)

Investor 3: $50,000 (50 percent)

Investor 4: $15,000 (15 percent)

If the investment manager were to buy EUR 1 million against dollars, it would be split as follows:

Investor 1: EUR 250,000

Investor 2: EUR 100,000

Investor 3: EUR 500,000

Investor 4: EUR 150,000

The advantage for the money manager is that he can trade a group of accounts as a single account. Clients will all receive the same execution price for the products traded, and profits and losses will automatically be allocated to each subaccount based on each account's share of the total pool. Any agreed commissions are automatically credited to the money manager's PAMM account. If a client were to withdraw his funds or a new client were to join the pool, the percentage allocation would alter according to the new pool of funds and the relative percentages of each investor.

Many money managers prefer to use MAM structures for their additional flexibility in trade allocation. MAM structures are typically used on MetaTrader, and they allow a manager to execute *block trades* and allocate those trades into subaccounts according to different parameters. Whereas PAMM structures allocate trades according to the size of the pool of funds, MAM structures can allocate trades in ratios according to a specified number of lots (one lot is typically 100,000 units of currency), a percentage allocation model (like a PAMM), or according to the leveraged position requested by the investor. They also allow for partial closeouts (again required for highly leveraged investors) so that the overall strategy is not disrupted by any single investor.

Things have come a long way from the days when a money manager was trading with LPOAs for a few accounts. MAM accounts can quickly distribute trades from managers using Expert Advisors (robots) and can service hundreds of trades across hundreds of accounts almost seamlessly. They are MT4 and MT5 brokers' sources of untold riches and a great source of income for successful money managers. Some clients do quite well, others less well. Needless to say, it makes MetaTrader a very sought after platform.

As with Facebook, 2006 saw a great many opportunities open up for MetaQuotes, and MT4 brokers started to pop up across the globe. Alpari, its original backer, gained licenses to offer FX and CFD trading in the United Kingdom. FXDD, another early adopter of MetaTrader, offered its products out of the United States. Avatrade saw its beginnings in Dublin. FxPro set up as EuroOrient Securities & Financial Services, Ltd., in Cyprus. GO Markets opened its doors in Melbourne, Australia.

THE SUCCESS OF EXPERT ADVISORS

MetaQuotes had a coup in December 2006 when it organized its first ever Automated Trading Competition (Table 7.1). There were 258 developers of Expert Advisors who competed in the 12-week trading contest for a prize fund of $80,000. The winner, Roman Zamozhniy, multiplied his starting "virtual cash" of $10,000 by 250 percent. The word was out, and trading robots were fast becoming a thing of "the now." MetaQuotes would organize an Automated Trading Competition again in 2007, in 2008, 2010, 2011, and 2012.

The year 2008 saw over 700 competitors vie for the top prize of $40,000. The panel of judges included Renat Fatkhullin and representatives from the online retail brokerages FXCM, Interbank FX, and FXDD. These companies would sponsor first, second, and third prizes.

The winner that year was Kiril Kartuniv of Bulgaria, who turned a virtual $10,000 into just under $170,000, exceeding the previous year's winning total of just over $130,000. The year 2010 saw a winning total of $77,102; 2011, a total of $113,115;

TABLE 7.1

MetaQuotes Automated Trading Championships Results

Year	Traders	Profitable	Percent Profitable
2006	258	43	17
2007	603	91	15
2008	705	128	18
2010	314	99	32
2011	395	77	19
2012	451	129	29
Total	2,726	567	21

and 2012, a little under $55,000. Impressive trading indeed, and magnificent headline results. Plenty for retail brokerages to shout about. But as ever, there was a twist. A deeper analysis of the results revealed that less than a third of the Expert Advisors in any of the competitions were profitable. In fact, in 2006, 2007, 2008, and 2011, fewer than 20 percent of the systems were profitable!

It is an admirable achievement that Renat Fatkhullin has created a medium for trading algorithms to operate on his platform. It is not really for him to monitor the ineptitude of some of the robots. Suffice to say if only 21 percent of robots make money, then 79 percent lose money. (In the 2006 competition, the losing robots lost five times more than the winners gained.) In 2010 (the robots' best year with 32 percent profitable), the losing robots still lost more than the winners. In 2012, it was the same story. The odds would appear stacked against anyone who wishes to follow a robot! Add slightly wider spreads, and the odds of winning diminish further—something, it has to be said, that is not lost on retail brokerages running B Books.

B BOOKS AND THE
STRAIGHT-THROUGH PROCESS

Licensing MT4 or MT5 and offering a suite of Expert Advisor trading algos that clients may follow while simultaneously running a B Book might seem a little like a conflict of interest when it is statistically very likely that clients will lose. And yet it is the modus operandi of many brokerages that offer MT4 and MT5. Other brokers may offer a more palatable *straight-through process* (STP) *model* whereby they charge a slightly higher spread between bid and offer and pass the risk of each particular trade to the bank or non-bank provider that pledged the quote.

There are merits to both systems of course. As Alpari, FXCM, and many other brokers found to their cost, when a trade is passed straight through to a counterparty, the client's position is held in the broker's name at the client's prime broker. If the client cannot pay her margin call, it is the broker's capital that needs to support that trade and any potential losses.

A comparison of a B Book versus a straight-through process is as follows. In this example, a client trades 1 million EUR/USD each with two different brokers and executes a buy trade followed by a sell trade. First, I cover the B Book methodology.

The B Book Process

There are only two parties involved, a client and a broker:

Client ↔ Broker

EUR/USD quote 1.10201/1.10213.

The client buys 1 million EUR at 1.10213. The client is long 1 million EUR; the broker is short 1 million EUR at 1.10213. Let's say the euro goes lower. The client sells 1 million EUR at

1.10013. The broker buys them from him. Both the client and the broker are square.

The client has lost 1.10213 – 1.100013, or 0.0020 or 20 pips × 1 million = $2,000. The broker has the other side of the trade and so therefore makes $2,000. If a broker holds hundreds of small accounts that are highly leveraged, the odds are that the broker will make a fortune as clients fail. Most clients will blow up by themselves. The evidence of robotic trading is that trading algos will also cause over 70 percent of clients to lose money.

The Straight-Through Process

Client → Broker → Price provider → Give up to broker's account at prime broker

In this instance, the broker adds a spread. The broker sees the quote as 1.10201/1.10213. The broker quotes the client a slightly wider euro spread. The EUR/USD quoted by the broker is 1.1020/1.1022. The client buys EUR at 1.1022 from the broker.

The broker buys EUR at 1.10213 from the price provider. The price provider gives up the trade to the broker's prime broker. The broker's electronic platform sends a corresponding trade to the broker's prime broker. The broker's prime broker matches the two trades: the broker versus the client and the broker versus the price provider. The broker's profit is 1.1022 – 1.10213, or 0.00007, or $70.

The Two Models Compared

The STP process is repeated on the sell side. The broker earns only the difference in spread. It appears to be a fairer system because the broker doesn't profit (or lose) by taking the other side of the client's trade (as happens in the B Book trade). In theory, it makes for a safer system for protecting the client's money because if all clients win, then a broker running a B Book model is vulnerable to losing his capital. Counterflip the scenario: if the clients lose, the broker collects the spoils. STP works very favorably for brokers if clients trade frequently. Spread capture is also magnified by leverage.

Paradoxically, STP as a system failed in January 2015, when the Swiss National Bank (SNB) unexpectedly unpegged the Swiss franc against the euro, causing several brokers to incur huge losses and subsequently file for bankruptcy. Customers holding long EUR/CHF positions and employing huge amounts of leverage on small cash positions exposed themselves and their brokers to catastrophic losses. The flash crash in EUR/CHF that followed the unpegging meant that stop-losses were filled several hundred pips from where they were left, resulting in many small retail investors facing margin calls in the millions of dollars.

It became clear very quickly that it would be impossible for some clients to meet these calls, and so many brokers in turn were left with massive margin calls at their prime brokers. While clearly it brought the dangers of excessive leverage to light, it also raised questions about which systems brokers should use to mitigate their risks. Ironically, those running B Books did not lose in this scenario. However morally abhorrent B Booking may be to some who compare retail brokers to casinos in terms of how they operate, it is actually the brokers who employed this model who suffered the least from the fallout in EUR/CHF.

The Swiss National Bank debacle has little to do with MetaQuotes save by association to FXCM and Alpari, two of its largest supporters that were both dealt grievous blows with the fallout of the Swiss franc. Alpari and FXCM ran straight-through processes, and both took crippling hits. Alpari filed for bankruptcy. FXCM took a large loan at a punitive interest rate to stave off the liquidators, and it managed to stay in business. Some people may level the blame at high-frequency traders for the rapidity and exaggerated move in the many Swiss franc currency pairs. But the HFTs in question were more of the institutional kind. The robots that trade on MetaTrader, in general, are not of the high-frequency variety. They have been developed by programmers to follow any number of trading signals and indicators, short-term oscillators being the favored kind.

THE DANGERS OF USING
EXCESSIVE LEVERAGE

It must be reiterated at this stage that trading FX is effectively a zero-sum game. That means that the odds of winning are 50:50 in a market with no spreads. So if spreads are involved, the odds of winning are less than 50 percent. Those who advocate trend following tend to follow longer-term trend following strategies employing sensible amounts of leverage. A sensible amount of leverage is between 2 and 4 times capital. An amount of 10 times leverage is high; 20 times is considered very risky; and 100 times means a drawdown of 1 percent, and capital will be erased. At 400-to-1 leverage, capital will be wiped out with a quarter percent move in the wrong direction. If spreads are involved, capital will erode that much more quickly when compounded by leverage.

A secondary point is about time frames. There are many of them. Traditionally traders might use hourly, four-hourly, daily, weekly, and monthly charts in their analysis. Nowadays, there are a lot of systems that trade on minute charts, 5 minutes, 15 minutes, and hourly. Some might argue that patterns can evolve in any time series. Others might counter this and say that more frequent trading allows for collection of more spread and commission earnings.

In the realm of Expert Advisor trading algorithms, there are many that employ short-term high-turnover models. It is extremely difficult to identify what, if any, competitive advantage these systems have. Some report incredible returns in the thousands of percent. A 1 percent favorable move leveraged 400 times does equate to 400 percent after all. And a 3 percent move therefore would equate to 1,200 percent. These are the kinds of headline returns that entice inexperienced traders to follow these systems, and in many cases they pay for the privilege.

TRACKING SOCIAL TRADING PERFORMANCE

Transparency is one of the aspects of social trading that win it enthusiasts. MetaQuotes technology allows Expert Advisors to register their systems and have their performance tracked. It allows traders to subscribe and follow some trading robots for free or by paying others a monthly fee. The fees are generally in the range of $20 to $100 per month. There are lots of transparent statistics about each trading signal. The headline information statistics are the name of the system, monthly subscription cost, percentage growth, how many subscribers, how many weeks the system has been running, how many trades, win percentage, and profit factor. A typical headline figure may appear as shown in Figure 7.1.

Algo Name						
$30	6,500%	135	12	901	66.7%	2.5
cost	growth	subscribers	weeks	trades	win	profit factor

Figure 7.1 Trading robot typical headline.

Drill down into the system, and you will find many more interesting statistics. These include account initial balance, current balance, leverage employed, best trade, worst trade, gross profit and gross loss, winning trades, and losing trades (Figure 7.2).

Initial deposit	$200
Current balance	$13,200
Leverage	1:200
Trades	901
Winning	601
Losing	300
Best trade	$601
Worst trade	$(803)
Average profit	$110
Average loss	$(176)

Figure 7.2 Trading robot typical statistics listing.

In the example in Figures 7.1 and 7.2, there are some telltale signs that the headline 6,500 percent growth is extremely vulnerable and that investors wishing to subscribe for $30 per month may expose themselves and their capital to a reversal of fortune in performance:

First, the level of leverage is frightening.

Second, the system has been up and running for only 12 weeks.

Third, while winning trades exceed losing trades by 2 times (601 compared to 300), the average losing trade at $176 exceeds the average profitable trade of $110 by a factor of 1.6 times.

Fourth, the worst ever trade of $803 exceeds the best ever trade of $601.

Fifth, this account started with only $200 and currently has only $13,200.

In summary, a rather cynical opinion of this hypothetical Expert Advisor is that it is a highly leveraged churning algo with poor risk management. Its performance is probably due to luck. The equity in the account is minimal, and the trades are unlikely to be scalable in any reasonable size. It might be quite fun to throw $100 at it to see if you can double your money, but you certainly should not invest $1 million. There, in a nutshell, really lies the problem with following trading algos. They are not built for scale! There are no doubt some very good (or lucky) algos out there that have produced astronomical results. But ask the question, "Can they do this in any scale?" and the answer is a categorical no!

To better explain my point, I will give a hypothetical example. Let's say we have a short-term trading signal that buys and sells on meandering trendless markets. Perfect for an algo built to trade on a combination of time and change of direction. Let's say the algo uses a 5-minute chart and a 15-minute chart and the system buys or sells when there is a crossover of a moving average on these two charts. Let's also say the system is designed to take a 10 pip profit and stop itself out on a 5 pip loss.

This very basic trading algo no doubt could be refined to add other parameters to enhance its performance. The algo might work stunningly well. There's no reason to say it shouldn't on a small amount of capital and on a liquid currency pair. So with $1,000 invested and 200 times leverage, it can quite easily trade USD/JPY $200,000 without having any effect on the market. At $10,000 invested, it's quite likely that there will be no material diminution of performance as $2 million USD/JPY will be quite easily absorbed into the market.

At amounts above $2 million and certainly above $5 million, the best available bid and offer prices are distorted and will start to widen. So with capital of just $25,000 employed in this trade, performance starts to trail off. This is certainly not the fault of the Expert Advisor, nor is it the fault of the broker who provides the price. It certainly has nothing to do with MetaQuotes or its platform. It is, however, a reality of the market. As trade size gets bigger, market makers need to widen their price to cover their risk. If we elaborate this example a bit more, we can add HFTs to the mix, and as explained in the previous chapter, the effects of "spinning the stack" by HFTs come into play (Figures 7.3 and 7.4). With just $500,000 invested, the system has the ability to trade $100 million. (This could be $200 million at 400 times leverage.)

Notice that the first $2 million can be covered at 120.212 and that to buy the whole $100 million, the price for the last $30 million is 120.27 (Figure 7.3). The *volume-weighted average price* (VWAP) should be 120.2472. This is 3.52 pips away from the buy signal. HFTs distort this price further. Once HFTs are involved, the last $30 million is covered at 120.28. The VWAP is 120.2568. There is slippage of 4.48 pips. (Figure 7.4)

If this trading algo were to manage $1 million and trade $200 million, it is fairly unlikely that it would be able to buy this amount without 10 points slippage from the best-offer price of

Currency Pair: USD/JPY			
Millions	**Bid**	**Offer**	**Millions**
2	120.2	120.212	2
3	120.198	120.218	3
5	120.193	120.223	5
10	120.185	120.23	10
15	120.18	120.235	15
15	120.175	120.24	15
20	120.16	120.25	20
30	120.15	120.27	30

Figure 7.3 Liquidity stack. The first $2 million can be covered at 120.212. To buy $100 million, the price for the last $30 million is 120.27.

Currency Pair: USD/JPY			
Offer	Millions	HFT Buy	HFT Sell
120.212	2	120.212	120.212
120.218	3	120.218	120.222
120.223	5	120.223	120.229
120.23	10	120.23	120.234
120.235	15	120.235	120.239
120.24	15	120.24	120.249
120.25	20	120.25	120.269
120.27	30	120.27	120.28

Figure 7.4 The effects of "spinning the stack" by HFTs.
Here you buy the last $30 million at 120.28.

120.212. The system cannot function because if the take profit were 10 pips away from the initial entry price, it would be slipped on the sell side too. It would end up losing more than 10 points in slippage against a 10 point profit objective. It is therefore a system that effectively creates a profitable trade but cannot trade it in any decent size whatsoever. Performance of algos with capital of just $50,000 or more will be impaired if they trade on short time frames with high leverage. If 79 percent of over 2,700 algos employed in six MetaQuotes trading competitions lost money with starting capital of just $10,000, it is most unlikely that anybody will become a currency millionaire, let alone a billionaire, by following one of these systems!

ZULUTRADE

The first Automated Trading Competition held in 2006 turned out to be a spark for an explosion in Expert Advisor development and in companies offering automated trading via PAMM and MAM structures. One such company that formed in Virginia in the United States in 2007 was ZuluTrade. Its founders, Greek entrepreneurs Leon Yohai and Kostas Eleftheriou, subsequently set up their headquarters in Athens, Greece. ZuluTrade is connected to 64 brokerages, and it offers what it calls a "peer-to-peer service." ZuluTrade predates the Expert Advisor subscriber and follower model of MetaQuotes, and in many ways it inspired MetaQuotes to set up its MQL5.com website and Trading Signals service, whereby investors can select and pay to follow Expert Advisor trading algos.

How it works with ZuluTrade is that in principle, ZuluTrade acts as an introducing broker to the 64 brokers it works with. If an individual wishes to subscribe to one of the Expert Advisors (EAs) that ZuluTrade promotes, he may do so. The client will then sign an agreement with the broker with whom he has an account to agree and acknowledge that a "pip rebate" goes back to ZuluTrade, which then disburses a proportion of that pip rebate to its Expert Advisors. In many ways this is a much more expensive way to trade than following an EA through the MetaQuotes route. The EAs on MetaQuotes charge a monthly fee. On Zulu-Trade, a commission is paid on every trade. It might not hurt, but it certainly pinches! And if trading is frequent, many pinches cause severe bruising to profits. What is also striking about some of the headline figures for EAs profiled on ZuluTrade is that they trade in single lots or fractions of lots. A single lot is equivalent to 100,000 currency units. A master account that trades in single lots will necessarily have a better performance than a slave or follower account that trades in larger quantities, pays a commission, and is subject to slippage.

METATRADER'S POPULARITY

Part of the reason for MetaTrader's popularity is the ease with which it can be licensed and its ability to run many thousands of trading algorithms. A properly marketed successful trading algorithm can bring thousands of dollars in monthly fees and possible spread rebates to its successful developer. This fact has not been lost on many companies that set up as "algo libraries." It is not lost on MetaQuotes either. There are many firms competing in the race to monetize this aspect of social trading. Companies such as Collective2, which offers 56,000 strategies developed by 18,000 traders whom you can follow at $99 per month, is one such example. To give credit to Collective2, they are a company that does give an explicit warning about following trading strategies. It reads as follows:

> Past results are not necessarily indicative of future results.
>
> These results are based on simulated or hypothetical performance results that have certain inherent limitations. Unlike the results shown in an actual performance record, these results do not represent actual trading. Also, because these trades have not actually been executed, these results may have under- or over-compensated for the impact, if any, of certain market factors, such as lack of liquidity. Simulated or hypothetical trading programs in general are also subject to the fact that they are designed with the benefit of hindsight. No representation is being made that any account will or is likely to achieve profits or losses similar to these being shown.
>
> In addition, hypothetical trading does not involve financial risk, and no hypothetical trading record can completely account for the impact of financial risk in actual trading. For example, the ability to withstand losses or to adhere to a particular trading program in spite of trading losses are

material points which can also adversely affect actual trading results. There are numerous other factors related to the markets in general or to the implementation of any specific trading program that cannot be fully accounted for in the preparation of hypothetical performance results and all of which can adversely affect actual trading results.

It's the same old story: performance dwindles with scale. In this case "lack of liquidity" could be defined as wider spreads associated with trading larger amounts or trading in less liquid currency pairs. Also, there are "numerous other factors." It is interesting that Collective2 implies that in some cases traders might not "adhere" to a particular trading program in spite of trading losses. In other words, traders are human and the human element might "override" the system. Optimism bias takes over!

Other variants on the same expert trader-advisor theme are "educators" and their websites. An FX education website, normally run by an ex-FX trader or expert, may boast of a superlative trading approach, may tutor on "risk management," and then might offer some kind of a hybrid oscillator with several entry, take-profit, and stop-loss levels, the high number of which will ensure daily activity in the market. The educator makes money in two ways: (1) she charges for her system, and (2) she links her website to preferred brokers. She will receive some kind of compensation when clients referred from her website sign up and trade with her preferred brokers.

Some innovative companies, such as Quantopian, employ a merit-worthy community-based approach whereby developers of trading code can communicate on a blog, and once they have developed their own algos, they can enter them in a monthly competition. It is not too dissimilar to MetaQuotes with its MQL5 community and the Automated Trading Championships. The differentiating factor is that Quantopian aims to back the best algorithms and find investor capital for them to trade in what it describes as a "crowd-sourced hedge fund." Quantopian will provide the capital, technology, legal, and compliance operations. The top programmers will provide the investment strategies. Quantopian will match top-performing managers with outside investor capital to fund their ideas. Quantopian uses Python as its coding language and supports Robinhood and Interactive Brokers.

With the many thousands of programmers and the abundance of incredible brain power working at beating the market, the chances are that there are some very good traders and Expert Advisors. Ditto FX has endeavored to harness some of what it considers to be "top managers with demonstrable track records," and it offers out their services for a connecting fee in what amounts to a similar model to other, more traditional algo libraries. Run by a successful former arbitrage trader, the company focuses on FX fund managers with at least $5 million under management. Track records run into years rather than weeks and months. Returns are real and not hypothetical. They are also attainable and sustainable rather than unbelievable and improbable. Typically its traders and their systems employ leverage of under three times, which in some ways explains why they have a chance of staying in the game. Naturally, they use Meta-Trader MT4!

THE VALUATION OF METAQUOTES

Inevitably, we arrive back at MetaQuotes. In March 2010, Meta-Quotes launched its MQL5 website for MQL5 application developers. The website had the explicit aim "to provide all visitors with an opportunity to freely communicate and discuss issues of programming in MetaQuotes Language 4 (MQL4) and MetaQuotes Language 5 (MQL5), trading, automated trading systems development, strategy testing, and using technical indicators in MetaTrader 4 and MetaTrader 5 platforms."

In June 2010, MetaQuotes launched its Metatrader 5 platform for trading FX, CFDs, and equities on the world's stock exchanges, and in October 2012, it launched Trading Signals, its own social trading network that can be accessed through both its MetaTrader4 website and the MQL5 website. There are already 800,000 MQL5.community users. It supports seven languages, and it offers over 7,000 trading applications, 4,000 Trading Signals for automated copy trading, and 6,200 free source codes. It provides access to 500 professional programmers who can be commissioned to create custom-made trading robots. The scale of MetaQuotes is immense relative to any of its industry peers. And it is growing!

It is difficult to put a value on MetaQuotes because of its massive potential worldwide. If Saxo Bank has 120 white label partners, then MetaQuotes has over 450 brokers who use the MQL platforms. If FXCM has 178,000 active clients, GAIN Capital 150,000, and CMC Markets 75,000, then MetaQuotes, through its partnerships has 7 million who use MetaTrader, of which over 1 million trade on mobile devices. If Collective2 offers 56,000 hypothetical strategies at a subscription charge of $99 per month, then MetaQuotes already offers 7,000 trading aps and 4,000 Trading Signals. It also has a following of 800,000 in its MQL5 community who can access 500 professional developers at any instance. On any metric you choose, MetaQuotes blows the competition away.

Of the retail brokers who have floated on the world stock markets, GAIN Capital as of February 2016 had a market capitalization of just over $330 million, at the low end of its range over the last five years. FXCM, similarly, is trading well below its $1 billion IPO valuation. CMC Markets floated on the London Stock Exchange in February 2016 with a value of GBP 691 million. At one stage, Australian broker Pepperstone was looking to float on the Australian ASX, with some pundits speculating that its valuation would be in the region of AUD$600 million. Pepperstone uses MetaTrader almost exclusively, and its main client base is in Asia Pacific. FxPro, another MT4 user, looked to float as early as 2011 with a valuation in excess of GBP 200 million. Alpari, which came unstuck in 2015 and was one of the original backers of MetaQuotes, missed out on an IPO. It claimed to have 100,000 clients as early as 2009.

It's a well-known fact in the world of retail FX that rough estimations of earnings can be made from a computation of retail client equity balances and number of active clients.

We can therefore develop a simple heuristic company valuation based on number of active clients, net revenue per client, and some kind of industry multiple. So, for example, 20,000 active clients earning a company $2,000 each in net revenues and multiplied by an industry price/earnings (P/E) ratio of 12 equates to a valuation of $480 million (20,000 × $2,000 × 12). If 50,000 clients were earning a company $1,000 each in revenue at a P/E of 12, that would equate to a $600 million valuation. There are obviously many other factors that contribute to the value of a company, not the least of which is the potential growth and intellectual property. One can only hypothesize about a valuation for MetaQuotes if it stood as a stand-alone company and was the sole provider of its platform. It would be billions!

The tangible aspects of a valuation for MetaQuotes are that it generally charges $100,000 to license MT4, and thereafter it charges $1,500 per month for ongoing maintenance and $750 to support mobile applications. In addition, it receives 20 percent of monthly subscription rates for Expert Advisors. It has been suggested that MT5, its new platform, can be licensed for $500,000.

Currently there are 450 brokers who offer MT4. They would have already paid up $45 million.

So monthly fees are $2,250 × 450, or just over $1 million per month, or $12 million per year.

Let's say they sell 50 new licenses per year for MT4 at $100,000, or $5 million.

And 20 MT5 licenses at $500,000, or $10 million.

Add revenues from aps, virtual hosting, and EA subscriptions and add, say, $3 million.

A guesstimate of $30 million doesn't seem so much. But what is the potential? And you might well attribute a multiple of 50 to 100 times earnings. The reasons are principally as follows:

1. A large proportion of the retail trading FX community depends on MetaQuotes for its software. It has millions of users.

2. The same goes for the programming community.

3. MetaQuotes charges are not high. They could be higher!

4. As yet MT5 is not the platform of choice. There may be a point in the future when MetaTrader MT4 is phased out and MT5 becomes the de facto trading platform for the MetaQuotes community.

5. There are 800,000 community members of MQL5.

6. MetaQuotes MT5 has passed conformance testing, and it has been certified on the Moscow Exchange, the Dubai Gold and Commodities Exchange, BM&FBOVESPA, Brazil's largest exchange, the Chicago Mercantile Exchange, the Warsaw Stock Exchange in Poland, the Australian Securities Exchange, Borsa Istanbul in Turkey, the Pakistan Mercantile Exchange, the Stock Exchange of Thailand, and the South African Futures Exchange.

7. MetaQuotes has representative offices in Turkey, China, Singapore, Japan, Australia, Brazil, United Arab Emirates, South Africa, Pakistan, and Thailand.

The reach, depth, and scale of MetaQuotes and its products are phenomenal. Based on the above, MetaQuotes could easily be worth several billion dollars. It seems to have entered markets where others have failed to venture. It has penetrated many emerging market countries. It has a higher proportion of retail traders trading on its platform than any other single retail platform, and it also has a high proportion of programmers who apply their Expert Advisors to trade automatically on MetaTrader. Smaller brokers are dependent on MetaQuotes. Others base their IPOs on the popularity of MetaQuotes. Renat Fatkhullin and his team have very nearly monopolized the whole industry by being smart. And monopolists, ultimately, can charge what they like!

SOCIAL TRADING NETWORKS

Although there is very scant information circulating about Renat Fatkhullin and his past, the Kazan connection does run very deep. The cofounders of Alpari, Andrey Dashin and Andrey Vedhikin, were both raised in Kazan. Dashin graduated from the Kazan State Institute of Finance and Economics in 1996. Vedhikin graduated with distinction from the finance and economics unit of Kazan State University in 1997 prior to picking up a PhD in economics. Metaquotes Software Corp. set up its first office in Kazan in the year 2000. It is run by Lenar Fatkhullin, although there is no reference to him as being a relation of Renat. Alpari linked arms with MetaQuotes in 2000 and executed the first ever trade through its platform in November of that year.

Now it seems that Cyprus is the new hotspot for software developers, programmers, and brokers. Cyprus is home to at least 50 brokers and also to MetaQuotes. Most of the brokering community offers MT4 and hosts social trading facilities. Typical social trading innovations include blogs, information about social community trading positions (sentiment), other information concerning conglomerations of stop-loss orders and limits (open orders), and transparent details of the trading performance of any number of Expert Advisors, which can be followed.

It seems that in some ways, the real-time communication of thousands of smaller traders is an effective tool in the decision-making process of that community and complements more traditional technical and fundamental analysis. Social trading networks are also forums where trading clubs can band together and trade in the same direction. Or where gurus with sufficient clout can direct their followers to trade. There is a real possibility that a significant retail-based network could actually move markets! Retail trading makes up about 8 percent of the FX market, and so while small, it is still significant relative to the whole. And its weighting is likely to grow.

A TRULY INNOVATIVE AND VISIONARY ENTREPRENEUR

Renat Fatkhullin is a genius, perhaps matched only by Kim Fournais and Lars Seier Christensen at Saxo Bank in terms of what they have provided for the retail FX trading public. (Saxo Bank added its own variant of social trading, launching TradingFloor. com in 2014.) Fatkhullin has focused on delivering a low-cost, scalable platform to a worldwide network of brokers and added functionality to cater to multiple product types. His telling innovation was to enable thousands of programmers to create trading robots to trade using his software.

Like many of his generation, he had a vision, and his was to be a professional software developer in the field of foreign exchange. Not only did he create exceptional software, he also created a coding language applicable to his platform. He worked with similar like-minded entrepreneurs and was able to quickly deliver a market-leading product. Perhaps two of his competitive advantages were that he could work with many experts in a low-cost environment and deliver a state-of-the-art platform at the genesis of online retail trading. Another might be that he focused solely on software development and let others indirectly market the platform on his behalf. He has been incredibly fair in licensing his product, charging relatively little to brokers who can connect directly with their client bases. At the same time he has captured an enormous market share of the online retail trading community.

His eureka moment was the inception of the Automated Trading Championship, which has taken retail FX trading to new levels. Just 258 traders took part in the inaugural competition in 2006, which has acted as a catalyst for an explosion in the growth in retail foreign exchange trading. Now, millions of people can follow Trading Signals or copy trading from hundreds of thousands of trading algos and trade through hundreds of brokers all connected to MetaQuotes MT4 or MT5 trading technology. Brokers trying to emulate MetaQuotes have a toss-up between trying to develop their own software and simply joining the bandwagon and purchasing a license to offer MT4 or MT5 to their clients.

Several brokers have made astronomical profits using a combination of MT4, trading robots, and elevated levels of leverage and by running B Books to profit from some less successful trading algorithms and retail traders. Some have even considered floating on world stock markets on the back of their impressive gains. Fatkhullin steers clear of controversially acting in the dual capacity of software developer and bookmaker, preferring to focus on what he does best in simply delivering his product to an ever increasing number of brokers, banks, and exchanges and listening and adapting his platform to meet the requirements of his clientele.

In an ever evolving, more scrutinized market, MetaQuotes delivers what the public wants and what brokers want. All Trading Signals have transparent track records, and social trading communities are capable of informing, educating, and guiding each other to make appropriate trading decisions. If there is a lesson that the trading public and novice investors should learn, regulators can pass that lesson down through brokers. A wary public should be aware that headline gains of several hundred or several thousand percent are not sustainable in the long term. In order to achieve those types of gains in the short term, huge leverage is involved, and slippage in following such systems is highly likely as is deterioration of performance proportional with larger investments. MetaQuotes is an enabler of trading. It is neither a robot nor a broker. There are many good sustainable profit making robots. However, scalability should always be a question that anybody has in mind when following such a system.

Fatkhullin, like all good traders or innovative entrepreneurs, has kept himself low key and secretive. He has built his business organically and resisted the need to issue an IPO. If he were to do so, his company would be worth billions. Fatkhullin and Meta-Quotes are to social trading what Zuckerberg and Facebook are to social networking. In the retail FX world, probably more than 80 percent of traders are touched by his influence. It is for that reason that it is an easy choice to name him Social Trading King.

Caveat Emptor: Tricks and Traps to Avoid When Trading Online

8

I n 2005, in an article published by the *Wall Street Journal*, Dror Niv, the then CEO of FXCM, commented, "I'd be surprised if 15 percent of day traders make money!"[1] It took the U.K. regulator, the Financial Services Authority, another 11 years to work out that what he opined was more or less accurate. Their survey suggested that 82 percent of retail traders lose money. And they will introduce measures in 2017 to curb leverage and strengthen risk warnings.

I commend Dror Niv for his candor, for it is his quotation that forms the basis of this chapter. Taken out of context, Niv's comment is a very daunting assertion from the CEO of one of the largest online FX companies in the world. It would prick the skin of any regulator and probably put butterflies in the stomach of any budding trader. And yet, if you analyze why he said it and compare it to new trading statistics published by FXCM, it is a remarkably straightforward, accurate observation from which any people considering "day trading" or trading retail FX or CFDs can gauge their likelihood of success if they choose to trade in a carefree manner.

This chapter analyzes the many ways that retail traders do not help themselves in their approach to trading FX and CFDs. It also highlights methods that brokers use to benefit from active retail trading accounts and also the role of Introducing brokers and how they, introducing agents and affiliates, can all prosper from the naïveté of fledgling FX participants. It is meant to be thought provoking and eye-opening. If this chapter points out glaring repetitive failures of typical FX newcomers in formulating a successful strategy, draws attention to certain trading blunders consistent with human behavior, and underlines some of the devious tactics of some market makers, then the following chapter attempts to redress the balance and guide the trading public to a far more disciplined and hopefully successful approach to trading and making money.

Niv's comments originated from a *Wall Street Journal* article published in 2005, covering the newfound popularity of FX trading.[2] They are perhaps more relevant today considering the explosion of Expert Advisor robotic trading algorithms and signals that are ubiquitous in the market. In 2015, FXCM published a paper titled "Traits of Successful Traders." To its credit, the paper examines what goes wrong with some traders' tactics and tries to explain why. It gives data on trading performance, comparing leverage to percentage of profitable trades and, interestingly, comparing deposit size to profitable accounts. It proposes time zones where day traders might avoid volatility in an effort to encourage profitable trading. FXCM, which operates a straight-through process for its clients' trading activities, would appear to have a palpable interest in their survival—something that is not consistent in the industry. Some brokers profit when clients lose or blow up! It cannot be very satisfying to be included in that metric. And nobody has to be. If people learn to trade smarter, they can significantly increase their odds of winning, which is what it is all about.

FOREIGN EXCHANGE INVESTMENTS
AS AN ASSET CLASS

Over the years there have been arguments that FX is an asset class in its own right, and proponents of diversified portfolios often squeeze in a 10 percent allocation to more "risky" investments in which somehow FX finds its inclusion. In times of equity market volatility, especially when markets are moving lower, FX seems a much more compelling investment and could indeed be considered an asset class. The unwinding of carry trades, consistent with smart money looking for safety, often leads to significant movements in emerging market currencies. Time and again when equity markets are volatile, currencies such as the Swiss franc and yen will appreciate.

Equity investments are meant to be safe and to go higher. Large capitalization public companies are expected to pay stock dividends and provide comfort to people who rely on them for income. A combination of capital appreciation and dividends is what gives people comfort and confidence in equity markets. When billions of dollars get wiped off the value of stock markets, naturally people get very nervous. They look for safer investments. Government bonds have long been considered the safest of investments, and they find popularity as both a complement and an alternative to equity investments. But while they might be a "store of value," they are hardly an attractive investment when they pay trivial amounts of interest or, worse still, when they pay no interest at all or even charge interest to be held. In the sense that every asset class has its day, FX is ever present.

Whether it be putting on or unwinding carry trades, currency hedging, trend following, or mere speculation, FX is more than just about spinning the roulette wheel and gambling. Holding currencies in a portfolio is becoming far more relevant in a world where bonds pay relatively little, equity markets are volatile, and precious metals and commodities don't seem to offer much in terms of upward momentum.

THE MARKETING OF FX INVESTMENTS

By now, anybody who regularly uses the Internet will have encountered some sort of banner that advertises FX trading. Click on the banner, and you will be transported to an FX website where you will be deluged by information about great award-winning platforms, breadth of products, tight spreads, charts, no-dealing desks, 24-hour live chat, feeble or zero commissions, free rollovers, and any number of other headline positives that might convince you to fill out an account opening application, whether that be for a demonstration or a live account.

Some brokers will offer incentives such as free cash to get you started or additional bonuses with certain deposits. Others may hold trading competitions offering lucrative prizes. There are plenty of advertisements, notably in Asia, that highlight how somebody has made outstanding returns in a short period trading FX. Everything you read, see, or click with regard to trading FX or CFDs online is an invitation to encourage you to open an account. Marketing is an essential element of a retail FX broker's business, and millions of dollars are spent in the enticement phase.

B BOOKS, A BOOKS, AND STP

Foreign exchange brokers make money in many ways, and in years past, the most obvious and quickest way was running a straightforward "B Book." The B Book is effectively one big bucket where all client trades are pooled. Some online retail brokers operating this tactic can be compared to *stock market bucket shops* outlawed in the United States in the early twentieth century in terms of how they take the opposite side of customer trades.

The contrast is that FX brokers are generally regulated, and those that run a B Book have an audited trail for each trade that they execute. They have to meet certain capital requirements and adhere to client money rules. In addition, trading "as principal" in FX against a customer is not illegal. Some brokers still operate B Books today. Others opt to "trade as agent" and operate a *straight-through process* (STP) and pass all trades to market making banks and non-bank counterparties. Some brokers operate a hybrid of the two. Passing trades via STP is often known as "A Booking." A Book clients tend to be successful. Once A Book clients have been identified as such, they are usually excluded from the B Book. It would make no sense to include continually successful traders in a book designed to benefit from taking the opposite side of trades that lose. A winning trader would impair profitability. Brokers, therefore, often follow A Book clients. Flow traders, having executed trades for these clients, will "go with the flow."

Traditionally the B Book took advantage of three common factors that, combined, gave brokers a winning edge:

1. Spreads tended to be wide; for example, EUR/USD might trade at 5 pips.

2. Customers would often overleverage, increasing the chance that many would lose.

3. For some strange reason, average traders would be quick to take profits and would tend to run losses to a far greater extent than their gains. This has been explained in *prospect theory*: people hate losing, and they experience far more pain in losing than they experience joy in winning an identical amount. Therefore, people

in general seek to avoid pain by putting it off (running losses). It creates an asymmetric profit profile for retail clients, which skews in favor of brokers who feel only joy at reaping the benefits of this peculiar human trait. In Hong Kong, there is even a phenomenon known as *locked trades*.

Clients somehow think it's unlucky to lose, so some brokers give them the ability to open a second trade in the same currency pair, equal in size and in the opposite direction to their original trade. The client then has to put up double the margin and pay or receive swap charges on both positions. The theory behind locked trades is that at some stage the client can close the original trade when it comes back into profit, but by then the second trade will have become a losing trade! It's a difficult logic to comprehend. Nowadays, spreads have compressed somewhat compared to, say, 15 years ago. But people, in general, trade with far too much leverage and still run losses far longer than they run profits, and of course, as online trading has evolved, retail clients tend to trade far more frequently.

Irrespective of whether a broker runs a B Book or an STP, the fact is that all brokers benefit by clients' overtrading. Spreads eat into account equity, and spreads and other transaction costs effectively become a wealth transfer between client and broker. Brokers have various tools in their arsenals that can help accelerate account degeneration. By and large these are more relevant to brokers that run a B Book than those that run an STP. The perfect scenario for a B Book broker who wishes to effect a complete wealth transfer from client to broker is that the client "blows up" any which way. By contrast, an STP broker benefits from high-trading turnover accounts that manage to stay alive. The longer the clients keep trading, the more commissions that are earned.

The events of January 2015, when the Swiss National Bank (SNB) unexpectedly unpegged the Swiss franc against the euro, have ignited much-heated debate about retail FX trading. A single event wreaked havoc in the market, caused many clients to wipe out instantaneously, bankrupted several brokers, critically wounded many others, and caused several prime brokers and market makers to incur multi-million-dollar losses. Since the event, many questions have been raised about adequate capitalization of brokers, corporate structures, leverage limits, B Booking versus straight-through processes, client suitability, client education, client monies, and risk warnings.

RISKS OF EXCESSIVE LEVERAGE

Above all, there now seems to be some consensus that there is a real danger to trading with excessive leverage and that clients who do so run a large risk of losing their entire account equity. FXCM must be commended for publishing "Traits of Successful Traders." In an era of heightened awareness about the dangers of trading FX and increased regulatory scrutiny in all markets, it doesn't make much marketing sense to promote drinking from a poisoned chalice. Even novice marketing professionals know that garnering referrals is one of the cheapest and most powerful tools in the marketing basket. If clients have a bad trading experience, they are more than likely to pass on information about their dissatisfaction to other people, which can then quickly pyramid into a consensus of negative sentiment about individual brokers and the industry in general.

Selecting a broker who is honest about the risks and hazards to profitable trading, who has a transparent pricing policy and a stable platform, who makes clear how it processes trades, who is adequately capitalized, and who has robust client money policies would seem to be a minimum comfort requirement for anybody considering commencing FX trading. The market is evolving into one in which informed traders appreciate straightforward commonsense tips to improve performance. There are enough forums and trading rooms now for rapid and effective communication. The retail crowd is not as gullible as it once was.

Niv's 2005 comments about retail traders' dismaying underperformance are backed up by FXCM's data (Table 8.1). The first statistic reminds us of the dangers of leverage. Just 17 percent of FXCM's clients win when they employ leverage of over 25 times. Only 22 percent of clients win when trading with leverage of between 10 and 15 times capital.

TABLE 8.1

Leverage Compared to Win Percentage

Leverage	Win Percentage
<5:1	40
5:1–10:1	29
10:1–25:1	22
>25:1	17

Source: FXCM.

Another interesting statistic seems to be that larger accounts tend to perform better, implying that they probably trade with less leverage (Table 8.2).

TABLE 8.2

Equity Compared to Win Percentage

Equity	Win Percentage
<$1,000	21
$1,000–$5,000	29
$5,000–$10,000	34
>$10,000	43

Source: FXCM.

If we compare this data to the results of the MetaQuotes Automated Trading Championships held between 2006 and 2012 (discussed in the previous chapter), we can form a certain idea of what are our likely chances of winning when trading with high amounts of leverage.

First of all, we must accept that FX trading is a zero-sum game: for every buyer of a currency, there is a seller. So for every winner, there is a loser. Our odds of winning, therefore, start at 50 percent. Include spreads, and they decrease to less than 50 percent. Add leverage, and our chances of success come down further. In the case of leverage of over 25 times, our odds of winning fall to roughly 20 percent. In the MetaQuotes Automated Trading Competitions (see Chapter 7), starting equity was a notional $10,000. In many cases Expert Advisors trading in the competitions used leverage in excess of 25 times.

The goal of course was to win the prize. But it turned out that overall performance "winning" percentages are not too dissimilar to those of FXCM's real clients: 21 percent versus 17 percent. Despite FXCM's contention that accounts of $10,000 and above trade with a 43 percent win rate, the danger of allocating a reasonable amount of money to an Expert Advisor is apparent. Performance will follow the same path as smaller accounts if trades are highly leveraged. Leverage is by far and away the most dangerous aspect of trading FX. And people throwing away easy money is by far the biggest reason that there are so many brokers offering the trading platform MetaTrader MT4. MT4 is a great platform and has superb functionality. It offers a great many tools to assist people in making money.

MetaQuotes' websites act as a forum for many automated trading robots. When people assign their trading to a third party, they are effectively electing to hand over "doing the work" to somebody else. It's fine if that is your strategy; it may well work for short periods of time and in small amounts, but take heed of the data about leverage and you might think again.

It must be pointed out that while excessive leverage is Killer number one, it is ably aided and abetted by its accomplice, "overtrading"! Together they form an outstanding team that can drastically reduce account equity in a very short space of time. There is a counterside to trading with large amounts of leverage. It can work both ways and multiply gains. However, there is no positive side for anybody who overtrades. In conventional STP setups, the degradation of performance due to self-churning is plain to see. On each trade, a commission or fee—whether it is an explicit charge or included in the spread—goes to the broker. That fee or commission varies from broker to broker, and it can grow according to whom the broker shares it with. The simple matrix in Table 8.3 shows the attritional value of spreads or commissions multiplied by leverage and number of trades. All things being equal, if a trader neither makes nor loses money, an account can quickly be wiped out by this dangerous duo.

To put this into perspective, 500 trades is one buy and one sell per day over a 250-day trading year. Work out how many times you trade per day and what is your average trading size. Consult the matrix with respect to commissions, and then you will have an idea of how much you have to outperform the market to just break even. Ask yourself what really is your competitive advantage, and you will start to have a reality check! If you have any doubt that your performance (both winning and losing) is anything other than luck, please take heed of the following interesting facts about investment performance:

- More than 50 percent of fund managers do not outperform an index. These people are considered experts in their field! In any given year, that statistic can add up to over 60 percent. It makes intuitive sense that if an index is an average of stocks or commodities, the average is made up of both winners and losers. Professional fund managers are paid to add *alpha*—that is, apply their professional

TABLE 8.3

Matrix of Commissions Multiplied by
Leverage and Number of Trades

Account Starting Equity: $10,000

Assuming a Commission of 0.1 Pip

Trading EUR/USD

Leverage	X5	X10	X20	X100	X200
Trade Size	50,000	100,000	200,000	1 Million	2 Million
No. of Trades					
1	$0.5	$1.0	$2.0	$10.0	$20.0
5	$2.5	$5.0	$10.0	$50.0	$100.0
10	$5.0	$10.0	$20.0	$100.0	$200.0
100	$50.0	$100.0	$200.0	$1,000.0	$2,000.0
200	$100.0	$200.0	$400.0	$2,000.0	$4,000.0
500	$250.0	$500.0	$800.0	$5,000.0	$10,000.0

expertise to pick winners that outperform a benchmark.
The fact is that over half of them can't. The truth is that
they also have to cover their salaries and overheads and
charge fees for their expertise. Fees eat into performance.
You'd be better off just buying the index, and try to do so
by paying as little commission as possible. If an index goes
down by 25 percent and a manager loses only 20 percent,
it still doesn't make any compelling reason to follow that
manager.

- In a paper titled "Trading Is Hazardous to Your Wealth,"
Professor Terry Odean and his colleague Brad Barber
contend that on average, active traders tend to produce
worse results than those who trade less frequently.[3]

These facts complement the findings of FXCM and the trading results in the MetaQuotes competitions. It enables us to create a general rule of thumb about leveraged trading:

- Unless we have a genuine competitive advantage, the chance of winning when using leverage of 25 times or more is roughly 15 to 20 percent.

SUREFIRE INVESTMENTS: NOT ALWAYS WHAT THEY SEEM

Beware of fail-safe, moneymaking, capital-guaranteed FX investment "funds" that crop up from time to time. A highly intelligent, white-collar working friend of mine once asked my opinion of an FX "fund" he had recently invested in.

The facts are below:

1. He was introduced by a broker to a "fund manager" to whom he assigned limited power of attorney.

2. His maximum investment was $20,000, and he had to pay a $500 up-front non-recoverable annual maintenance fee.

3. He could open any number of accounts of $20,000 and pay the same fee.

4. If he made monthly profits of less than $2,500, he would not pay a performance fee, but on amounts between $2,500 and $3,000, he would pay 30 percent of profits; between $3,001 and $4,000, 40 percent of profits; $4,001 and $5,000, 45 percent of profits; and above $5,000, 50 percent of profits.

The "fund manager," in its agreement with him, assured him of "complete protection of his initial capital investment" and said that it employed very low degrees of leverage and that it did not take "unsustainable" or "reckless" amounts of leverage.

I asked to see a record of the "fund manager's" trades that had been taken on his behalf. Sure enough, he was being bounced in and out of the markets at 100 times leverage, and although remarkably he was in the black, with many small winning trades, there were some losing trades that were of far greater magnitude than his average winning trades:

- My opinion, from reading the prospectus literature, was that it certainly wasn't a fund, just an elaborate hoax to give my friend the sensation that he was investing his money with a professional outfit.

- After having taken a look at the "fund's" license, I saw nothing other than a commercial business license. There was no evidence whatsoever that the "fund" even had the bare minimum in terms of compliance and risk personnel and procedures in place. Nor that it was regulated.

- There was absolutely no guarantee that my friend's investment was safe. He had sent his money to the bank account of the company that held the commercial business license.

It occurred to me that my friend had been hoodwinked into sending his money to a dubious source who doubtless allocated his funds to a trading robot and who benefited from overtrading the account to extract commissions (an unethical and in some jurisdictions illegal practice known as *churning*) and charging outrageous performance fees on the off chance that the account made money. I couldn't quite figure out how the company guaranteed my friend's capital and could only assume that it made enough money from the $500 administration fee, commission rebates, and performance fees to have a pool of funds to distribute to disgruntled clients who didn't get off to a winning start.

A more detailed look at the trades executed on behalf of my friend revealed the following:

- He had opened two accounts of $20,000 in mid-August 2015.

- By the end of August, he had executed $40 million of trades.

- September was more prolific: $86 million.

- October, $20 million.

- November, $30 million.

- There were often occasions when one account would buy a currency pair and the other account would simultaneously sell the same currency pair. The two trades would be closed at the same time.

- The biggest drawdown in one of the accounts was $13,000.

His starting equity of $40,000 had traded $176 million, or an account turnover of 4,400 times! By the end of November, one of his accounts stood at $23,000 and the other at $27,000. He had paid about $4,000 in performance fees. My estimation was that in this period, he had paid roughly $18,000 in hidden commissions. He had also paid $1,000 to maintain the two accounts. My considered advice was that he should withdraw his money while he still had a chance, as the "fund" would probably blow up and he would lose all of his investment.

There were other irregularities insofar as there were ambiguities in trade reporting. My friend told me he did not have real-time confirmation of trades and that he got his trade confirmations one or two days later. My biggest fear was that he had invested in some kind of Ponzi scheme. My friend was unconvinced and said he was happy because he was making money. He even went on to tell me that he had referred some of his friends and also had an acquaintance who had opened eight accounts each of $20,000. The story ended well for my friend. After a profitable month, he withdrew the bulk of his profits. While he left $40,000 at risk, he at least would never lose all his cash in the scheme. I was not sure that everybody would ultimately have that experience.

Aside from what we know about the likely winning chances of trading with exaggerated amounts of leverage, it is fairly clear that my friend could have better protected his "client money"— that is, his investment—by placing those monies with a properly regulated broker. In addition, we know that money managers on average have no investment edge. There are more bad ones than good ones! There are thousands of Expert Advisors with transparent track records who can be followed by paying $20 or $30 per month.

My friend could have selected any Expert Advisor himself and had the same probability as the "fund" manager of picking out a profitable one. He would have saved himself thousands of dollars in performance fees. In addition, by selecting a broker of his choice, he would have had an accurate real-time notion of the spreads he paid. In the "fund" manager scenario, he had no real-time trade confirmations and no idea whatsoever how much slippage he paid on every transaction. The "fund" manager had at least done his homework in one respect: he had understood that his trading performance would diminish with a trade size of over $1 million to $2 million, which is why he kept the deposit size down to $20,000 when leveraging up. The "fund" manager's $500 maintenance fee or 2.5 percent over and above $20,000 gave him a small chance of initiating a positive trading performance.

Everything said and done, it was not dissimilar to a model employed by a bona fide fund that functioned several years ago when interest rates were a few percentage points higher. That particular fund would accept much larger deposits (in the millions of dollars) and offer capital-guaranteed performance. What the fund did was buy zero-coupon bonds, such as Treasury bills, at a discount to par value, say, paying $950 for a bond that matured at $1,000. The fund would use the $50 per $1,000 to massively leverage foreign exchange positions in the futures market, paying excessive execution and clearing fees and receiving a rebate into an introducing broker account. If their FX positions turned out to be winners, they would earn a performance fee on top of their management fee.

The fund kept its total risk limited to the $50 per $1,000 it saved on its bond purchases. In effect, it had a free 5 percent to gamble. All the while it got a kickback in commission charges. Clients were happy because they had a capital-guaranteed product. Brokers were happy because they saw plenty of business. The hedge fund had a win-win situation. It won when it genuinely made money, and it also won when it lost money with all the rebated brokerage commissions! The target market, naturally, was unsophisticated retail and high-net-worth investors.

There is a small moral in the above two examples, and that is that surefire investments are not always what they seem. Neither of these two so-called fund managers had any competitive advantage or any real incentive to outperform the market save to say that they could churn accounts even more aggressively. Their sole purpose was to ruthlessly and unrelentingly extract as much in commission rebates as they possibly could from their investors' capital, which they did without compunction. And if they ultimately did turn out to be lucky and post positive returns, they had the additional benefits of charging performance fees.

It would pay to ask yourself the following questions before you allocate your capital and delegate trading authority to a trading robot or, indeed, to any money manager:

1. What is the robot's or money manager's competitive advantage (beyond luck)?

2. What is the frequency of trading?

3. How much leverage is employed?

4. What spreads am I paying?

5. What performance fee am I paying?

If you assign power of attorney to anybody who trades on your behalf, it is best if you do so knowing all the relevant facts that may hinder a positive return on your capital. You may save yourself a lot of pain if you approach trusting the investing skills of a third-party manager with a large touch of skepticism. If you trade with a basic plan and some modicum of discipline, you are just as likely to achieve the same if not better results with your money.

If investors forgo the easy option of assigning trading authority to a third person and actually follow a disciplined self-trading plan, they are much more likely to avoid some of the more insidious abuses of their capital. There's an old saying in exam taking technique that if you read the question, it is equivalent to half the answer. Similarly, developing a cogent applicable and sustainable trading plan is a far better starting point for any trading strategy than just having a whimsical flutter on the markets. There has to be a start point, an end point, and a purpose behind the strategy. Otherwise it will end in disaster.

CHOOSING THE RIGHT BROKER

That said, we now come across the often difficult decision-making process of choosing the right broker. We have a choice between those brokers who offer a straight-through process and those who rather contentiously trade against us. On the one hand, we can elect to use the services of a broker and be somewhat assured that she has our best interests at heart, someone who might even add value to our trading experience.

On the other hand, we are pitching our wits and money against a much larger opponent who doesn't necessarily have any interest in our ability to win and one that almost certainly has a conflict of interest in providing best pricing. Ironically, B Book operators often offer slightly better pricing than their STP rivals. They have done their homework of course on the performance metrics of clients who lose money. They can offer *choice pricing* if they wish (no spread at all—a price where the bid and offer are the same and you "choose" whether to buy or sell). After all, in the long run, if clients overleverage and overtrade, these brokers know the odds of winning are massively in their favor.

Most FX strategies, particularly those that incorporate technical analysis, can be back tested. If the results are positive, then the strategy can be applied to live markets. In any live environment, a common human flaw is to override a system that has been carefully conceived, developed, and tested. Excluding the "human factor" is what John Henry sought especially hard to do. He was intuitively aware of the "optimism bias" and how human intervention can spoil a perfectly good strategy. Anybody who wishes to create a technical trading strategy and apply it algorithmically can pay for the services of a programmer who for relatively small fee can produce a trading program to the exact specifications of the trader. A custom-made trading algorithm may be worth the investment, and $500 spent up front to ensure trading discipline might be money well spent.

Stop-Loss Orders

Another great lesson we learned from John Henry and also from Turtle trading is that not all trades are successful. Both these superlative trading systems had more or less a 40 percent win rate, which means about 60 percent of their trades were "stopped out." Any trading robot that shows an excessive ratio of winning to losing trades is normally creating an illusion of success. It is important to compare the average winning trading profit to the average losing trading loss. If losses are run longer than profits, the system is flawed.

Any trading manual will tell you to do the converse. "Run winners" and "cut losses." If a system trades in and out three times for a 10 pip gain and has one trade that loses 12 pips, it may well show a 75 percent win ratio. The fact is, it is still losing money. In a longer-term trading strategy, such as trend following, with wider profit-and-loss parameters, it is essential that stop-losses are incorporated, and it is vitally important to focus on letting winning trades run. An absence of human intervention can aid this process immensely. Humans are notoriously bad at picking tops and bottoms. And there are plenty of false summits and troughs in the FX market.

Stops are part of the game and can invoke painful emotions and reactions. It is foolhardy to trade without a stop in place. And people who override their trading system and move stops are just as irresponsible. There are millions of stories of traders who get stopped out only for the market to move back in their direction. *Hindsight bias* can lead these people to say "I knew that was going to happen!" And it might even convince them to trade without stop-loss orders in place. The fact is, these people will be thankful the next time if their "stop" is filled before the market collapses 100 points from where they left their order.

In the interbank market, where millions of dollars change hands every second, it is very unlikely that seasoned investors trade without stop-losses. Stops can also be used as entry points to the market. Some funds use this practice and place stops at support or resistance levels to initiate trades on breakouts of support and resistance.

Dealers have mixed opinions about stops. They either love them or hate them. If a dealer has to watch a limit order and he loses concentration but the market shoots up through the limit level, the dealer escapes without penalty for not watching and acting. In fact, he makes money! For example, if a client leaves an order to sell EUR/USD at 1.1201 and the market spikes up to 1.1210, the dealer will make an additional 9 pips in profit because he will have bought from the client at 1.1201 and sold to the market at 1.1210. However, the converse is true for stops. Dealers have to watch stops like hawks. If a stop-loss in EUR/USD is left to sell EUR/USD at 1.1195 and the market shoots lower, say, to 1.1185, the dealer is obliged to buy from the client at 1.1195. If he were to sell at 1.1185, he would lose 10 pips.

There is a widely accepted protocol in the market that dealers will try to keep customers in their positions in the hope that markets bounce back in their clients' favor. Therefore, if a stop is left at 1.1195 and the market trades there, it is more than likely that a professional dealer will not elect to fill the stop in hopes that it will bounce back. If EUR/USD trades lower, say, to 1.1194 or 1.1193, then the dealer may keep the client in his position or may at that time fill the stop.

Another generally accepted protocol is that for all their efforts in looking after clients' stops, dealers tend to take a pip profit for themselves. The 1.1195 stop may end up being filled at 1.1192, so the dealer may end up filling the stop at 1.1193 and take 1 pip profit. In trading in larger amounts with larger brokerages, it pays to have a good relationship with dealers. In their order books, dealers will have many stops and limits around the stop price.

If a dealer is watching a stop for 10 million EUR/USD at 1.1195 and is watching a limit for 20 million EUR/USD at 1.1194 and the market falls to 1.1185, she may very well fill the stop at 1.1194, in which case the customer of the stop has a very good fill. In this example, the dealer buys 10 million EUR/USD at

1.1194 (where she fills the stop) and also sells 20 million EUR/USD at 1.1194 (other side of limit). She may then buy back 10 million at 1.1185. The dealer makes $9,000 on 10 million EUR/USD (9 pips). The stop-loss client is happy. The limit order client should also be happy as his order is a take-profit order.

Slippage of stops causes much frustration for clients and can create rancorous relationships between clients and brokers. Most people have a good idea of when they are being given a fair price and when they are being taken for a ride. An illicit practice that was once quite prevalent in the market was *stop hunting*. In thin illiquid markets where large stop-loss orders were looming, dealers would "squeeze" up (or down) the market to take out the stops, only for markets to fall back in line. Dealers would then take profit on the large positions they had accumulated. Slippage of stops is not limited to the interbank market. It can happen at a retail level too. It pays to keep an eye on where the markets trade. Electronic market makers can take out stops in the blink of an eye.

When stops are filled, it can cause many anxious and emotional moments for some traders, but the fact is that it shouldn't. Average golfers don't play golf like Tiger Woods, and average tennis players don't play tennis like Roger Federer. There is no need for an average golfer or tennis player to swear, throw golf clubs, or smash tennis rackets on the sporting field, and neither is there any need for traders to have tantrums, smash calculators, or throw pencils in the trading world. If more than 50 percent of trades are destined to be losers, it's best to be mentally prepared to embrace stop-losses as a matter of course.

Choosing a Broker on the Basis of Stop-Loss Order Management

Returning to the decision of which broker we should choose, it could be argued that stop-losses should be better filled at brokerages that operate B Book structures. As we know, a B Book operator, by definition, profits when we lose. The broker has the opposite side of our initial trade and therefore will close out his position against us either when we take profit or when we are stopped out. Therefore, the broker has a high incentive to put through a stop-loss order in a timely manner.

Evidence to support this assertion is clear from the aftermath of the decision of the Swiss National Bank to abort its policy of supporting the euro against the Swiss franc. Several STP brokers were critically wounded, whereas many B Book competitors hardly suffered at all. It is somewhat ironic, the extent to which stops were slipped by B Book operators. But of course they were at liberty as to where they set their stop-loss levels. STP brokers got their client fills from where they were filled at their own counterparties. If that happened to be 10 percent away from the previous price, that was the fill they passed on to their clients. STP, which might be considered a more honorable practice, did not work in favor of the many brokerages that were bankrupted on that fateful day.

Having said that, the logic of passing client trades "straight through" that were leveraged at 400 times must be called into question. (Several brokers offered extremely leveraged positions in long EUR/CHF to retail clients so that they could take advantage of a minute carry trade.) If 80 percent of clients who are leveraged at 25 times are likely to fold, that statistic must be nearly 99 percent for those leveraged at 400 times! It was the millions of dollars that these sorts of clients lost that crippled the brokers. The debt was passed on to the brokers when the clients couldn't meet their margin calls.

Many B Book operators also offer *guaranteed stops* at an additional cost. For B Book operators, any client stop-loss is conversely a *limit* or *take-profit order*. They are more than happy that clients pay for the privilege. It's extra profit for them! Guaranteed

stops may give peace of mind in situations such as the unpegging of the Swiss franc, but that was a statistically highly unlikely
event. In 99.9 percent of circumstances, guaranteed stops are a
luxury good, and normal stops will suffice. If stops are continually slipped, consider using an alternative broker.

Choosing a Broker on the Basis of Fees and Charges

Avoiding paying hidden (and not so hidden) fees and charges can
add percentage points to performance. One of the original and
easiest ways for all retail brokerages to skim free money off clients is by offering what is known as *click-and-confirm trading*,
which is akin to asking a broker for an *at-best price*. Say a client
wishes to buy 100,000 EUR/USD. She enters the details of her
trade into some kind of blotter and creates a market order. She
then clicks and confirms, and the order is sent. It will be filled *at
market*—that is, at wherever *best offer* is trading at that moment.
That best offer can be skewed ever so slightly in the broker's favor, obviously to the detriment of the client. We have already discussed slippage of stop-losses. Stops are generally left as resting
orders in the market. The B Book brokerage is at liberty to fill
stops where it likes. STP brokers will pass on stop levels where
they are filled at their counterparties and perhaps take a pip or
two for themselves.

All brokers have the ability to skew pricing and also to monitor and manage accounts on an individual basis. Some platforms
have *intelligent pricing servers*, which effectively means that
brokers can skew pricing on individual or groups of accounts.
Therefore, brokers can influence the price their clients receive by
moving it away from the market price. Subtle distortions of price
add up to big profits for brokers. Nowadays clients expect fifth
decimal pricing. But it was not so long ago that fourth decimal

pricing was the norm. Brokers still received fifth decimal pricing, but they would round up or down their pricing to clients to provide a fourth decimal bid/offer spread, taking the difference as a profit for themselves. If individual clients are fully utilizing all available leverage to hold an open position, the only trade they have is a trade in the opposite direction, whether that be a limit or a stop. It is quite easy, therefore, to skew the price of an exit trade as the broker already knows what the client has to do!

Rollovers, or *tom-next swaps* (tomorrow to the next day), are also a considerable money earner for retail brokerages. If you are long a currency that has a higher interest rate than the U.S. dollar, for example, the New Zealand dollar, you should receive interest in the form of a positive rollover payment. Similarly, if you are short a currency with a higher interest rate than the U.S. dollar, you will pay a rollover charge.

B Book brokerages traditionally made large amounts of money by "crossing up all their long and short trades" and paying interest minus a "haircut" to clients. So, for example, a B Book brokerage has client positions of long 100 million NZD/USD and client positions of short 99 million NZD/USD. The brokerage has a net position of short 1 million NZD/USD against clients who are net long 1 million NZD/USD. The brokerage will pay a rollover minus a haircut to its clients who are long and will charge a rollover plus a haircut to its clients who are short. If the haircut is half of 1 percent on each side, the brokerage will effectively make 1 percent on 99 million NZD/USD for one day or one-360th of a year (assuming a 360-day trading year). The brokerage's net interest payment is only on 1 million NZD/USD. The STP brokers will still take a haircut, but they may not have the luxury of crossing up their client trades.

Brokers generally post rollover rates on their websites, and so it is a relatively simple process to compare what brokers pay and charge on positions. Investors thinking of operating a carry trade strategy (such as long AUD/USD or long NZD/USD) would be wise to check benchmark interest rates and then work out how much interest they will receive by comparing what individual brokers pay on rollovers. For significant positions, it may also be wise to trade with a larger brokerage that may offer the facility to swap positions out to longer maturities—say, three months, six months, or one year.

All brokers, particularly those operating in jurisdictions that have a positive interest rate environment, also benefit from interest they earn on client funds not utilized in trading. Dormant accounts with excess money in the account contribute to a pool of funds on which brokers can earn overnight interest. Clients can request to receive part of this interest, but in general if you do not ask, you do not receive it, and brokers that do share will once again charge a haircut on what they receive and what they pay out.

TRADING ABUSES

If and when trading accounts become larger, it is generally a positive sign as the likelihood is that the account is winning. There are one or two malpractices that are prevalent in the market that can affect larger accounts. Every investment bank or brokerage courts what they call *home run accounts*—that is, trading behemoths such as sovereign wealth funds (SWFs), pension funds, mutual funds, large hedge funds, commodity trading advisors, large high-frequency traders (HFTs), ultra-high-net-worth individuals, and high-net-worth individuals. These are the sorts of accounts on which sales executives can earn excellent sales credits and commissions and traders can optimize useful flow and information. Unfortunately, in a culture of greed, certain abuses of privilege frequently come to light, and they tend to center on large customer orders or trades.

Some of the more common abuses are known as *market manipulation, trading on inside information*, and *front-running*. HFTs have come in for much criticism for the way that their algorithms can seemingly get in front of orders and push the market away from larger clients (and for that matter, smaller ones). Larger clients are obviously furious that their performance is degraded in what many consider some kind of legalized front-running. Efforts are therefore again being made to trade outside of the realms where HFTs can influence pricing, in essence reintroducing voice-brokered dealing.

Long before HFTs were around, and of course before the many electronic communication network (ECN) platforms were put into use, large orders could be executed through smaller brokers who would trade among themselves. Ultimately portions of those orders would find their path to even larger market makers that effectively ran huge risk books. One legendary trader in London had the capacity and pluck to make choice prices in $1 billion USD/DEM (dollars versus deutsche marks). However, he would generally have a good inclination as to which direction the client was trading and pitch his choice price accordingly. He could then offset his risk by trading with other large market makers in the interbank market.

The original ECNs, such as Electronic Broking Services (EBS) and Reuters Dealing 2000, definitely made it easier for brokers to offset smaller trades, but best pricing in amounts of $50 million and above would most certainly be found at some of the bigger banks. Many brokers had the capacity to deal with larger amounts than $50 million, but if trades of $200 million to $500 million went through a broker's hands, probably 10 or 20 other market making brokers would get a piece of the action.

One way or another, the market would move as brokers offset their risk. Orders of under $50 million could generally ripple through with little effect on the total market. If abuses in front-running were likely to occur, it would potentially be at the broker who received the original order, who might trade for himself first in front of a client buy order, get several calls out to "fill" tranches of the client order, and then sell his position to the client as the final tranche of the fill given to the client. If 100 or 200 million was going through the market, it would be quite possible for markets to move for a few seconds as market making dealers disseminated the order.

Great efforts are made inside financial institutions to prevent so-called inside information from reaching sources who might benefit from using it. *Chinese walls* are prevalent in investment banks, and their purpose is to restrict information from being transferred from separate groups of employees. The fact is that humans talk, and there are many sources of information that can affect markets. It's not just market orders. It can be any sensitive announcement, whether it be on interest rates, employment, inflation, a referendum, impending war or conflict, natural fuel disruption, or any other relevant information that can impact an economy or group of economies. "Inside information" in an FX trading sense can lead to front-running and a worse deal for the client.

In recent months, many examples of *market manipulation* have hit the headlines, and once again, it is generally home run accounts that suffer. Individual traders and cartels of individuals can collude to secretly doctor markets to keep them from finding their natural equilibrium. While some market "fixes," such as LIBOR, gold, and FX fixes, have come into question, it is fairly unlikely that the FX market can be manipulated to the detriment of the vast majority of traders. It pays to be aware of market abuses, and if you fall victim to such malpractices, institutions should have detached unbiased compliance officers who can be alerted to your concerns. Firms are obliged to correctly supervise their staff and their conduct, employ fit and proper persons, and have effective controls in place. Failure to do so can put them in regulatory breach. Regulators have complaints departments that are an alternative means for you to use to report your anxieties.

Larger accounts tend to demand large and stable banks and brokers as counterparties, and as if there weren't enough risks inherent in the system, the risk of a brokerage or bank blowing up when your money is with it is about as distressing an outcome as there can be. It's tough enough to make money, and that money of course should be protected and properly segregated. There are certain taboos in the market, but banks and brokers digging into client funds to support their operations is about as reprehensible as it gets. Some brokerages have fallen foul of this basic principle of trust.

The Dodd-Frank Act and the Volker Rule have effectively eliminated most proprietary trading activities undertaken by commercial banks and their affiliates, therefore reducing potential trading calamities and some conflicts of interest in that sector. The industry as a whole is suffering from ever decreasing transaction charges and therefore income streams, increased supervision and operational costs, and competition for capable staff to work in alternative vocations. It may become a question of survival of the fittest, and more and more, it definitely pays to transact with trustworthy and well-capitalized partners.

As can be seen, there are many contributing factors to substandard trading performance in the FX market. The biggest factors by far and away are self-inflicted. By now we should all be aware of human weaknesses in trading. To coin a pearl of wisdom from the film *Highlander*, we turn to Egyptian sage Ramirez, the mentor of MacLeod. He says, "Never overextend your thrust, you are vulnerable and off balance!" and "If you lose your head, the game's over." When trading FX, it pays to continuously ask the question, "Am I overextended?" Be ultraconscious of overtrading, overleveraging, and overriding stop-losses. If you fail to take heed, you will very quickly lose your head!

Secondary factors that can impair performance find themselves centered on the market makers with whom we transact. Almost every single FX trader I know has at one time or another suffered from receiving shocking execution of orders despite the fact that the majority of brokerage and bank sales staff list "best execution" as one of the principal strengths on which they pride themselves. Slippage of stops is an incendiary point and causes intense aggravation to those who are victims of this dubious practice. Most people are unaware that market orders are slipped too and that HFTs getting in front of orders can cause slippage on trading amounts of as little as $2 million. Brokers who take the opposite side of customer trades have no incentive to offer best pricing. Watch out for rollover costs and payments. Ask yourself if they are fair.

Assigning power of attorney to a third party is something to consider very carefully before contracting to do so. It's a simple exercise to ask what the transaction fees are and what the performance fees are, but in addition, it may be well worthwhile to try to fully understand what the trading agent's true competitive advantage is. The chances are that he has none. For those who choose to follow trading robots (Expert Advisors), it is a lot easier to drill down into all sorts of trading metrics reported in a transparent way on the many websites that sponsor them. Cast aside the fantastic headline returns for a moment and look for "assets under management" and the frequency of trading, and compare average winning trades to average losing trades, and also average trade size. This will give you a fair idea as to the scalability and long-term survival of most trading strategies. From what we know about leverage, it will also pay to discount your odds of winning in the longer term if anybody to whom you entrust your funds trades with leverage in excess of 5 to 10 times.

Choosing an adequately capitalized broker, in a reputable jurisdiction, will inevitably aid in preventing sleepless nights worrying about client monies disappearing in the event of a broker default. Historically and ironically, some of the largest bankruptcies of banks and brokers, some of them household names, have occurred in the United States. However, there are many undercapitalized brokers in less stringently regulated jurisdictions that give cause for concern. The Dodd-Frank Act and the Volker Rule have also restricted most proprietary trading activities of commercial banks. In addition, there have been several high-profile court cases in recent months focusing on addressing certain corporate and individual practices of market manipulation and insider trading. Together, these efforts help make the markets a safer environment in which to trade.

The good news is that money can be made in the FX market. In an interview with the *International Business Times* in 2011, FXCM's then CEO Dror Niv commented that Hong Kong investors' profitability fluctuated around 50 percent, due in large part to the imposition of a maximum 20 times leverage by the Hong Kong Securities and Futures Commission. In Hong Kong the minimum account size for FX accounts is also higher at HK$10,000 or about US$1,300. FXCM's "Traits of Successful Traders" suggests that short-term trading tactics employed in off-peak hours with the absence of market announcements can lead to improved performance in some European currency pairs. Their data showed performance levels of above 50 percent, although there was a caveat to warn that past performance cannot be relied upon for the future.

There seems to be a perceived wisdom that larger accounts, trading with less leverage and in nonvolatile markets, can outperform small, highly leveraged frequent-trading accounts. Therefore, investors who are serious about trading FX should post sufficient margin with a reputable trading partner. In addition, they should have access to multiple products such as spot, forwards, options, futures, and NDFs. Trading performance can be significantly enhanced by trading smarter—that is, employing rigid discipline and sticking to a trading plan. The merits of different trading methods will be discussed in the final chapter. Ultimately it is an individual choice as to what to trade and how to trade it. My hope is that many more people, however small their account is or however new they are to trading FX, will now endeavor to become winners!

Top Tips to Improve Performance

Over the last few chapters, we have seen how some of the greats of foreign exchange trading have made their billions. In each case the individuals, or groups of individuals, have had some sort of competitive advantage that they have put to good use to extract riches from the global markets.

Soros developed his own behavioral "theory of reflexivity," which he applied to a global-macro approach in taking down the Bank of England. Henry researched and back-tested a hundred years of past futures prices to figure out that the markets are people's expectations and these expectations manifest themselves as price trends. He also restricted his algorithm to avoid human intervention, apart from executing its trading signals, and he followed his model with rigorous discipline over many successful years. Schwarzenbach was an early adopter and original market maker in selling option strategies. Cruddas, Fournais, Christensen, and Stevens were all early adopters and market makers in retail foreign exchange. Simons recruited a superlative multitalented team of quants, and he applied science, artificial intelligence, and lightning speed to take advantage of inefficiencies across a wide range of markets. Fatkhullin focused on delivering a magnificent multifunctional and multiproduct trading platform to the masses and also created a simple programming language to promote algorithmic trading on his platform.

All these men had a vision and a plan, worked hard at implementing their vision, stayed resolute through ups and downs, and came out on top. We can learn a lot from them!

Making a fortune in the foreign exchange market might seem a daunting prospect, and for sure, a lot of good luck is required. But with a well-researched and solid plan, a disciplined approach, adequate capital, and prudent risk management, most people can start off on the right footing. Scaling up a legitimate competitive advantage can lead to the outsize returns that make people millionaires and ultimately billionaires.

DISCIPLINE AND FOCUS

There is no surefire way to extract scalable consistent winning returns, save in a limited capacity from arbitrage trading. There are some who advocate trading only certain currency pairs or particular time zones, and it is possible that there is a logic behind this that may add to improved performance. There are, however, several simpler techniques that we can adopt to make sure we stay in the game and continue to be there when luck shines on us. Chiefly these revolve around maintaining discipline and focus.

The fundamental elements in giving yourself a winning chance come down to doing just that: remain focused and disciplined; block out noise, rumors, and opinions; and follow whatever strategy that you consider your best winning chance. If markets are efficient, then for every winner, there is a loser, which is certainly true in foreign exchange. Remember that over 50 percent of fund managers cannot beat an index. Therefore, confidence in yourself and your plan is as good as any one single piece of advice. Yes, you should do plenty of research, and yes, you should understand some basic economics and technical analysis.

But no, it is not entirely necessary to entrust your capital to the skills of another in order to make money. Statistically, you have exactly the same chance, and maybe an even better chance, when you cut out hidden fees and charges, as well as management and performance fees.

Being adequately prepared to make a structured start in beating the markets is where we must focus our attention. I believe that being prepared mentally and physically is a good starting point. And if I were to advise any novice potential foreign exchange trader, I think four to six weeks preparing mind and body before you commit to any trade will be time well spent.

MY OWN PREPARATION FOR TRADING

As I recall my own initiation to foreign exchange trading, I remember it as being quite structured. First, there was a gruff, no-nonsense risk warning of an introduction, almost as if to scare me about the dangers of the market. This was followed by several weeks of on-the-job training and patient answering of my questions about the many peculiarities of how and why people trade.

I cannot say that my arrival at Prudential Bache was met with a fanfare and fireworks. I felt more like a recruit in an army boot camp, such was the unfriendliness of my welcome. My colleagues were not intentionally rude. They were just working at 100 miles per hour. That's how it was in the 1990s. Full on! All day long! After having been shown around the dealing room and getting a few grunts of acknowledgment from my new colleagues, I was shown my seat, which was second from the right in a line of five dealers.

My colleague on my left, who would become my mentor, briefly took a few seconds off from answering phones to fire a volley of choice words in my direction. "Don't screw up! If you screw up, tell somebody! And don't take sick days!" After that, he was back on the phones, barking numbers across the desk, continuing to frantically scribble out trading tickets, only lifting his head momentarily to say, "Oh, by the way, the last person who sat in your seat got sacked!"

"Oh, why?" I responded, instinctively half knowing the answer.

"She screwed up! She ran an error trade. Never run errors! They always screw up!"

I spent the next six weeks, from 7 a.m. until 5 p.m., only taking a break to go get the lunches, with my ear pinned to a phone listening to live conversations between salespeople and clients, then watching the interaction between salespeople and traders, then back to the conversations between salespeople and clients as deal upon deal was struck. There was never a dull moment. It was always busy, and on the few minutes either side of any economic announcement, it was extremely busy. I cottoned on quickly to the FX jargon, how to make prices, how to communicate, how to write tickets, and crucially how not to screw up!

My mentor was at the epicenter of the business. Incredibly sharp, sometimes irascible, but always on top of his game, reliable, intelligent, humorous, and all in—just a great guy to have next to you. Each week, armed with calculator in hand, I would be grilled by the head of sales, who would fire question after question at me, get me to calculate cross-currency prices, swap prices, futures prices, and invert bids and offers, while generally trying to confuse me as much as possible so that I was at last prepared, in his mind at least, to pick up the phones myself and deal with clients in a quick-fire hostile environment.

I must admit to being terrified making my first price to a client and similarly when making a market to much larger clients. Part of it was because I was paid so little, and an error could be as much as my annual wage. Part of it was knowing that the previous incumbent of my seat had been fired. I didn't wish that to happen to me because I already loved what I did. The group of guys and women I met at Prudential Bache were the funniest and most eclectic, sharp-witted bunch of people I've ever had the pleasure of working with. It was the best apprenticeship I could have dreamed of, and I learned so much from them all.

YOUR PREPARATION FOR TRADING

The initial advice I received is probably as good advice as anybody seriously contemplating trading can get. If I can rephrase it in a polite way, it might sound familiar. Be serious about what you do (don't take sick days!). Stick to your strategy (don't screw up!). And always cut your losses quickly (never run errors!). Anybody who follows these three tips will have a far better chance than the majority of traders out there.

While the noise of working in a busy dealing room with the additional pressure of making markets in millions of dollars can fine-tune concentration levels, it also pays to stay focused when trading online on a computer. It is quite easy to become laissez-faire, particularly if you have had a few quick victories. Markets have a tendency to move savagely against the unaware. I have touched upon the trading characteristics of fatal overoptimism— namely, overriding, overtrading, and overleveraging—in the previous chapter. We can add overconfidence to that list. Always remember that the risks are ever present. Stay alert!

Having gotten the don'ts out of the way, it is now time to focus on the dos. It's a great deal harder to make money than people think. And learning with hindsight is not a very satisfying experience, particularly if your account equity has halved. It is a far better starting point to go into trading fresh and prepared. And just as if you were preparing to run a marathon, it is important to get some pre-trading training. It's called "doing the work." Or, in other words, preparing self and strategy.

Six weeks should do it. You can learn a lot about yourself in six weeks. In particular, you can assess your ability to follow a regime, whether it be a diet, a fitness regime, a course of study, meditating, getting up on time or half an hour earlier, reading the financial section of a respected daily newspaper, or giving up a bad habit. I would suggest you do all of these. It will all help you prepare mind and body for the hard work that follows. If you falter on any one thing that you set for yourself, you may well have to ask yourself whether you have the discipline or aptitude to be a successful trader.

This is not about creating superheroes. It is about testing oneself. All the above activities can and should be pleasurable, and they need not eat horrendously into your time. Meditating might not be everybody's idea of fun, and it's certainly not compulsory, but simple meditations can last for just 20 to 30 minutes. They can open up your mind (and soul) and significantly increase the positive sense of well-being. Similarly, committing to exercising for 40 minutes to an hour a day (or every other day) will boost energy levels. A diet doesn't have to be overly constraining. Avoiding one or two obviously unhealthy eating choices or even just organizing your eating habits in a different way can reduce weight and aid considerably in general energy levels and concentration.

There is wisdom in the saying "Eat breakfast like a king, lunch like a prince, and dine like a pauper." If you have meditated or if you have done a workout first thing, then a good breakfast will set you up for the trading day. Small healthy snacks will maintain energy levels. Take a break—some air and something nourishing—for lunch. Avoid excessive carbohydrates and heavy foods at night. You will sleep better for it! Similarly, the weekend starts on Friday in most countries, so avoid excessive partying on Thursday night (or any other night that precedes a trading day). Reading a good-quality financial newspaper over the weekend and keeping abreast of important political and economic events should become your focus.

At the beginning of the six-week period, I would suggest that all budding traders open a live demonstration account. I would also suggest that this demonstration account be opened before the beginning of the first week of any given month. Next up, download an economic calendar for the month, which is something we'll come back to. Make sure it covers economic announcements in the United States, the eurozone, the United Kingdom, Japan, Australia, New Zealand, and Canada. The second part of our preparation phase is to follow the markets' reaction to the release of economic data. The six-week period should cover at least two nonfarm payroll employment announcements, which are released on the first Friday of the month at 8.30 a.m. Eastern Standard Time.

FORMULATING GOALS AND STRATEGIES FOR TRADING

Before we rack ourselves with worry about becoming the next economic guru, it is time to take a step back and think for several moments, hours, or even days about what type of strategy we wish to follow. The **first element** of our plan is for us to think about what and how we want to trade. What are our objectives? How much capital do we envisage commencing with? What are our profit expectations? How much are we prepared to lose, if it starts off badly, in pursuit of those profits?

In the preceding chapters we have several examples of billionaires who adopted different strategies in making their millions and billions. Can we replicate any of those strategies? What barriers are there to entry? What more do we need to know? What, if any, competitive advantage do we have? Is it scalable? What strategy would make us feel most comfortable and not stress us out morning and night? How serious are we about all this?

Whatever type of strategy you adopt, whether it's spot trading, pairs trading, technical trading, trading specific time zones, market making, futures trading, or options trading, it is important to follow at least one monthly cycle of economic releases before you commence, which is the **second element** of our preparation plan. There are some announcements that are considered timelier and to have greater impact on the markets than others. It is an extremely interesting activity to watch a trading system when economic numbers are released. It will give you an idea of how markets move and in what magnitude. It will start to attune your instincts to the sensation of "noise" or lack of it.

The important thing to achieve here is to start to get a feeling for the market. You may well have a temptation to trade. But do not do so just yet! Unless you have real-time information, the best you can do for now is watch how the market reacts to economic announcements. By following an economic calendar, looking at a particular set of data that is due for release, and studying the consensus view of the many economists who dare to predict an outcome, and only then turning your attention to your trading platform, you can compare where the market was prior to the announcement and its activity during and after the announcement. It is well worth keeping a diary during these few weeks. After each announcement, you should take time to record what you have just witnessed. It is something you can consult in the months going forward.

The **third element** to our preparation plan is to read up as much as possible about FX and trading in particular. There are some great books out there, and depending on your focus and strategy, you can attune your reading list to point you toward the trading style you wish to adopt. I would advise you to read some books of a more humbling nature. You can learn a lot from other people's failures too. You may also choose to read books on behavioral economics. They will give you an idea of how humans tend to react to stimuli, both good and bad. Make sure you have a good book at hand for the next six weeks. Try to set yourself a target of reading one relevant book per week. That's about 40 or 50 pages of reading per day.

So in the next six weeks we have the following schedule to pursue and several targets to achieve:

1. Commit to a fitness, diet, and well-being regime.

2. Download an online trading demonstration platform.

3. Download an economic calendar.

4. Buy a diary.

5. Buy six good books on the financial markets.

There is no gauge of success or failure in this preparation phase. If you break your regime, you can always start again. But try to understand where you went wrong. If you need more time, then so be it. Take the time that you feel is necessary.

If you are struggling with any element of your schedule, it can sometimes be helpful to have a "will-do list" at hand. A will-do list obliges you to do something. It is stronger than a "to-do list," which is effectively a wish list. Write down what you *will* achieve the next day. Consult your list frequently, and if the first thing on your list is getting up at a certain time, consult your list last thing at night. At the end of this six-week period, you might find yourself mildly surprised at your progress. One thing is certain: if you haven't traded, your cash will still be safe—and you may know a little more about the markets and a good deal about yourself.

One of the things I have found inspiring about researching the traders who are mentioned in this book is that they all come from different backgrounds and cover the spectrum of education levels from having no academic qualifications through to having PhDs in math. All of them specialized in a distinct element of the FX business, and they all had different capital commitments to back their foray into the foreign exchange market. Peter Cruddas started CMC Markets with just GBP 10,000, and John Henry launched his firm with $100,000. Urs Schwarzenbach originally traded a small amount of capital for his father. George Soros started Quantum Fund with under $5 million.

It took Henry about 12 years to be running over $1 billion in assets, and it took Soros about 16 years. FXCM listed on the New York Stock Exchange with a value of $1 billion just 11 years after the company was formed. Peter Cruddas had an estimated net worth of over $1 billion in 2005, 16 years after setting up CMC. Saxo Bank, arguably, has a value in the billions of dollars. MetaQuotes was set up in 2000, and I believe it must have a valuation in excess of $1 billion. What that says to me is that it is possible for anybody with an innovative scalable strategy to start from a relatively small capital base and—provided that he or she has a modicum of luck, appropriate investment, and time—become an FX billionaire. It's worth thinking about!

Unfortunately, that will not be all of us. If destiny is not calling us to be the next FX billionaire, we can at least try to avoid some of the common pitfalls that can eat into our capital, confidence, and well-being. It is absolutely essential, therefore, to focus on your own FX strategy. You can do this alone or as part of a group; there are merits to both. However, if you trade with a group, it is important that your vision is aligned with that of the other members of the group and that you all follow the rules that you set yourselves. Remember, the human tendencies are to be lazy, greedy, and impatient. Be doubly sure with whom you partner. And set yourself achievable targets.

ECONOMIC INDICATORS

Back to economic announcements! Most people, unless they adopt a specific pairs trading strategy, will inevitably trade something against the U.S. dollar. And so being abreast of what is going on in the United States with regard to its economy is a useful starting point in commencing to trade FX. Obviously, world events, other economies and markets, and particularly commodities markets can affect how currencies move against each other, but a few basics about what drives the U.S. dollar are highly relevant in helping you form an FX strategy.

Common to all countries is the way in which growth and inflation interact to affect interest rates. In simplistic terms, growth is good for a country, and coupled with a small amount of inflation, interest rates can be set to maintain a sustainable trajectory that keeps growth and inflation in balance. If an economy grows too fast or inflation starts to get out of control, interest rates can be raised to control inflation. Similarly, interest rates can be depressed to stimulate growth and inflation. Cheaper borrowing costs imply that money will be invested to start or fuel business growth. In economies in which interest rates are low, a small sign that those economies are starting to enter an expansionary phase is that small incremental increases in interest rates may follow. Foreign investment may flow into those economies, attracted by rising equity markets and business opportunities. Cash will earn interest.

Currency traders look to compare how economies are faring against each other. Among other things they will compare growth, inflation, and interest rates and what factors drive these variables. Smart money tends to flow where it will grow. Economic indicators can provide traders with clues to the strength or weakness of certain economies and therefore how best to invest their money.

U.S. ECONOMIC ANNOUNCEMENTS

In the United States, over the course of a month, a good deal of economic information is released. Most reports, surveys, and indicators are released monthly, but others, most notably gross domestic product (GDP), are released quarterly. During the month, bit by bit, information is released that can be pieced together to assess how the domestic economy is doing. Remember, we are looking for signs of growth and inflation that will ultimately influence the direction of interest rates. Higher interest rates, in general, tend to draw money from investors. Interest rates that are higher than the rate of inflation mean that the value of money grows in real terms. Currency investors will look at interest rates of pairs of currencies. If a currency pair is trading at a certain level at current interest rate differentials, then all things being equal, an interest rate increase in one currency relative to another will tend to strengthen the currency in the country where the interest rate hike occurs.

By focusing on the beginning of the month in the United States, we encounter four timely growth indicators straight off the bat. These are the Institute for Supply Management's (ISM) survey of U.S. manufacturing activity, or the ISM Manufacturing Purchasing Managers Index (PMI) on the first business day of the month; nonfarm payrolls on the first Friday of the month; and the ISM nonmanufacturing PMI survey on the third business day of the month. The fourth indicator, the ADP Research Institute's nonfarm employment report, sneaks in two days before the Bureau of Labor Statistics nonfarm payrolls report Both employment reports and the corresponding unemployment percentages give clues to whether the economy is in expansion or contraction mode. In general, the more people who are employed, the higher the confidence numbers and the larger the retail sales. All good signs for growth in GDP.

The ISM indexes are business activity indexes. They are diffusion indexes based on responses to questions to purchasing and supply executives of over 400 companies in the case of the manufacturing PMI and 370 companies in the nonmanufacturing PMI. The diffusion indexes are calculated as the percentage of respondents reporting higher activity, plus half of the percentage reporting no change. A reading of 50 means there are equal numbers of respondents indicating higher or lower activity. A reading above 50 is considered expansionary and therefore positive for GDP and the U.S. dollar.

The excitement that heralds the nonfarm payrolls announcement is the financial markets' equivalent to that of spectators waiting for the start of a major sports event. The flurry of noise and activity that blasts through the market in the first few seconds after the announcement can make for joy or misery for those bold enough to trade the numbers. As well as the headline number, it is well worth watching out for the unemployment rate percentage and any revisions in the previous month's number. If there is an extreme variation from what was previously reported and the headline number is benign or as forecast, markets can move equally viciously. Payrolls are great fun to watch, but they are tricky to trade. The safe option is to be a spectator!

The middle of the month brings one more significant "growth" number and several "inflation" gauges. Retail sales reports are often anxiously awaited. They are the foremost indicators of consumer spending or consumption, and retail sales makes up about one-third of GDP. We are looking for positive readings or surprises that will contribute to dollar strength. The University of Michigan Index of Consumer Sentiment and the Philadelphia Federal Reserve manufacturing index also help build the picture of how robust the U.S. economic situation is. Add to this the reports on new and existing home sales at the end of the month, as well as the durable goods report, and most people can get a fair idea of whether the prospects for GDP are good.

On the inflation side, the Producer Price Index (PPI) and the Consumer Price Index (CPI), released midmonth within days of each other by the Bureau of Labor Statistics, are two of the foremost inflation indicators. The PPI measures the change in the prices of goods sold by domestic producers. The CPI is a monthly index for prices paid by consumers for a representative basket of goods and services. Positive percentage changes mean that there is some level of inflation in the economy. The PPI can be affected by energy prices. Lower energy prices should in theory lower the cost of production, which can then be passed on to consumers. The converse is also true insofar as cost increases will inevitably find their way to consumers. Any strong inflationary number will indicate that an interest hike is in the cards, and so generally the dollar will appreciate.

Other U.S. inflation announcements include the Personal Consumption Expenditure (PCE) Price Index, at one stage considered the favored measure of inflation used by the Federal Open Market Committee (FOMC) of the Federal Reserve Board, whose role it is to determine monetary policy. Core PCE excludes volatile food and energy prices. The PCE Price Index is also the largest contributor to the GDP Price Index. Inflationary employment costs can be gauged in the Employment Cost Index (ECI) report, which is released quarterly on the last Thursday of the month following the survey month. The report includes the most up-to-date costs as of the 12th day of the survey month. So the December 12 data will be included in the January report. The ISM Prices Paid report, which represents business sentiment regarding future inflation, is released on the first of the month, and the average hourly earnings report, released at the same time as nonfarm payrolls, help complete the inflation picture.

In the United States, there are several important numbers at the beginning of the month, in the middle of the month, and at the end of the month. The periods in between tend to be a bit quieter, although the FOMC meets eight times per year and releases its minutes about three weeks later. In addition, GDP is released quarterly, and there are monthly announcements about advanced estimates.

For those who wish to trade in the quieter moments using a pairs strategy and hoping for nothing more than a meandering trading range, a study of relevant announcements in the countries of your chosen trading currencies may point toward potential periods of higher and lower volatility. Range trading pairs in periods with an absence of economic releases may have more likelihood of success.

Having said that, there are many external factors that affect currencies irrespective of domestic announcements, and the global calendar is incredibly full. In all countries we are looking for clues about growth and inflation and how they will impact GDP and interest rates. Interest rate announcements are exciting in themselves, especially if there is a hint of a potential move. Minutes of meetings are also potential market movers. If there is discord on a board or committee as to the direction of interest rates, it is something that may have more influence in future meetings. We should also be looking for relative moves in interest rates. A half-point drop in a country with interest rates at 10 percent is only half as much as a half-point drop in a country with interest rates at 5 percent.

OTHER COUNTRIES' ECONOMIC ANNOUNCEMENTS

We have covered the U.S. dollar, but for what are described in foreign exchange vernacular as the other "major" currencies—namely, the Australian dollar, New Zealand dollar, British pound, Canadian dollar, Japanese yen, Swiss franc and euro—there are many similar announcements to those that are released in the United States. Below are some of the more important announcements to watch out for.

Interest rate announcements are top of the list. The United Kingdom and Australia announce interest rates once a month (Australia skips January); the United States, Canada, Europe, and Japan, eight times per year; New Zealand, seven or eight times per year; and Switzerland, four times per year. In any given month there may be anywhere between two and eight announcements among the majors.

GDP is reported quarterly in all of the above countries. And similar indexes with regard to retail sales, inflation, manufacturing, confidence, and housing are all released either monthly or quarterly. In the eurozone, it pays to keep an eye out for German economic indicators and also the ZEW survey, which is a monthly survey of economic sentiment from 350 or so German economists.

In Japan, the quarterly announcement of the Tankan survey released by the Bank of Japan is a much awaited poll of business growth. The "large manufacturers' index" element of the Tankan is considered a leading economic growth indicator. Any speech by a central bank leader can also cause market volatility. Other significant market moves usually follow economic announcements from China. Several economies, particularly those that export commodities to China, will see their currencies bounce around when China reports its growth numbers. Any net importer or exporter of oil can see its economy and currency affected by changes in the price of oil.

There are thousands, if not millions, of people trying to predict the course of market movements on the back of economic announcements and the future course of interest rates. Many people will have their preferred statistics or batch of statistics that they use to formulate trading decisions. It is arguable to whether we can derive any immediate competitive advantage from studying them. A great many hindsight traders can say that they correctly predicted a move after an event but didn't trade it; and after a period of strongly trending economic figures, a great many traders can comment about how obvious a particular currency's strength is as a result. But ask these people to tell you which way a currency is going to trade in the next day, month, or year, and we're back to a 50:50 bet. Depending on your trading style, you might never look at an economic announcement at all. Some people try to combine economic analysis with technical analysis to choose better entry and exit levels for their trades.

Whatever methodology you use, there are three possible outcomes for a currency pair immediately after an economic announcement is released: it can go up, go down, or stay where it is. Frequently, markets jump and then revert to where they were before an announcement was released. It is well worth monitoring this because it can form a trading strategy in itself. James Ax, one of Renaissance Technologies' original traders, was a proponent of a mean reversion strategy, especially if markets had moved sharply on the open from the previous night's close.

In other cases, if, for example, an interest rate change occurs that is largely expected by the market, the market can move up in the days, hours, and minutes before the announcement and then trade lower soon afterward. This fits into what traders call "buy the rumor, sell the fact." Before the release of any important announcement, it is worthwhile to read up on what the consensus estimate is. Remember, though, that this is generally a consensus of economists and not traders and also that the sample is still small relative to the absolute size of the market. The market, if it is efficient, has priced in all knowledge about economic events and therefore trades at its current level because it has absorbed all news, views, and positioning.

Announcements, unless way out of line, in reality should not disturb the status quo of the market. That is why we should take time to watch how currency pairs move when economic announcements are released. In the course of six weeks, we can get plenty of practice. And writing down the market reaction immediately after any announcement may inspire many future potential trading strategies. Trading directionally on individual data releases can be hit or miss. I would urge caution. With economic announcements, it pays to be aware of when they are due for release, and they can certainly help in reinforcing a macroeconomic view. There are many numbers to trade over a month, but trading all of them is not advisable.

Trading non-U.S. dollar pairs of currencies can be an effective alternative strategy—for example, limiting trading to, say, EUR versus GBP or AUD versus NZD or any other pair of currencies. The influence of the U.S. dollar can be virtually removed, therefore allowing the trader to focus full concentration on just two currencies and their economies. It is still important to monitor what's going on elsewhere because moves in the yen and dollar can effect cross-currency pairs such as EUR/GBP and AUD/NZD. In periods of bond or equity market turmoil, the yen strength is sometimes a factor, as it certainly was in 1998 (Russia default) and 2008 (global financial crisis). As yen crosses were sold off, both EUR/GBP and AUD/NZD appreciated.

On the subject of the Japanese yen and the New Zealand dollar, there have unfortunately been a number of devastating earthquakes in both these countries. The 1995 Kobe earthquake and the 2011 Tohoku earthquake and resulting tsunami brought tremendous pain and suffering to the people of Japan, as did the 2010 and 2011 Christchurch earthquakes to the people of New Zealand. The resulting currency moves were initial weakness in local currency followed by strengthening of the currency due to repatriation of yen and New Zealand dollars to rebuild infrastructure. As ghastly as wars may seem, the Swiss franc tends to be a winner in such situations. The Swiss franc is known as a safe haven currency, and it strengthened notably during the buildup to the first and second Gulf Wars.

SHORT- AND LONG-TERM STRATEGIES

For most traders new to FX, attention will typically be drawn to trading with some sort of technical strategy or delegating trading authority to a third party that uses some sort of technical strategy. My view is that economic cycles happen in years, not in minutes or ticks; therefore, technical trading strategies, which in some ways tend to reflect economic fundamentals, will evolve over years too. That is to say, any technical indicator that is applied to monitoring short-term ebbs and flows in the market is merely monitoring noise. If somebody tosses a fair coin and heads turns up eight times in succession, the odds of heads turning up a ninth time are 50:50. Similarly, if EUR/USD ticks up eight seconds in a row, or eight minutes, or even eight hours, it's totally possible that this can continue for eight days. Trading short time frames with any accuracy is a game of chance. All the pretty charts and fancy jingles are just color and noise.

Trend following is a longer time frame strategy that involves huge amounts of patience and discipline. It is also worthwhile to note that longer-term trend following strategies should also utilize less leverage due to the fact that drawdowns can be large. Successful traders and their systems, such as John Henry and Turtle trading, initiated trades with low amounts of leverage, and they incrementally increased leverage as successful trades moved more into-the-money. At any one time, it is unlikely that they had capital leveraged by more than 8 to 12 times. Once a trend was caught and it was in force, they traded with trailing stop-losses. They let their winners run and didn't take short-term intuitive profits.

What does this mean for any would-be trend follower? It means we can do the same. First of all, if you are looking at charts, focus on longer time frame charts, such as monthly, weekly, and daily. Choose the currency pair you wish to trade. Look to see if there are any economic fundamentals that might influence your trade (although strictly speaking, they should be ignored). Have a strategy in place for initiating your trade, adding to it, and stopping it out if the trade goes wrong. Do not overleverage or double down on losing trades. Have the courage to run winners, which means that you have to have a written exit strategy in place and stick to it.

On the subject of drawdowns, John Henry had several peak-to-trough drawdowns in the region of 20 percent to nearly 40 percent. These normally followed periods of superlative out-performance. It makes sense that by incrementally ratcheting up leverage as performance improves, both gains and losses can be magnified. But a stop has to be in place, whether that be on initiation of the trade or a trailing stop. Once the stop is elected, the trade is over. If the stop is not triggered, toughing out a drawdown is part of the deal for any trend follower.

Trading options can be difficult as a retail FX strategy, primarily because you will overpay for the options you buy and you will not receive enough premium for the options you sell. The overriding advantage of buying options as part of an FX strategy is that if one is long an option, the temptation to trade in and out of the spot market can be negated. Therefore, while buying an option may be expensive, it may work out to be cheaper in terms of transaction costs than continually trading spot.

If you have a propensity to overtrade—and many people do—trading options may be the tool you need to instill trading discipline. Options give your position time to move in the direction you want, and so they can also take away part of the trauma of being stopped out. But remember the dual value killers of overpriced volatility and time decay! Implied volatility is higher for out-of-the-money options than for at-the-money options. Time decay starts to increase more rapidly from about six weeks out until option expiry. Short-term options can quite quickly lose their value, and so it may be best to purchase options of longer duration. Selling options has its dangers, and it requires deep pockets if a naked selling strategy is adopted. A big move against you can quickly wipe out all premium and leave you substantially out of pocket if the option is in-the-money and is exercised.

Selling options could be incorporated as part of a strategy if a spot position has significant profits. Say, for example, you are holding a long AUD/USD position that has 500 to 600 pips profit. A short duration out-of-the-money AUD/USD call could be sold to benefit from collecting premium. The hope would be that the spot price would move higher than, but not as far as, the option strike. If the option expires worthless, you collect the premium. If the option reaches the strike and is called away from you, it will act as a take profit on your spot position.

NON-DELIVERABLE OPTIONS (NDOs) AND NON-DELIVERABLE FORWARDS (NDFs)

A market that is evolving is the *non-deliverable options* (NDO) market, which is effectively a market based on non-deliverable forward currencies such as the Indian rupee, the Malaysian ringgit, the Chinese renminbi, and the Brazilian real, among others. Arbitrage opportunities exist in some of these options versus their exchange-traded counterparts. To effect any arbitrage, however, generally at least two brokerage accounts need to be held and sufficiently funded. Brokers and banks in many cases are somewhat reluctant to allow clients to write options. Any option that is traded needs to be in a market amount, and so it is unlikely also that unless an option is of sufficient size—a minimum of, say, $500,000 to $1 million—a broker will be prepared to offer this facility. As account size gets bigger, a meaningful brokerage relationship is formed, and clients demonstrate the necessary expertise, options can add a useful alternative means of trading.

Non-deliverable forwards (NDFs), in my opinion, are as yet little-known trading products that clients should consider trading as part of an FX portfolio. There are risks of course, and the chief one is volatility. Anybody who witnessed the collapse in the Russian ruble in 2015 or the significant devaluation in the Brazilian real would understandably advise trading such currencies with extreme caution. I would urge the same; while both Russia and Brazil have interest rates in excess of 10 percent, their currencies can weaken by more than 10 percent in a month.

Having said that, in defense of trading non-deliverable forwards, I would argue that they offer exposure to BRIC and emerging market economies via a currency play, and they offer attractive rates of interest. Furthermore, nowadays most western equity markets take their cue from growth in emerging markets, so trading NDFs is an easy way to access these countries without having to buy into a fund. Trading EUR/CHF with 400:1 leverage to earn a pitiful positive interest rate carry turned out to be one of the riskiest trades of the century. Perhaps trading Indian rupee or Chinese renminbi with very small amounts of leverage of only two or three times may offer a slightly less risky alternative with commensurately better returns.

I do not advocate excessive leverage in any form of currency trading unless the competitive advantage is legitimate, clear, and properly risk managed. But in all markets, in the current climate, in order to make returns of even 5 or 10 percent, some degree of risk, or in other words an acceptance that losses are now part of the game, must be incorporated into the strategy. Equity markets are a case in point—single stocks can move in excess of 10 percent in a day, up or down, and indexes can move by as much or more in a month.

Currencies are no different, and in fact, in many cases, they are much more stable. A clue to how risky it is to trade individual NDF currencies lies in the interest rates they offer (Table 9.1). If a long NDF trade moves in your favor, the benefits are capital appreciation and positive interest rate carry. The downside risk is that in some instances certain NDFs can halve or more in value over the course of a year, which makes some NDFs as risky to trade as crude oil. The upside is that they can therefore appreciate by similar amounts. Before trading any currency pair, it pays to be aware of the risks. It is probably useful to check trading charts to see where a currency is trading with respect to its historical trading range. Try to work out what significantly affects a currency's strength. Always trade with sensible amounts of leverage. Especially with NDFs.

TABLE 9.1

Major NDF Currencies as of September 2016

Currency	ISO CODE	Central Bank Interest Rate, Percent
Latin America		
Argentinian peso	ARS	29.25
Brazilian real	BRL	14.25
Chilean peso	CLP	3.50
Columbian peso	COP	7.75
Asia and Russia		
Chinese renminbi	CNY	4.35
Indonesian rupiah	IDR	6.50
Indian rupee	INR	6.50
South Korean won	KRW	1.50
Malaysian ringgit	MYR	3.00
Philippine peso	PHP	3.00
Russian ruble	RUB	10.50
Taiwanese dollar	TWD	1.38
Vietnamese dong	VND	6.50

Access to NDFs may be difficult to obtain in all but a few brokerages. Futures are offered in some of the above currencies and can be traded on exchange. There was a big push by several exchanges, notably the CME in 2012 and the SGX in 2013, to offer INR futures due to their popularity in Dubai and the fact that there was an arbitrage between the exchange-traded INR and the NDF. There are certain reporting requirements to trade NDFs as they are considered derivatives. Whether they can be traded as a contract for difference (CFD) is open to debate.

QUESTIONS TO ASK YOURSELF BEFORE YOU TRADE CURRENCIES

Five important questions to consider when thinking about trading currencies are (1) how serious are you about making money, (2) how much capital do you wish to commit in terms of margin, (3) how much money do you wish to make and (4) over what time frame, and (5) how much are you prepared to risk (or lose) in pursuit of your profit objectives? Answering these five questions will help you form part of a workable trading strategy.

If we analyze the returns of George Soros, John Henry, and Jim Simons, who are among the best of the best, we can see that consistent annual returns of 20 to 40 percent can compound to enormous gains over time. Nobody should be of the opinion that they can make 50 percent or 100 percent several years in a row. Making an enormous return may happen as a one-off, but it is unlikely to be sustainable without commensurately taking huge risks. Neither Henry's funds nor Soros's were impervious to losses either. Soros's fund took a hit in 1981 of nearly 23 percent after achieving returns of nearly 103 percent in 1980.

Henry regularly had drawdowns of 20 percent and more and once racked up 9 months of consecutive losses in a period of 14 monthly losses out of 15. The fact is that both men controlled their risk and leverage, and so the drawdowns were relatively small compared to the outsize gains they both made. As a rule of thumb, in FX trading, we should be prepared to risk about half of what we expect to earn. So if 30 percent is your target, then be prepared to risk 15 percent. People who trade equities are getting used to 10 or 20 percent drawdowns in the value of their portfolios, and so it should be no different in trading currencies.

It is up to each individual to set his or her capital and risk levels. If the capital-at-risk limit is hit for any one year, then it is advisable to stop trading and take time out to reassess both strategy and aptitude for trading currencies. A break will do you good. It may also be a good idea to reduce capital employed in trading by an amount similar to your loss. For example, if you lose 10 percent of your account equity, it may be advisable to trim off another 10 percent of account equity and recommence trading with 80 percent of your original investment. This is a tactic that was employed successfully by Richard Dennis's Turtle traders. If, of course, the strategy is successful, the gains can be reinvested and compounded.

A quick look at compound interest can also help in setting a reasonable time scale for achieving required returns:

> A compound return of 5 percent will double capital in a little over 14 years.

> A compound return of 8 percent will double capital in about 9 years.

> A compound return of 10 percent will double capital in a little over 7 years.

> A compound return of 15 percent will double capital in 5 years.

> A compound return of 26 percent will double capital in 3 years.

Once you have an idea of your target annual return and your overall goal, you can now break down your trading strategy to work out how you might best achieve your targets. For example, if you wish to make 15 percent annually, it might amount to five winning trades making 3 percent or just one of 15 percent. (A 3 percent move in a currency with five times leverage can achieve this goal.) It may be several smaller trades. Pure trend followers will have to keep a figure in mind and ride the trend both upward and downward. If you wish to make 15 percent, be prepared to lose 7.5 percent. If you wish to make 26 percent, be prepared to lose 13 percent. Just by doing this exercise, you will see that you do not need to trade every single day or on every economic announcement each month in huge multiples of your capital.

Setting an overall loss limit that is acceptable to you will help you be mindful of your capital and hopefully avoid the disaster of exaggerated losses. A loss of 50 percent of your capital means you have to make 100 percent to get back to even. A loss of 75 percent means you have to make 300 percent to get back to where you started.

On the subject of getting back to par, there are some advocates of what is known as a *Martingale strategy*—that is, doubling down exponentially to double your original stake. For example, a gambler bets on the toss of a fair coin. He bets 1 unit on tails, and it comes up heads. On the next toss, he bets 2 units, then 4, then 8, 16, 32, and so on until tails comes up. On his bet of 32 units, he wins 32 units, which covers his loss of 31 units and gives him a 1 unit profit. This is a strategy for the bold who have deep pockets. Whoever uses it must also assume that currency trading ranges revert back at least to where they started. It is not going to work in trending markets if you are on the wrong side of the trade. If you consider the sequence 1, 2, 4, 8, 16, 32, 64, 128 and replace the word "unit" with "times leverage," you will quickly see that risk and danger quickly mount. Thus 128 times leverage requires less than a 1 percent move against you to wipe you out.

DECIDING HOW MUCH
CAPITAL TO INVEST

A large question that should be on everybody's mind is exactly how much capital to invest in currency trading, and there is no straightforward answer to this. It really depends on what you are looking to achieve and what sort of commitment you wish to focus on the project. Is your idea to earn some extra income, earn a living out of trading, become a fund manager, write trading programs, or run your own brokerage?

FXCM's statistics support the notion that small accounts of less than $10,000 tend to perform less well than those of more than $10,000. Billionaire Peter Cruddas started what became CMC Markets with a GBP 10,000 investment, although it has to be said he was somewhat of an inter-dealer broker with a good client base before becoming an online currency broker. John Henry had an initial investment of $100,000 and made 9.93 percent, 20.66 percent, and 61.55 percent in his first three years of trading. If you have an audited performance of three years of positive returns, then in many instances, you have a marketable track record. Henry's assets under management grew 15 fold in his fourth year of trading.

Trading giants Ken Griffin of Citadel and George Soros started trading with assets of between $4 million and $5 million. They have made billions. My view is that whatever capital you commit to trading, you should use it as capital to win. If you wish to be frivolous with your money, then don't trade. You can use it for better purposes. As Ed Seykota once remarked, "Win or lose, everybody gets what they want out of the market. Some people like to lose, so they win by losing money."[1] I once took a friend of mine to the casino in Monaco. He said he had 200 GBP to lose. Sure enough, he lost it. Try not to make the same mistake trading FX.

If becoming a market maker or broker is your wish, $1 million might capitalize your own brokerage in certain jurisdictions, but then you will have to commit as much and more to staff it correctly and market your brand. A $5 million to $20 million investment may bring you into the realm of being a small brokerage with your own prime broker in better-known jurisdictions and enable you to offer a greater array of products. You will have plenty of competition and regulatory scrutiny.

ALLOCATING YOUR CAPITAL

If professional trading is your goal, I think you need sufficient capital to diversify your risks. I believe you need access to a whole suite of products—namely, spot, futures, options, NDFs, and NDOs. This may mean you need to have more than one brokerage account. Be mindful of whether your broker acts as agent or as principal to your trades—that is, does the broker pass your trades straight through to other market makers, or does he or she take the opposite side of your trades? The choice is yours. Larger accounts tend to prefer a straight-through process to avoid conflicts of interest in pricing from their broker.

There is certainly money to be made in FX, and all styles of trading have their moments of success. A diversified portfolio with percentage allocations to different strategies may offer a path to superior performance. It will in some ways aid in stemming volatility compared to one single trading theme. For example, you might allocate 20 percent of your capital each to five different strategies, such as a macroeconomic view on a pair of currencies, trend following, carry trading, mean-reversion trading on economic figures, and non-U.S. dollar pairs trading. If you apply leverage of 2 times capital to each strategy, you will arrive at 10 times leverage for the whole portfolio, which is an ample amount of risk to take.

If you have sufficient capital, training, and expertise, strategies involving options, NDFs, and NDOs can be embraced. It can be a very useful undertaking to diarize your trades before and after trading. What is the logic behind the trade? What are the profit objectives, and where is the stop loss? How did it work out? What lessons did you learn? It might seem like a pain to do this for every trade, but it will instill trading discipline and check the temptation to overtrade.

Arbitrage has proved to be a successful strategy for many who have the resources and speed to capture price anomalies between exchanges and the spot or NDF market. Arbitrage requires either intense concentration or a speedy computer algorithm, normally connected via API. It is highly unlikely that a broker will allow you to connect to his liquidity via API if your tactic is to arbitrage. Picking off the banks in a latency arbitrage strategy can quickly lead to no liquidity at all. If a trader engages in an arbitrage strategy, it must be properly risk managed to monitor trade rejections that do occur from time to time.

MANAGING STRESS

Whatever your approach to trading and however much your initial investment, one thing for sure is that you will have a better feel for the risks you are taking if you manage your own money. The more "skin" you have in the game, the more acutely you are likely to feel the joy of winning or the pain of losing. Strictly speaking, you should keep your emotions in check and stay focused on your strategy because if emotions creep into the equation, it can change the dynamics of your trading tactics, and you may become less rational in your trading decisions.

At the outset, your initial investment and your stop trading limit should be of an amount that you are comfortable managing. And your profit objectives should be realistic and attainable.

If they are not, then you are likely to be stressed before you start, and your decision-making processes may become impaired. As your account grows, you must continually try to stay focused and rational and apply the same discipline to your trading however much money you are managing. For some people it will come more naturally than to others. Two of the greatest traders for managing pressure are George Soros and John Henry. Huge P&L swings can unnerve all but the best traders. These two men traded colossal amounts and had P&L swings in the multimillions, but both came out on top. It's an entirely different skill set to contend with, but staying focused under pressure is no less relevant to small than to big accounts.

BEING GUIDED BY THE FOUR PRINCIPLES

At the beginning of this book, I suggested that there were four basic principles that when followed contribute to trading success in the foreign exchange market: do the work, cultivate a competitive advantage, work out how scalable your trade is, and manage the size of the risk so that it is appropriate and effective for the size of your trade.

This chapter, in essence, has been about applying yourself or setting yourself up to do the work. Previous chapters have described styles of trading or innovation successfully employed by the Currency Kings and other smaller market participants to reap untold riches from the market. I hope that they will inspire budding traders or entrepreneurs to focus intensely on ways they consider they can compete with and beat the market. By "beating the market," I mean winning and adopting a serious attitude to winning. A competitive advantage should not be confused with a lucky streak, and we should all be humble enough to know the difference. That said, if anybody has a legitimate competitive advantage, it should be scaled up for maximum effect.

The dangers in the market are clear, and the most glaring danger is the individual trader to himself or herself. Overleveraging and overtrading go counter to effective risk management. If there is such a thing as a traders' graveyard, most of its occupants got there by doing the above or letting bad trades ruin them.

Many brokers have done their homework, and they have made their money by taking the opposite side of trades of foolish investors. There are of course many other leakages in the system that can contribute to underperformance, and these include spreads, commissions, and financing charges. Slippage or poor execution of market orders that can be exacerbated by the influence of high-frequency traders can also degrade overall returns, which therefore make the chances of winning less than 50:50. Delegating power of attorney to Expert Advisors or trading robots is unlikely to yield superior returns in terms of either the likelihood of winning or the scalability of winning. It is arguable that any single trader has a better chance to win than by passing that authority to a third party, especially when management and performance fees are included.

It is imperative that we go into foreign exchange trading with our eyes open. If we choose to self-trade, then we should do so with a well-thought-out strategy. Currently the statistics are poor among retail traders, with only about one in five making money. I hope that by reading this book, many new budding traders shift that winning percentage to 40 percent and above. It can be done!

While I have been inspired by many of the greats of trading, I have also taken inspiration from the many humble smaller traders I met during my time in Dubai. In many ways, these people did everything right in their application of the four basic principles mentioned above. They discovered a market where they had a competitive advantage and exploited it to the fullest. In their case, it was an exchange versus NDF arbitrage. What it tells me is that there are some very smart, intelligent traders out there who can become the next great FX giants. Everybody has to start somewhere, and without doubt there will be many more self-made currency millionaires and even billionaires.

There are several other great traders who could quite easily have made the grade as Currency Kings and whom I have not mentioned in this book. These people have also utilized trading styles and run businesses similar in type to those mentioned in the previous chapters, whether it be global macro trading, futures trading, trend following, option trading, carry trading, arbitraging, building software, or running brokerages. While I admire the courage and determination of the big hitters, I'm no less in awe of the operators who make small relentless profits, and I also respect the brokers and software providers who create a market where millions of people can try their hand at trading FX.

My single biggest hope is that the market remains fair for all participants, and in that respect, I believe people should be properly briefed and aware of the risks before they start to trade. I believe the onus is on brokers to provide a fair market and regulators to work with brokers to make sure this is the case. I'm firmly of the belief that more FX education would be helpful, and I urge budding traders to seek it out. FX is a fascinating market and there are many ways to access it and to make meaningful profits.

Preparing, mind, body, and strategy will certainly aid with the mental challenges that lie ahead. Preparation is one thing, discipline is another, and perhaps for those who make it big, luck plays a part. What sets the Currency Kings apart is their unrelenting pursuit of excellence. Courage, tenacity, willpower, and perseverance are all key traits. Tactics, competitive advantage, discipline, and risk management are others. What made these men billionaires was scale, and that can be seen either in Soros's blockbuster GBP trade or in the prevalence of Fatkhullin's MT4 platform. Ultimately scale is the differentiating factor between small and large gains.

It is worth repeating John Henry's maxims because they are inspiring and relevant:

- One must have a valid personal philosophy.

- There is no Holy Grail to trading.

- Discipline is more important than genius.

- Persistence is more important than talent.

- Performance is more important than capability.

- Ability to create value is more important than ability or creativity in any realm.

- Continue to look for ways and to think about how you can create value.[2]

It tells me that it is possible for anybody with the right attitude to become a successful trader. The last maxim is akin to George Soros's maxim to "stay ahead of the curve." Innovation, looking for value, and looking for ways to win must always be present in any successful business or trading strategy. We have plenty of products to trade.

We also now have an idea of how the Currency Kings started, how they applied themselves, and how they made their money, whether that was in speculating, market making, arbitrage trading, or building software. They are all inspirational, and they have made the market what it is today. Now it is our turn. Good luck, and good trading! I look forward to reading or writing about the next Currency King!

NOTES

Chapter 2

1. George Soros, *The Alchemy of Finance: Reading the Mind of the Market*, 2d ed., Wiley, New York, 1994, p. 25.
2. Michael T. Kaufman, *Soros: The Life and Times of a Messianic Billionaire*, Knopf/Random House, New York, 2002, p. 142.
3. *Black Wednesday, BBC News*, 1997, https://www.youtube.com/watch ?v=K_oET45GzMI.
4. John Ramkin, personal interview with Ben Robson, 2014.
5. Ross Donaghue, personal interview with Ben Robson, 2014.
6. *Black Wednesday, BBC News*.
7. Ibid.
8. Unnamed Prudential Bache Dealer, personal interview with Ben Robson, 2014.
9. Ross Donaghue, personal interview with Ben Robson, 2014.
10. *Black Wednesday, BBC News*.
11. Jim Trott quoted in the *Guardian* newspaper, September 13, 2012.
12. John Ramkin, personal interview with Ben Robson, 2014.
13. Ross Donaghue, personal interview with Ben Robson, 2014.

Chapter 3

1. Robert D. Edwards and John Magee, "In Memorium," *Technical Analysis of Stock Trends*, 7th ed., CRC Press, Boca Raton, FL, 1998.
2. Ibid.
3. "John W. Henry," *Wikipedia*.
4. Michael Peltz, "John Henry's Bid to Manage the Future," *Institutional Investor*, August 1996.
5. Michael Covel, *Trend Following: How Great Traders Make Millions in Up or Down Markets*, Prentice Hall, Upper Saddle River, NJ, 2004.

6. Michael Peltz, "John Henry's Bid to Manage the Future."

7. Curtis Faith, *The Original Turtle Trading Rules*, 2003, http://bigpicture .typepad.com/comments/files/turtlerules.pdf. As quoted in Richard Dennis in Jack D. Schwager, *The New Market Wizards: Conversations with America's Top Traders*, HarperBusiness, New York, 1994.

8. Ibid.

9. Ibid.

10. Ibid.

11. "John W. Henry," *Wikipedia*.

12. "John Henry: Holding on to Dreams," *Profit & Loss*, March 2005.

13. Curtis Faith, *The Original Turtle Trading Rules*.

14. "John Henry: Holding on to Dreams."

Chapter 4

1. Jean Rafferty, "A Palace Fit for Nonroyalty," *New York Times*, November 11, 2008.

2. *The Dolder Grand Fifth Anniversary Magazine*, March 2013.

3. "The Dolder Grand: Suburban Retreat with Artistic Credentials," *Highlight in Hotels, Centurion Magazine*, December 2015, https:// centurion-magazine.com/travel/hotels/europe/switzerland/zurich -dolder-grand.

4. Mark O'Neill, personal interview with Ben Robson, 2014.

5. Mintao Fan and Richard Lyons, "Customer Trades and Extreme Events in Foreign Exchange," in *Monetary History, Exchange Rates, and Financial Markets*, edited by Paul Mizen, Edward Elgar Publishing, Camberley Surrey, U.K., 2003, chap. 6.

6. Mark Davison, personal interview with Ben Robson, 2014.

Chapter 5

1. David Teather, "Cockney Croesus Who Still Craves Recognition," *Guardian*, January 12, 2007.

2. "Refco and Saxo Forge Online Trading Pact," *Finextra*, July 21, 2003, www.finextra.com.

3. Saxo Bank A/S press release, "Saxo Bank Goes to China," *Marketwire*, August 16, 2007.

4. Pat Mathieu, "Gain Capital Opens Beijing Office," May 11, 2011, www.stockbrokers.com.

5. "Citi and Saxo Bank to Launch CitiFX Pro for Private Client Access to World Class FX Trading," November 20, 2007, www.citigroup .com.

6. Janet Whitman, "What Caused the Financial Crisis?" *National Post*, January 27, 2011, http://www.nationalpost.com/related/topics/what +caused+financial+crisis/4179621/story.html.

7. James Quinn, "Greenspan Admits Mistakes in 'Once in a Century' Credit Tsunami," *Telegraph*, October 23, 2008.
8. Philip Stafford, "FXCM Pushes into Algorithmic FX Trading," *Financial Times*, June 14, 2012.
9. Craig Karmin and Michael R. Sesit, "Currency Markets Draw Speculation, Fraud," *Wall Street Journal*, July 26, 2005.

Chapter 6
1. Unnamed Societe Generale trader, personal interview with Ben Robson, 2014.
2. Hal Lux, "The Secret World of Jim Simons," *Institutional Investor*, November 1, 2000.
3. Ibid.
4. https://www.gsacapital.com/.
5. Virtu Financial, Inc., Form S-1 filed with the Securities and Exchange Commission, March 10, 2014, https://www.sec.gov/Archives/edgar/data/1592386/000104746914002070/a2218589zs-1.htm.
6. Ibid.
7. Rakesh Daryani, personal interview with Ben Robson, 2014.
8. Hal Lux, "The Secret World of Jim Simons."

Chapter 7
1. "Yet More Talent," *FX-MM*, December 20, 2013, https://www.fx-mm.com/article/31634/yet-more-talent/.

Chapter 8
1. Craig Karmin and Michael R. Sesit, "Currency Markets Draw Speculation, Fraud," *Wall Street Journal*, July 26, 2005.
2. Ibid.
3. Brad B. Barber and Terrance Odean, "Trading Is Hazardous to Your Wealth: The Common Stock Investment Performance of Individual Investors," *Journal of Finance*, vol. 55, no. 2, April 2000.

Chapter 9
1. Jack Schwager, *Market Wizards*, HarperCollins, New York, 1989, p. 172.
2. "John Henry: Holding on to Dreams," *Profit & Loss*, March 2005.

INDEX

ABOUT THE AUTHOR

 **Ben Robson** has over 20 years' experience in the financial markets in the fields of fixed income currencies and commodities. After having served as an officer in the British Army's elite Brigade of Guards, Robson embarked upon a financial career, first as a repo-funding analyst at Goldman Sachs International and then as a foreign exchange dealer at Prudential Bache International, both in the City of London.

Robson subsequently set up CMC Markets Asia Ltd. in Hong Kong before running MF Global's Asia Pacific Foreign Exchange and Bullion business operating out of Singapore and with offices in Hong Kong, Japan, Australia, India, and Dubai.

From 2011 to 2015, Robson created and acted as CEO of Fixi Plc's proprietary FX and arbitrage businesses based in Singapore and Dubai.

Robson holds an MBA in finance from the International University of Monaco and a bachelor of science in land management from the University of Reading in the United Kingdom.